INSIDERS'GUIDE®

FUN WITH THE FAMILY™ SERIES

fun WITH the Family™

INDIANA

HUNDREDS OF IDEAS FOR DAY TRIPS WITH THE KIDS

MARGARET GISLER

FIFTH EDITION

INSIDERS'GUIDE®

GUILFORD, CONNECTICUT

AN IMPRINT OF THE GLOBE PEQUOT PRESS

The prices, rates, and hours listed in this guidebook
were confirmed at press time. We recommend, however, that you call establishments to obtain current
information before traveling.

INSIDERS'GUIDE®

Copyright © 1995, 1998, 2000, 2002, 2004 by Margaret Gisler

Insiders' Guide is a registered trademark of The Globe Pequot Press.
Fun with the Family is a trademark of The Globe Pequot Press.

Text design by Nancy Freeborn and Linda Loiewski
Maps created by Rusty Nelson © The Globe Pequot Press
Spot photography throughout © Photodisc

ISSN 1540-1510
ISBN 0-7627-2978-3

Manufactured in the United States of America
Fifth Edition/First Printing

To my wonderful family—Les, Tricia, Ann, Mark, and David, and my mother Patty White—with whom I have had so much fun exploring Indiana. Thank you for helping me write this book! I truly appreciate all your efforts and the wonderful memories we all have from our many adventures throughout Indiana.

INDIANA

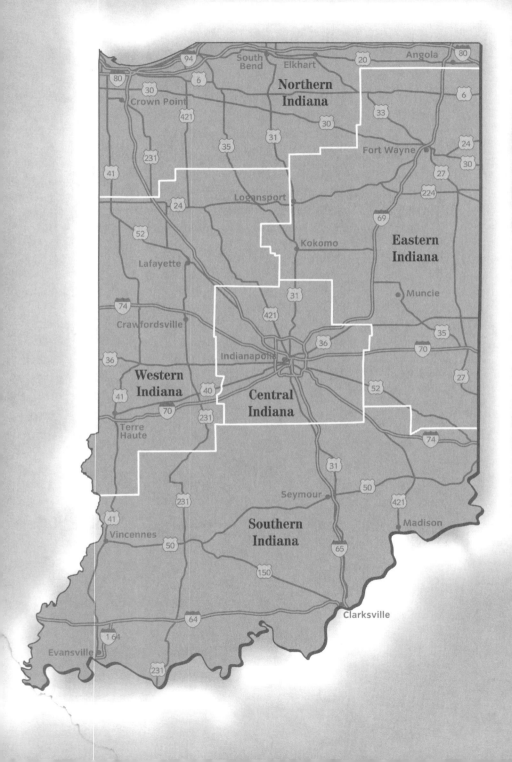

Contents

Acknowledgments

I would like to thank the following people for their help in putting together this book: Maria P. Olson, Ann M. Gisler, Mark L. Gisler, David A. Gisler, Michael Urban, and Maria Patricia White. I would also like to thank Kevin Crider for his help researching and updating the information in this book.

Introduction

I have lived in Indiana all my life and have many wonderful memories of my childhood adventures in the state. Nonetheless, it was not until I returned from living in Germany that I began to seriously investigate things for my own four children to do in Indiana. Over the years my family and I have had the opportunity to gather memories from almost every place mentioned in this book. I have climbed the steps at the Soldiers' and Sailors' Monument on Monument Circle in downtown Indianapolis, struggled over sand dunes to reach Lake Michigan, taken a boat trip through an underground cave, and thoroughly enjoyed every adventure.

To help you begin exploring Indiana, I have grouped the descriptions of the family attractions into five areas: Northern, Southern, Central, Eastern, and Western Indiana. Each area is introduced by a map that highlights the towns you will want to visit. Then the towns with family spots of interest are grouped together so that you will be able to plan to see as many attractions as you have time for in a certain area. Hotel and restaurant listings are provided for most of the cities so that you will be able to plan overnight excursions. Some of the towns have a great number of places to visit; others have only one special attraction. I have described some of the things you can do at each spot to ensure an enjoyable visit. Many of these places are so much fun that you will want to plan a return trip. I hope you and your family will have as much fun exploring Indiana as I have had with my family.

Before taking off to visit any or all regions of Indiana, visit the state's tourism Web site at www.indianatourism.com.

Attraction Rates

Dollar signs represent general per person rates, including the range for adults and children. Always inquire about family and group rates and package deals that may include amusement park tickets, ski area tickets, and tickets for concerts and other performing arts events.

$	less than $5
$$	$5 to $10
$$$	$10 to $15
$$$$	more than $15

Attractions Key

The following is a key to the icons found throughout the text.

SWIMMING		**FOOD**	
BOATING / BOAT TOUR		**LODGING**	
HISTORIC SITE		**CAMPING**	
HIKING / WALKING		**MUSEUMS**	
FISHING		**PERFORMING ARTS**	
BIKING		**SPORTS/ATHLETICS**	
AMUSEMENT PARK		**PICNICKING**	
HORSEBACK RIDING		**PLAYGROUND**	
SKIING /WINTER SPORTS		**SHOPPING**	
PARK		**PLANTS/GARDENS/NATURE TRAILS**	
ANIMAL VIEWING		**FARMS**	

Northern Indiana

Beaches in Indiana? Yes! Northern Indiana has a lengthy coastline on Lake Michigan. And this area that abounds in tall sand dunes is only thirty-five minutes from Chicago's Loop. This is just one of the places where your family can have fun in an area that stretches across northern Indiana between Illinois and Ohio. You can visit Amish settlements, explore the historic sites in the area, enjoy cultural events, visit museums, see a world famous university, and enjoy outdoor fun both summer and winter.

TopPicks for fun in Northern Indiana

1. Indiana Dunes National Lakeshore and State Park

2. Mount Baldy, Michigan City

3. Amish Acres, Nappanee

4. Washington Park Zoo, Michigan City

5. University of Notre Dame, South Bend

6. Pokagon State Park, 5 miles north of Angola

7. Potato Creek State Park, North Liberty

8. Potawatomi Zoo, South Bend

9. Hannah Lindahl Children's Museum, Mishawaka

10. Lake Maxinkuckee, Culver

NORTHERN INDIANA

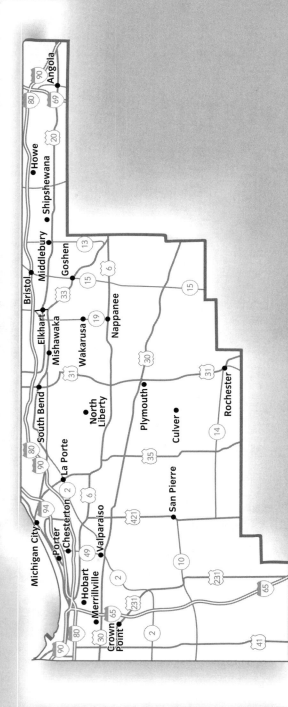

Angola

Heading north on I–69 out of Fort Wayne you will arrive at the town of Angola, the county seat of Steuben County.

Take a walk through the streets of downtown Angola, and you will be surrounded with history. You will see old-fashioned street lamps, attractive specialty shops, and many historic landmarks, including the county jail and courthouse. And right in the center of town, there is the Soldier's Monument erected in 1917 to honor county soldiers who served in the Civil War. Steuben sent more men per capita to the war than any other county in Indiana.

Pokagon State Park (all ages)

Just 5 miles north of Angola at 1080 West State Road 727; (260) 833–2012.

Does your family enjoy outdoor activities such as hiking, swimming, fishing, camping, and exploring nature trails? Come spend a day or more at Pokagon State Park and enjoy all these activities. The park is located on the shores of Lake James and Snow Lake. From the full-time naturalist staff you can learn all you want to know about the animals, trees, flowers, and even weeds as you hike through the beautiful woods. If you wish to extend your visit in this wonderful park, family cabins are available. Besides the activities already mentioned, you can rent a horse, play tennis, or water-ski. In the winter months, a ¼-mile-long, side-by-side toboggan slide provides chills and thrills for the entire family. Just imagine sliding at speeds up to 60 miles per hour. Ice skating and cross-country skiing are additional winter fun options.

Fun Spot Park (all ages)

2365 North Highway 200 West; (260) 833–2972; www.funspotpark.com. Open Thursday through Sunday late May through late August 10:00 A.M. to 5:30 P.M. Admission $$$.

For even more family fun in Angola, there is the Fun Spot Park. Here you can ride a roller coaster that is one of only four "after burner" roller coasters in the world as well as the largest roller coaster in Indiana. If you have some golfers in your family, they can select from one of the seven challenging courses for a game.

Indiana **Trivia**

Where is Tri-State University located?

What is the most populated U.S. city founded during the twentieth century?

Where was the Studebaker automobile built?

Angola, Gary, South Bend

Where to Eat

Baker Street Restaurant. 7265 North Baker Road; (260) 495–9884. Open twenty-four hours serving breakfast, lunch, and dinner. Full-service menu, all meals served at any time, from sandwiches to full entrees. The place to go if you are hungry—any time of the day or night.

Caruso's. 2435 North 200 West, exit 150 off I–69 (north 1 mile); (260) 833–2617. A family tradition since 1976, Caruso's offers a unique blend of fine Italian and American cuisine in a warm, comfortable atmosphere. Homemade pizza and home of the famous "Torpedough" sandwich and sausage roll. Family Room open 4:00 P.M. daily; restaurant closed Monday and Sunday, but open Tuesday through Friday for lunch 11:00 A.M. to 2:00 P.M. Dinner hours are Tuesday through Thursday 4:00 to 9:00 P.M., Friday and Saturday 4:00 to 9:30 P.M.

Captain's Cabin. 3070 West Shadyside Road; (260) 665–5663. Located on the south end of Crooked Lake, this restaurant offers steaks, seafood, and the best prime rib in northern Indiana. Enjoy casual dining in the downstairs lounge area or fine lakefront dining upstairs. A northern Indiana favorite. Open Wednesday through Saturday at 5:00 P.M. during the winter, Monday through Saturday at 5:00 P.M. during the summer.

Where to Stay

Budgeteer Motor Inn. 4980 North State Road 127; (260) 665–5694. Twenty-four rooms. Small pets are allowed.

Best Western. 3155 U.S. Highway 20 West; (260) 665–9561. Ninety-four rooms; two stories; complimentary breakfast, including coffee; outdoor pool; restaurant and lounge. Within easy access to shopping center. Children younger than 12 stay free with adult.

Camping

Circle B. Campground. 340 Lane 100 Hogback Lake; (260) 665–5353. Approximately 150 RV and tent sites. RV sites have water and electricity. Swimming, playground, fishing, and shower facilities. Open April 15 through October 15.

Menefee's Camp Sack-In. 8740 40 South; (260) 665–5166.

For More Information

For more information on the Angola area contact **Steuben County Tourism Bureau, Inc.** at 207 South Wayne Street, where you will be able to obtain information on Steuben County, home of 101 lakes and Pokagon State Park. You can also call (800) LAKE–101 and have information sent to you. Check its Web site at www.lakes101.org.

Howe

Twin Mills Camping Resort (all ages) 🌊 👫 🎣 🚲
1675 West State Road 120; (260) 562–3212; www.twinmillscamping.com.

More than just a shaded campsite with full hookups, this resort has a friendly staff that is proud of its Woodall's Four-Star rating and wants to make your stay the best possible. For families who are looking for a quiet getaway, you can enjoy the river, wooded nature trails, and lake—complete with a private beach. For those looking for more activity, there are three challenging public golf courses only fifteen minutes away. For those who like to fish, Twin Mills rents both boats and canoes to take out onto the lake. Other fun areas to be found at the resort include a heated pool, kiddie pool, recreation hall, eighteen-hole minigolf course, basketball court, shuffleboard court, mountain bike trail, and pond for kiddie fishing. Reservations are available for groups, clubs, or individual families.

Where to Eat

Town Square Restaurant. 407 Third Street; (260) 562–3584.

Where to Stay

Super 8 Motel. 7333 North State Road 9; (260) 562–2828. Handicapped accessible rooms, pets allowed, nearby restaurants and shops.

Travel Inn. 50 West 815 North; (260) 562–3481. Thirty-eight rooms.

Bristol

Bonneyville Mill (all ages) 🏛
53373 County Road 131; (574) 535–6458. Open daily 8:00 A.M. to 8:00 P.M. April, May, and September and until 9:00 P.M. June, July, and August.

You and your family will get a chance to see history when you explore the rustic gristmill that is the oldest continually operating mill in Elkhart County Park. You can also purchase freshly ground grains and picnic in the park surroundings.

Where to Eat

Buck's Deli and Ice Cream Shop. Corner of State Roads 15 and 120; (574) 848–1307. Serves its famous "Bristol subs" with salads, homemade soups, or chili and nachos. For your sweet tooth, try the flavor-of-the-day frozen yogurt served in a dish or a cone. Sugar-free yogurt is also available. Open 10:30 A.M. to 4:00 P.M. Monday through Friday. Closed weekends.

River Inn. 304 East Vistula Street; (574) 848–7438. The River Inn's menu features lake perch, slow-roasted baby-back ribs, a variety of burritos, pasta dishes, pizza, and sandwiches. Children's menu is available.

Where to Stay

Eby's Pines Campground. 14583 State Road 120; (574) 848– 4583; www.ebyspines.com. A great family camp-ground in northern Indiana for families who are looking for adventure and a variety of things to do. Besides all the usual things that most parks have, such as playgrounds, trails, and campsites, Eby's Pines also has a swimming pool, fishing, convenience store, basketball and tennis courts, hayrides, roller skating, and a restaurant. Eby's offers both tent and RV camping, with full hook-ups. Rustic log cabins are available to rent. Pets must be kept on leashes.

Elkhart

In historical downtown Elkhart, you can enjoy shopping in many unique stores. The town also hosts frequent cultural events and festivals for the whole family. It is also a museum lover's paradise, as the town has several very different museums for your family to explore.

Appropriately, Elkhart, the band instrument capital of the nation (producing more than one-half of all band instruments), has many music-filled activities. In the summer every Tuesday evening from June through mid-August, the **Elkhart Municipal Band** gives a free summer concert in the **Arthur Singleton Band Shell** in **McNaughton Park.** In the latter part of June, jammin' jazz greats from across the country come to play in the **Elkhart Jazz Festival.** The three-day **Rhapsody in Green Festival** is held each year in mid-June at Island, Bicentennial, and High Dive parks. Besides music, there are craft booths, food stands, volleyball tournaments, tumbling exhibitions, and much more.

A festival that truly makes waves is the **Head of the Elk Regatta** in early November on the **Upper St. Joseph River** in which collegians from across the nation compete in their crafts. A street dance, dinner, and activities are part of the festival. In early December, **Winterfest** is kicked off with a parade and the remainder of the weekend is filled with holiday activities including breakfast with Santa.

For more information on these and other events in the area, call the visitors' bureau at (800) 860–5949, or visit Elkhart's Web site: www.elkhartindiana.org.

RV/MH Heritage Foundation Hall of Fame (all ages)

810 Benham Avenue; (574) 293–2344. Open Monday through Friday 9:00 A.M. to 4:00 P.M. Free.

Here is a museum devoted to the history of American recreational travel, from early camping trailers of the 1930s to today's house trailers and camping accessories. You can also see a photo collection covering the entire history of recreational vehicles and manu-factured homes. Visit its Web site at www.rv-mh-hall-of-fame.org.

Indiana **Trivia**

From what Indiana city was the first submarine launched?

Michigan City

Midwest Museum of American Art (all ages)

429 South Main Street; (574) 293–6660. Open Tuesday through Friday 11:00 A.M. to 5:00 P.M. and Saturday and Sunday 1:00 to 4:00 P.M. Closed Monday. Admission $. Free admission on Sunday.

This museum is a showcase of nineteenth- and twentieth-century American art. A permanent collection can be viewed along with temporary exhibits located in a restored bank building. Some of the highlights at the museum include Norman Rockwell lithographs and originals and an impressive collection of photographs, plus works by Grandma Moses and Alexander Calder. Phone ahead to find out what special exhibits are on display.

National New York Central Railroad Museum (all ages)

721 South Main Street; (574) 294–3001; www.nycrrmuseum.org. Hours are Tuesday through Saturday 10:00 A.M. to 4:00 P.M., and Sunday noon to 4:00 P.M. Admission $.

Any railroad buffs in your family? Well, if so, this is just the place to visit. Most of the museum is in an old New York Central freight house. There are displays, a video view room, a 1930s stationmaster's office, two model railroad layouts, and a variety of memorabilia. A New York Central "Mohawk" steam locomotive, the last surviving piece of that particular class, is part of the museum's rolling stock collection.

Ruthmere Museum (all ages)

302 East Beardsley Avenue; (888) 287–7696; www.ruthmere.org. Guided tours are Tuesday through Saturday at 10:00 A.M., 11:00 A.M., 1:00 P.M., 2:00 P.M., and 3:00 P.M.; Sunday at 1:00, 2:00, and 3:00 P.M. Open year-round. Admission $. Sunday tours are free.

Members of your family may have their interest in architecture increased through a visit to the Ruthmere Museum, a magnificent mansion built in 1908 by Albert R. Beardsley in memory of his only child Ruth. It features a combination of Beaux Arts and Midwestern Prairie School architecture. Here you can see some of the china used by presidents Hayes, Jackson, and Harding. Call ahead to find out about special events at the museum.

"Time Was" Museum (all ages)

125-A North Main Street; (574) 293–6005. Open Thursday through Saturday 10:00 A.M. to 2:00 P.M., other times by appointment. Free.

Have you ever wondered about the past residents of old homes you have visited? Well, this museum may satisfy some of your curiosity. Housed above a circa 1899 retail building, this attraction offers a look back at the ever-changing city of Elkhart. Photos of all downtown structures can be found along with individual histories of their occupants. Elkhart yearbooks from 1900 and city directories from 1864, along with local industrial publications and advertising memorabilia, can be found in this distinctive collection.

Where to Eat

Bob Evans. 2915 Brittany Court; (574) 264–1890. Family-style restaurant. Open Sunday through Thursday 6:00 A.M. to 10:00 P.M., Friday and Saturday 6:00 A.M. to 11:30 P.M.

DaVinci's Pizza and Family Restaurant. 2720 Cassopolis Street, just off I–80/90, exit 92; (574) 264–6248. Casual dining, classic Italian cooking with some American dishes. Open Sunday and Tuesday through Thursday 11:00 A.M. to 9:00 P.M., Friday 11:00 A.M. to 10:00 P.M., Saturday 4:00 to 10:00 P.M.

Ramada Inn. 3011 Belvedere Road, just off I–80/90, exit 92; (574) 262–1581. Family dining specializing in steaks, seafood, and pasta. Open Monday through Friday 6:30 A.M. to 2:00 P.M. and 5:00 to 9:00 P.M., Saturday and Sunday 7:00 A.M. to 2:00 P.M. and 5:00 to 9:00 P.M.

Where to Stay

Ramada Inn. 3011 Belvedere Road; (574) 262–1581; www.ramada.com. Full service hotel with 145 rooms. Indoor and outdoor pools, live entertainment, handicapped accessible rooms, **free** newspaper.

Red Roof Inn. 2902 Cassopolis Street; (574) 262–3691. www.redroofinn.com. Eighty rooms, **free** coffee and newspaper, pets are allowed, rollaways and cribs available upon request, handicapped accessible rooms.

Signature Inn. Exit 92 off I–80/90; (574) 264–7222; www.signature.com. **Free** breakfast express buffet and complimentary copy of *USA Today* offered Monday through Friday. One hundred twenty-five rooms.

Holiday Inn Express. 330 North Pointe Boulevard; (574) 262–0014; www.holiday inn.com. **Free** breakfast bar; indoor, heated pool; and hot tub.

Quality Inn. 3321 Plaza Court; exit 92, off I–80/90; (574) 295–0280 or (800) 228–5151; www.hotelchoice.com. **Free** continental breakfast and indoor heated pool. Pets allowed.

For More Information

City of Elkhart. www.elkhartindiana.org.

Michigan City

Lighthouse Place Outlet Center (all ages)
Sixth and Wabash; (219) 879–6506. Open Monday through Saturday 9:00 A.M. to 9:00 P.M. and Sunday 10:00 A.M. to 6:00 P.M. Closed Christmas and Easter. In the winter, the center closes each evening at 6:00 P.M.

This is the place to go if you enjoy shopping, especially bargain shopping. Shop until you drop at more than 120 stores operated by the country's top retailers. There is sure to be something that each family member needs. Besides shopping, the center offers a wide variety of restaurants and has an ice cream parlor. For weary shoppers, there is an old-fashioned trolley used as a free shuttle.

Washington Park Zoo (all ages)
On the lakeshore at the end of Franklin Street; (219) 873–1510. Open October through April 10:30 A.M. to 3:00 P.M. Between May and September, the zoo stays open until 6:00 P.M. Hours vary by the seasons. Admission $. Free for children age 2 and younger.

Are the members of your family animal lovers? Do they love to pet and feed animals? They will enjoy a day at the Washington Park Zoo. With more than 260 animals and a huge petting zoo, this zoo is one of Indiana's oldest and largest.

Indiana's Only Lighthouse (all ages)
On the shores of Lake Michigan; (219) 872–6133. Open 1:00 to 4:00 P.M. Tuesday through Sunday, March through December. Admission $. Free for preschool-age children.

Washington **Park**

With one child who is an animal lover, my family was never able to pass Washington Park without a yell from her to get out and see all the animals at the Washington Park Zoo. While Washington Park is one of the largest and oldest zoos in the state with more than 260 animals, the children really love the large petting zoo that is located as you walk into the park. Our children enjoy petting and feeding all the animals, from little billy goats to large horses. After touring the zoo, we usually hike up the sand dune to the observation tower for spectacular views of Lake Michigan and the lakefront. On the way back to the car, the children love to run along the water, go out on the fishing piers, and watch the boats. Oftentimes we pack a picnic meal and sit on the beach or in a picnic area and eat on the grounds before heading home for the night.

Besides seeing zoo animals at Washington Park, you can hike up a dune to the observation tower for spectacular views of Lake Michigan and the lakefront. This ninety-acre park also has a beach, picnic areas, pier fishing, a boat launch, and trails. You'll see the original lighthouse that was built in 1858 and eight display rooms of Lake Michigan history, shipwrecks, the era of sailing ships, and local history.

Mount Baldy (all ages)

The entrance is located approximately 2 miles west of downtown Michigan City, just off U.S. 12. Free.

Mount Baldy is a part of the Indiana Dunes National Lakeshore and is a "living" sand dune that actually moves south 4 or 5 feet each year from the drifting sands and blowing winds. For an exhilarating rush, climb to the top of this 123-foot-tall dune and let gravity help you down to the water's edge.

Creek Ridge County Park (all ages)

7943 West 400 North; (219) 326–6808.

Creek Ridge County Park consists of seventy-six acres along Trail Creek, a tributary of Lake Michigan, a few miles south of Michigan City. A 400-foot boardwalk alongside the creek allows anglers and outdoor enthusiasts easy access to the salmon and trout runs during spawning season. There are also a variety of accessible nature trails and picnic facilities that are great for family reunions.

Alyce Bartholomew Children's Museum (all ages)

450 St. John Road in the Marquette Mall; (219) 874–8222. Open Wednesday through Saturday 10:00 A.M. to 4:00 P.M. Admission $.

A hands-on, interactive museum offering programs and exhibits where kids can explore science principles, nature's architecture, sounds, music, color, light, and culture.

The Great Lakes Museum of Military History (ages 5 and up)

360 Dunes Plaza, West Highway 20; (219) 872–2702; www.militaryhistorymuseum.org; e-mail: militarymuseum@niia.net. Open Tuesday through Friday 9:00 A.M. to 4:00 P.M., Saturday 10:00 A.M. to 4:00 P.M., and Sunday noon to 4:00 P.M. Closed Monday. Admission $. Free for children 7 and under.

Displays of military memorabilia from all eras, including military vehicles and armament, uniforms, photos, edged weapons, posters, medals, firearms, research library, and more.

Lange's Old-Fashioned Meat Market (all ages)

218 West Seventh Street; (219) 874–0071. Open March through December, Tuesday through Saturday 9:00 A.M. to 6:00 P.M. and Sunday 10:00 A.M. to 4:00 P.M. Closed January and February. Free.

Tasty homemade sausages, ham, smoked turkey, U.S.D.A. prime steaks, beef sticks, and more. Yesteryear atmosphere, sawdust on the floor, and a character behind the counter.

Art Festival (all ages)

Washington Park, Lake Front in Michigan City; (219) 874–4900 or (800) 634–2650. Held in August.

More than 125 artists from more than fifteen states participate, with displays and art items of all kinds for sale.

Red Arrow Equestrian Center (ages 8 and up)

3848 Academy Road; (219) 872–2114. Trails are open May through October 9:30 A.M. to 5:30 P.M. Winter hours are 9:00 A.M. to 4:00 P.M. Lessons are by appointment. $$.

Do you want a horseback riding adventure? You will be able to enjoy riding on wooded trails, hayrides, and lessons in hunt- or western-style riding for a fee.

The Royal Acres Equestrian Center (ages 5 and up)

9375 West 300 North; (219) 874–7519. Open Sunday through Saturday 9:00 A.M. to 6:00 P.M. Free.

The most modern, technologically advanced stable in the Midwest. Set on forty-six acres; specializing in English riding lessons, boarding, training, and sales. Visitors welcome.

Barker Mansion (ages 5 and up)

631 Washington Street; (219) 873–1520. Guided tours are conducted at 10:00 A.M., 11:30 A.M., and 1:00 P.M. Monday through Friday between June and October. Closed holidays. There are also tours on weekends at noon and 2:00 P.M. Admission $. Free for children 3 and under.

This thirty-eight-room mansion is the former estate of John H. Barker, a founder of a railroad car company. The home has a mirrored ballroom, hand-carved marble fireplaces, and many works of art. During the month of December, there is a special Christmas celebration at the mansion.

Don't leave Michigan City without going on the Historic Barker Area Walking Tour. The tour will take you by eleven places of interest in the city including the Lighthouse Place Mall, the Barker Mansion, Top Dog, and the 5th Street Deli.

Michigan City Mainstreet Farmers Market (all ages)

Eighth and Washington Streets; (800) 634–2650. Open 8:30 A.M. to 1:30 P.M. May through October. Free.

A recent tradition on Saturday mornings. Local farmers bring their own vegetables, fruits, flowers, jams, and arts and crafts. Also enjoy a not-for-profit bake sale.

Where to Eat

Top Dog Restaurant. Seventh and Washington Streets; (219) 874–3647. Open seven days a week 10:30 A.M. to 3:00 P.M. Have you ever had a "Chicago Dog"? This means enjoying a hot dog nestled in a poppy seed bun with (piled on in this order) yellow mustard, bright green relish, freshly chopped onion, garden fresh tomato wedges, and a kosher dill pickle spear. Hamburgers and roasted chicken also available.

5th Street Deli. 431 Washington Street; (219) 872–5204. Do you enjoy a good sandwich? This deli offers delicious gourmet specialty sandwiches and hamburgers, homemade soup, and scrumptious desserts. You can eat in or carry the food out if you want to enjoy a picnic on the beach. Open Monday through Saturday 10:00 A.M. to 8:00 P.M., Sunday 11:00 A.M. to 6:00 P.M. in the summer with shorter hours in the fall and winter.

Ye Olde Benny's. Highway 12 at Karwick Road; (219) 874–3663. Italian specialties with an American flair. Families welcome. Seven days a week 11:30 A.M. till 1:00 A.M.

Swingbelly's. 100 Washington Street; (219) 874–5718. Family-style restaurant with sandwiches, all-you-can-eat crab legs on Wednesday nights, fresh perch on Friday.

Where to Stay

The Creekwood Inn. At Routes 20 and 35 at I–94; (219) 872–8357. If you're planning to be in the area for several days, you may wish to stay in a country home nestled in thirty acres of trees that offers a slower pace for a getaway stay. This small inn has twelve large rooms, lawn croquet, and bicycles available for guests.

Hampton Inn of Michigan City. 4128 South Franklin Street; (219) 879–9994. Five miles south of Lake Michigan, this hotel offers complimentary continental breakfast buffet, cribs, and an outdoor (heated) pool. Pets are not allowed. There are 107 rooms and two floors.

Holiday Inn Executive Conference Center. 5820 South Franklin Street; (219) 879–0311. Whirlpool, indoor pool, and suites available.

Knights Inn. 201 West Kieffer Road; (219) 874–9500. One hundred three rooms, one floor, outdoor pool, complimentary coffee in the morning, weekly rates, and kitchenettes available.

Golden Sands Motel. 4411 East U.S. Highway 12; (219) 874–6253. Thirty-one rooms with daily or weekly rates. Pets are allowed with a deposit.

Camping

Indiana Dunes National Lakeshore Dunewood Campground. U.S. 12 and Broadway; (219) 926–7561. Seventy-nine RV and tent campsites, showers and rest rooms available, handicapped accessible. Open April 1 through October 31.

For More Information

LaPorte County Convention and Visitors Bureau. 1503 South Meer Road; (800) 634–2650; www.laportecountycvb.com; www.michigancity.com.

LaPorte

With its beautiful maple trees lining its streets, LaPorte is often referred to as the "Maple City," and it is known as an antiques mecca, with three antiques malls and numerous antiques stores and shops. LaPorte serves as the LaPorte County seat, and the downtown is a historic district with preserved Victorian storefronts.

Door Prairie Auto Museum (ages 5 and up)

2405 Indiana Avenue; (219) 326–1337. Hours are Tuesday through Saturday 10:00 A.M. to 4:30 P.M.; Sunday noon to 4:30 P.M. Admission $. Free for children ages 9 and younger.

You and your family will be able to enjoy seeing classic automobiles, airplanes, antique toys, and historic facades spanning a hundred years of automotive history.

Hesston Steam Museum (all ages)

1000 North; (219) 872–7405. Open weekends, noon to 5:00 P.M. from Memorial Day through Labor Day. Admission free, except Labor Day weekend.

Three gauges of steam trains give rides around 155 wooded acres. Steam crane, sawmill, traction engines, power plant, and more. Free parking.

LaPorte County Historical Society Museum (ages 5 and up)

809 State Street; (219) 326–6808, ext. 276. Open Tuesday through Saturday 10:00 A.M. to 4:30 P.M. Free.

With more than 80,000 items on display, this museum houses LaPorte County family heirlooms and the W. A. Jones collection of antique firearms and weapons.

Quail Ridge Farm (all ages)

3382 East 1000 North; (219) 778–2194. Open 9:00 A.M. to 5:00 P.M. seven days a week, May 1 through October 31. Admission free.

Thousands of perennials and herb plants, display gardens, and an unusual gift shop. Quail Ridge has been designated an "Indiana Hidden Treasure"!

Whispering Winds Carriage Service (all ages)

2898 West 450 North; (219) 326–9147.

Make your special occasion even more memorable with a unique horse-drawn carriage ride. Carriage services offer unlimited use and are great for scenic tour rides, lunch and dinner packages, and weddings.

Willson's Nursery and Landscape (all ages)
2602 East Highway 2; (219) 362–8169. Open 8:00 A.M. to 5:00 P.M. seven days a week. Free.

Two hundred acres of unusual and rare landscape plants and supplies. Certified landscape architects to assist with residential or commercial projects. Garden center to pick and choose plants.

LaPorte City Parks (all ages)
250 Pine Lake Avenue; (219) 326–9600. Each of the eighteen parks is open from sunrise until 10:00 P.M. Call or visit park headquarters for information.

Whether you enjoy baseball, softball, golfing, or sunbathing, the LaPorte City Parks offer a variety of activities for people of all ages and interests.

Soldiers Memorial Park (all ages)
Grangemouth Road and Waverly Road. Open from sunrise to 10:00 P.M.

This sixty-acre scenic park hugs Stone Lake and borders Pine Lake, the city's largest. A favorite for picnics, hiking, and fishing, Soldiers Memorial Park is also a perfect spot to view the many water sports that take place throughout the year, as well as some breathtaking sunsets.

LaPorte County Parks (all ages)
County Complex, State and Michigan; (219) 325–8315, ext. 223.

The LaPorte County Parks are made up of three parks: Bluhum, Creek Ridge, and Luhr.

Bluhum County Park (all ages)
3855 South 1100 West Westville.

The colorful acres of the Bluhum County Park offer opportunities for your family to enjoy walking the miles of trails that wind through the park. Your family can enjoy biking, hiking, or horseback riding, and in the winter, cross-country skiing.

Creek Ridge Park
7943 West 400 North.

Creek Ridge encompasses seventy-seven acres and is located just south of Michigan City. A series of accessible boardwalks allows all visitors a chance to experience the entire trail system. This property is host to deer, fox, raccoons, and rabbits that live in the park's open-field prairies, wetlands, and hardwood forests. An annual steelhead migration also occurs along Trail Creek. The park offers picnicking, shelter rentals, rest rooms, playground equipment, volleyball nets, horseshoe pits, and fishing on Trail Creek.

Luhr County Park and Nature Center (all ages)
3176 South 150 West; (219) 324–5855.

Just south of LaPorte, Luhr County Park boasts a unique marshland boardwalk, wood-chipped nature trails, cozy picnic areas, and a fishing pond. Children and adults of all ages are fascinated by the educational displays and wildlife windows of live creatures at the Nature Center.

Where to Eat

Roskoe's. 1004 Lakeside Street; (219) 325–3880. This is the place for fun entertainment. Choose from the lunch or dinner menu; you can view picturesque Pine Lake on the outdoor patio during the summer months. Well-known for its prime rib and barbecued ribs. Children's menu available. Open Monday through Saturday 11:00 A.M. to 9:00 P.M. Closed most major holidays.

B & J American Café. 607 Lincolnway; (219) 362–3474. Home-cooked breakfasts and lunches in an authentic 1940's decor cafe. Enjoy swing-era music and movie memories. Open 5:30 A.M. to 2:00 P.M. daily, Sunday 7:00 A.M. to 2:00 P.M.

Where to Stay

Holiday Inn Express. 100 East Shore Court; (219) 326–7900.

LaPorte Super 8 Motel. 438 Pine Lake Avenue; (219) 325–3808. Fifty-one rooms (including handicapped accessible).

Pine Lake Hotel & Conference Center. 444 Pine Lake Avenue; (219) 326–4585, (800) 575–3880. A flotilla of staterooms and cabins that offers an adventure in lodging. These boathouses, with private decks, are sure to make your stay a true adventure. Pontoon rentals and seasonal dock space available.

The Blue Heron Inn. 1010 Lakeside; (800) 575–3880. A fourteen-room, European-style inn offering comfort and luxury. Each lakeview room boasts hot tubs for two, fireplaces, private baths, and outside decks and patios. Most rooms are outfitted with dataports and large desks. No pets allowed. Call ahead to be sure family rooms are available.

For More Information

LaPorte County Convention and Visitors Bureau. 1503 South Meer Road; (800) 685–7174; www.laportecountycvb.com.

Chesterton

Chesterton is a quaint town. When you are in the Old Downtown area located at Calumet Road and Broadway, you will see many unique businesses that are housed in renovated buildings restored nearly to their original appearances. You may wish to visit St. Pat's Church, which is now a historical landmark. Stop at the public library at 200 West Indiana Avenue to get information on taking a historic walking tour through the town, or call (800) 283–8687.

Chesterton Art Gallery (all ages) 🔲

115 South Fourth Street; (219) 926–4711. Open weekdays 11:00 A.M. to 4:00 P.M., weekends 1:00 to 4:00 P.M. Free.

At this gallery in a renovated machine shop you will see the work of more than one hundred different area artists. For further information about demonstrations, workshops, or classes call the gallery.

The Yellow Brick Road Gift Shop and Oz Museum (all ages) 🔲

109 East 950 North; (219) 926–7048; www.yellowbrickroadonline.com. Open Tuesday through Saturday from 10:00 A.M. to 5:00 P.M. and Sunday 11:00 A.M. to 4:00 P.M.

Learn more about Dorothy, Toto, and the Wizard at this museum featuring memorabilia donated by cast members or their heirs from the MGM movie *The Wizard of Oz.* There is a modest admission charge.

All-Steel Historic Home (all ages) 🏛

411 Bowser Avenue; (219) 926–3669. Open May 1 through October 31, Tuesday through Sunday 1:00 to 5:00 P.M. or other times by appointment. Call for more information. Free.

In the late 1940s, houses of this type, known as the Lustron home, were made entirely of porcelain enameled steel. All the parts, more than 3,000, were produced on an assembly line and then shipped to a site where the home was erected. The idea was to produce affordable housing for returning World War II veterans. The interior and exterior design reflected the trend of 1930s architecture toward mirroring the transportation industry by emphasizing a sleek, smooth, streamlined style. One of the unique features of this home is all the built-in steel furniture, from kitchen cabinets to a bedroom storage unit. To top it all off, the most appealing aspect of this house may be that you only need to wipe it off with a damp cloth to keep it clean!

Where to Eat

Duneland Pizza. 520 Broadway; (219) 926–1163.

Northside Diner. 100 North Calumet Road in downtown Chesterton; (219) 926–9040. Open 5:00 A.M. to 4:00 P.M. Monday through Saturday; 5:00 A.M. to 2:00 P.M. Sunday. Serving customers just like family since 1934. An authentic fifties and sixties diner serving a variety of breakfast and lunch meals, not to mention homemade pies baked fresh daily!

Port Drive-In. 419 North Calumet; (219) 926–3500. Seasonal. Chili dogs, homemade root beer, and car hops.

Where to Stay

Econo Lodge. 713 Plaza Drive (State Road 49 and Indian Boundary Road); (219) 929–4416. To get to the hotel from I–94, take exit 26A to U.S. 49 South, turn right at the first traffic light. To get there from 80/90 Toll Road, take U.S. 49 North, and the hotel will be on your left at the third traffic light.

Indian Oak Resort & Spa. 558 Indian Boundary Road; (219) 926–2200, (800) 552–4232; www.indianoak.com. One hundred guest rooms, complimentary continental breakfast, indoor pool and fitness center, no pets allowed. Call ahead to get seasonal rates.

Super 8 Motel. 418 Council Drive; (219) 929–5549. Free coffee and donuts in the morning, handicapped accessible rooms, cribs available.

Camping

Sandcreek Campground. 1000 North County Road 350 East; (219) 926–7482. The 99 RV and tent sites are open April 15 through October 15. Pets allowed.

Indiana **Trivia**

What Indiana University has had a marching band in continual existence since 1845?

Where were the Jackson Five born?

Notre Dame, Gary

Porter

Indiana Dunes National Lakeshore and State Park (all ages)

🏨 🏕️ 🎣

1100 North Mineral Springs Road; (219) 926–7561, ext. 225.

Does your family like the beach? Then pack the car with your favorite picnic foods and head to the Indiana Dunes, on the shore of Lake Michigan. Here your family will enjoy the sights and sounds. You will have fun slipping and sliding as you clamber over the dunes, which move back several feet from the lake each year. The largest dune is more than 120 feet high. Also in the beautiful 15,000-acre park is a nature center where you can learn more about the lakeshore's plant and animal life. For hikers there are more than 30 miles of trails. You can also enjoy camping, swimming, and fishing, as well as cross-country skiing in the winter.

Where to Eat

Buck Horn Family Restaurant/Truck Stop. 1600 West U.S. 20; (219) 926–8566. Weekend breakfast buffet, kids ages 10 and under eat **free.** Open twenty-four hours.

Santiago's Mexican Restaurant. 124 Lincoln Street; (219) 926–6518. Authentic Mexican food. Open Sunday through Thursday 11:00 A.M. to 9:00 P.M., Friday and Saturday 11:00 A.M. to 10:00 P.M. Closed major holidays.

A Gisler **Adventure**

If we are heading toward the northern part of the state, we always throw our swimsuits, towels, suntan lotion, and a picnic lunch in the car in hopes it will be sunny and warm enough to head for the beaches at Indiana Dunes National Lakeshore and State Park. The park holds various types of activities that fit the needs of everyone in the family. In the warmer months, we like to hike through the park's ten trails, ranging from easy to difficult, and then sit down at one of the many picnic sites and have lunch. Then we slip and slide as we try to tackle the more than 100-foot-tall sand dunes that surround Lake Michigan. Once along the shore of Lake Michigan, we get a family game of soccer or kickball going before taking a dive into the brisk waters of the lake.

Where to Stay

Spring House Inn. 303 North Mineral Springs Road; (219) 929–4600, (800) 366–4661. Fifty rooms, breakfast included in rate, indoor pool, whirlpool, sauna, and exercise room. No pets allowed.

For More Information

Porter County Convention, Recreation, and Visitors Commission. (800) 283–8687 or www.casualcoast.com.

Merrillville

Deep River Waterpark (all ages) 🎢
4½ miles east of I–65 on U.S. 30; (800) 928–7275. $$$.

Great water fun for the entire family. Some of the special features are body slides, wave pool, and a playland for kids.

Merrillville Community Planetarium (all ages)
At Pierce Middle School, 199 East Seventieth Street; (219) 650–5486. Open 7:30 A.M. to 3:30 P.M. on school days or by appointment. Admission $. Reservations recommended.

Visiting one of the finest planetarium facilities in the state is a great way for children to learn more about the stars, planets, and galaxies. This is a unique theater for presenting programs on astronomy and space to groups of children or the entire family.

The Celebration Station (all ages) 🎢
8121 Georgia Street; (219) 769–7672. Open Monday through Thursday 4:00 to 9:00 P.M., Friday and Saturday 11:00 A.M. to 11:00 P.M., and Sunday noon to 9:00 P.M.

A family fun center. Here your family can enjoy a thirty-six-hole miniature golf course, kiddie and adult go-carts, batting cages, and carnival game midways. But that's not all: There's a pizza parlor themed with animation.

Where to Eat

Joe's Crab Shack. 2757 East 80th Avenue; (219) 942–4554. Lots of fun and food. Kid's menu available.

J. Gingers. I–65 and U.S. 30; (219) 769–6311. American, seafood menu. Serves breakfast, lunch, and dinner.

Baker's Square Restaurant and Pies. 1675 U.S. 41; (219) 322–0027. Serves breakfast, lunch, and dinner.

Where to Stay

Comfort Inn. 1915 Mississippi Street (I–65 exit 255 and Sixty-first Avenue); (219) 947–7677, (800) 228–5150. Indoor pool/spa. Complimentary breakfast. Complete cable with HBO. Spa suites and presidential suite. Nonsmoking and wheelchair-accessible rooms available.

Fairfield Inn. 8275 Georgia Street (I–65 and U.S. 30); (219) 736–0500. Deluxe complimentary continental breakfast. Free local telephone calls, cable television with HBO, and indoor pool.

La Quinta Inn. 8210 Louisiana (I–65 and U.S. 30); (219) 738–2870, (800) 531–5900. Free deluxe continental breakfast with cereal, fruit, bagels, pastries, and more. Free local calls. Located across from Southlake Mall. AAA and AARP rates are available.

For More Information

Lake County Convention and Visitors Bureau. 7770 Corinne Drive, Hammond; (800) ALL–LAKE; www.alllake.org.

Hobart

Wood's Historic Grist Mill (all ages) 🏛

9410 Old Lincoln Highway in Deep River County Park; (219) 947–1958. Open daily May through October 10:00 A.M. to 5:00 P.M. **Free.**

Here is a restored mill where you can actually see grain being ground. After watching the grinding of the grain on the first floor, you view typical room settings of the late 1800s on the second floor. The third floor is filled with various rotating exhibits. Your family will also want to take a walk around the beautiful grounds of the mill. Surrounding the gristmill is a Victorian gazebo, gardens, brick walkways, and an 1830s sawmill. This family outing will be one that everyone remembers.

Hobart Historical Society Museum (ages 5 and up) 🏛

706 East Fourth Street; (219) 942–0970. Open Saturday 10:00 A.M. to 3:00 P.M. **Free.**

While in Hobart you can continue learning more about the past at this archive, library, and museum of local history in this 1914 Carnegie building, which is a National Historic Landmark. Andrew Carnegie donated the money for libraries across the country.

For More Information

Hobart Chamber of Commerce. 18 West Thirty-seventh Avenue; (219) 942–5774; www.hobartchamber.com.

San Pierre

When your family visits **Lomax Station** on Toto Road in San Pierre, everyone will enjoy a quiet country getaway at this historic railroad and pipeline town. There is always something happening at the station, from special events to line dancing, fishing, and hiking. You can stay in cabins with bedrooms and sleeping lofts, fireplaces, and kitchenettes that guarantee your privacy. You will also enjoy the home cooking at **Jeanie's Diner.** Call (800) 53–LOMAX for information and reservations.

Crown Point

If you are in the historic community of Crown Point, you should take a look at **The Grand Old Lady,** the courthouse that was built in 1878. This is the courthouse where celebrities such as Ronald Reagan, Muhammad Ali, and Rudolph Valentino received their marriage licenses. There are shops around the courthouse where you can browse, and you can sample a Sheik ice-cream delight at **Valentino's.** The square around the courthouse has even more shops and ethnic restaurants. If you like festivals, visit the town during the **Hometown Square Festival** in June or the **Octoberfest** held at the Lake County Fairgrounds.

For More Information

For more information about the town of Crown Point and its festivals, call (219) 663–1800 or visit www.crownpoint.net.

Valparaiso

Porter County Historical Society Old Jail Museum (all ages) 🏛
152 South Franklin Street; (219) 465–3595. Open Sunday, Wednesday, and Saturday 1:00 to 4:00 P.M. **Free.**

Here's your chance to visit a jail—only it's not a jail now. The museum has many different artifacts from the area, and a visit will foster your children's interest in the past. There is a World War II monument, intricate artwork known as pectoral marquetry, souvenirs from the Wild West donated by Bronco John (Buffalo Bill's partner), and dresses worn at Abraham Lincoln's inaugural ball. Call to learn more about this unique museum.

Where to Eat

Valpo Velvet Shoppe. 55 West Monroe; (219) 464–4141. Valpo Velvet ice cream, homemade soups, and salads.

Dawn's Diner. 1717 Calumet Avenue; (219) 531–0606. Family-style dining, all-you-can-eat fish dinner on Friday from 3:30 to 7:30 P.M. Children's menu available. Open Monday through Saturday 6:30 A.M. to 2:30 P.M., closed Sunday.

Suzie's Cafe & Catering. 657 South Washington; (219) 462–5500. Homemade bread, cinnamon rolls, soup, and specials. Open Monday through Wednesday and Saturday 5:00 A.M. to 3:00 P.M., Thursday and Friday 5:00 A.M. to 9:00 P.M. Live music on Friday.

Where to Stay

Courtyard by Marriott. 2301 East Morthland (U.S. 30); (219) 465–1700; www .courtyard.com. From I–65 take the exit for U.S. 30 East/Valparaiso. Follow approximately 14 miles to Valparaiso. Courtyard is on the left. Heated indoor/outdoor pool, restaurant open for breakfast.

Fairfield Inn. 2101 East Morthland (U.S. 30); (219) 465–6225, (800) 228–2800; www.marriott.com/fairfieldinn. From westbound 80/94, take the exit for State Road 49 South off U.S. 30 West. Turn right at first light, then left. Hotel is on the right. Complimentary continental breakfast, indoor pool, exercise room, guest laundry.

Super 8. 3005 John Howell Drive; (219) 464–9840; www.super8.com. Continental breakfast and indoor pool.

North Liberty

Potato Creek State Park (all ages) 🏕️ 🚴 🥾 ⚓

25601 State Road 4 in North Liberty; (574) 656–8186. Open daily year-round 7:00 A.M. to 11:00 P.M. Admission $.

State parks are always fun for a family outing, and this one is an excellent place to take out those bicycles and ride. The park has miles of bicycle and bridle trails, including easy trails for beginners and more advanced trails for those liking a challenge. You'll also find the usual park offerings, such as camping, hiking, fishing, and picnicking, in addition to a nature center with a full-time staff to answer any questions your family might have. In the winter the park offers activities like cross-country skiing and ice fishing.

South Bend

University of Notre Dame (all ages)
U.S. 31/33; (574) 631–5726; www.nd.edu. Free tours in summer. Call for schedule.

One of the most beautiful college campuses in the country. Are you interested in college football? Do you have a teenager who is looking for a college to attend? Or are you just interested in seeing one of the most intriguing college campuses in the country? A tour of this historic campus is a must when in South Bend. Visit the famous football stadium, the Golden Dome, Sacred Heart Church, and Snite Museum of Art.

College Football Hall of Fame (ages 5 and up)
111 South Saint Joseph Street; (800) 440–FAME; www.collegefootball.org. Open year-round 10:00 A.M. to 5:00 P.M. Closed Thanksgiving, Christmas, and New Year's Day. Admission $$. Children under 5 are free. Group rates and yearly passes are available. Call for details.

Visitors feel like they are part of the action when they tour the Hall's 360 degree stadium theater and training center. You will be able to make these football heroes come alive for your children through photo galleries, memorabilia, and the hall of champions.

Copshaholm (ages 10 and up)
808 West Washington; (574) 235–9664. Open Tuesday through Saturday 10:00 A.M. to 5:00 P.M. and Sunday noon to 5:00 P.M. Admission $.

Copshaholm is a unique mansion built in 1895 by Joseph Doty Oliver. The Oliver family were the founders of the Oliver Chilled Plow Company, a major international manufacturer of farm implements and equipment. You will be dazzled by the beauty of the furnishings, which are original to the thirty-eight-room mansion and range from the mid-seventeenth to the mid-twentieth century. The house, its two and a half acres of landscaped gardens, and carriage house are listed on the National Register of Historic Places.

Potawatomi Zoo (all ages)
500 South Greenlawn; (574) 235–9800. Open 10:00 A.M. to 5:00 P.M. April through October; 10:00 A.M. to 4:00 P.M. November. Closed December to March. Admission $. Children younger than 3 get in free.

See animals from around the world living in both indoor and outdoor naturalistic exhibits on more than twenty-two acres. Everyone in your family should find an animal that is fascinating. You can see how the animals are fed and what they enjoy eating plus attend all the daily shows.

Northern Indiana Center for History (ages 5 and up)
808 West Washington Street; (574) 235–9664. Open Tuesday through Saturday from 10:00 A.M. to 5:00 P.M., Sunday noon to 5:00 P.M. Admission $.

You and your family will be able to enjoy visiting Copshaholm, a Victorian mansion, and Worker's Home, a restored 1870s cottage. In the Voyages Gallery, you'll discover legends of the St. Joseph River Valley, from explorer Sieur de LaSalle to industrialist Joseph Oliver. Also enjoy the Kidsfirst Children's Museum, gift shop, and special exhibits.

Stanley Coveleski Regional Stadium (all ages)

501 West South Street; (574) 235–9988; www.silverhawks.com. Call for the game schedule and ticket information.

Take yourself out to the ball park to watch the South Bend White Sox play. Buy yourself some peanuts and Cracker Jacks as you watch this Class A franchise team of the Chicago White Sox. Between April and September the team plays seventy home games.

South Bend Motor Speedway (ages 5 and up)

25698 State Road; (574) 287–1704. Every Friday at 8:00 P.M. April through September; demolition derby Saturday at 7:00 P.M. $$.

Vroom! Vroom! Go out to the speedway and see auto stock racing, formula Indy cars, late-model stock cars, and IMCA modifieds. The Saturday demolition derby is a thrill.

East Race Waterway (ages 5 and up)

301 South St. Louis Boulevard; (574) 233–6121. Open June through mid-August Saturday noon to 5:00 P.M., and Sunday 1:00 to 5:00 P.M. Canoe or kayak on the course for a fee, or watch the action, even national and international races, for free.

You usually have to find a wild river to race through rapids. But believe it or not, you can have this thrill right in downtown South Bend on a 2,000-foot course of artificial white water!

Where to Eat

Tippecanoe Place Restaurant. 620 West Washington Street; (574) 234–9077. Reservations recommended. Monday through Friday lunch 11:00 A.M. to 1:30 P.M., dinner 5:00 to 10:00 P.M., Saturday dinner 4:00 to 10:30 P.M., Sunday brunch 9:00 A.M. to 1:30 P.M., dinner 4:00 to 8:30 P.M. Football home games reservations required. Dining in the traditional manner at Tippecanoe is a heritage handed down by the famous Studebaker family, who built the mansion a century ago. Located on historic West Washington, the restaurant revives the gracious spirit of the past. Its forty rooms are filled with fine antiques, massive fireplaces, and handcrafted woods. That special tradition can still be found in the casual elegance of Tippecanoe Place Restaurant. Its award-winning fare and beautiful interior will provide a feast for the palate and the eyes.

Honkers Restaurant. 3939 South Michigan Street; (574) 291–2115. Breakfast, lunch, and dinner. Family style dining featuring fresh-baked goods, slow-roasted roast beef, juicy pot roast, and made-from-scratch pancakes. Open 6:30 A.M. to 10:00 P.M. daily. Closed on Christmas.

Sorin's, University of Notre Dame. On the Notre Dame campus; (574) 631–2020. The terraced dining room offers the finest dining in the region. Enjoy the true spirit of Notre Dame. Breakfast, lunch, and dinner served daily. Open Monday through Saturday 7:00 A.M. to 8:30 P.M., Sunday 8:00 A.M. to 8:30 P.M.

Indiana **Trivia**

Where was the first metal clarinet made?

Where did Singer Sewing Machine open a factory in 1868?

Elkhart, South Bend

Notre Dame dining areas. (574) 631–6902. Enjoy the relaxed atmosphere of Greenfields' Cafe on Notre Dame Avenue or take a break at "The Huddle" food court in the LaFortune Student Center.

Siam Thai Restaurant. 211 North Main Street; (574) 232–4445. World-class Thai cuisine designed to excite your senses: sweet, sour, salty, spicy, and natural. Lunch Sunday to Friday 11:00 A.M. to 2:00 P.M., dinner Monday to Saturday 5:00 to 9:30 P.M.

Where to Stay

Hampton Inn & Suites. 52709 U.S. 31 North; (574) 277–9373; www.hampton inn.com. Choose from traditional guest rooms or fully equipped suites. Indoor pool and exercise room. **Free** continental breakfast served daily 6:00 to 10:00 A.M.

Holiday Inn–Downtown. 213 West Washington Street; (574) 232–3941; www.holiday inn.com. One hundred seventy-seven spacious guest rooms and suites located in downtown South Bend. Casual dining.

Holiday Inn–University Area. 515 Dixieway North; (574) 272–6600. Gipper's Cafe & Lounge depicts the Notre Dame 1988 football national championship.

The Inn at Saint Mary's. I–80/90 exit 77; (574) 232–4000; (800) 947–8627. One-hundred-fifty-room inn located at Saint Mary's College campus, adjacent to the University of Notre Dame. Large exercise facility with whirlpool and sauna; complimentary continental breakfast. No pets allowed.

Residence Inn. 716 North Niles Avenue; (574) 289–5555. All-suite hotel designed to accommodate long-term guests. Suites include fully equipped kitchen, large sitting area, and queen-size bed. Also included are complimentary breakfast and hospitality hour.

For More Information

South Bend/Mishawaka Convention and Visitors Bureau. 401 East Colfax Avenue; (800) 282–2330; www.ci.southbend.in.us or www.livethelegends.com.

Mishawaka

One of Indiana's fastest-growing communities, Mishawaka balances a variety of historical and cultural attractions with the region's most popular shopping area and quality dining establishments.

Hannah Lindahl Children's Museum (all ages)
1402 South Main Street; (574) 254–4540; www.hlcm.org. Open Tuesday through Friday 9:00 A.M. to 4:00 P.M. Admission $.

Everyone always has a good time here. This is a place where you can learn about the geologic history of the region from the glacial period to the early 1900s. You will discover how the glaciers transformed this area. Other displays change throughout the year, and there are special exhibits. Turn your children loose in the hands-on section so they can touch different surfaces that were affected by the glaciers.

Where to Eat

Friday's. 4730 North Grape Road; (574) 271–8443. Open Monday through Thursday 11:00 A.M. to midnight, Friday and Saturday 11:00 A.M. to 1:00 A.M., Sunday 11:00 A.M. to 11:00 P.M. Family fare with children's menu available.

Doc Pierce's. 120 North Main Street; (574) 255–7737. Steakhouse with a few chicken items. No children's menu. Open Monday through Saturday 11:00 A.M. to 2:00 P.M. for lunch, Monday through Thursday 4:30 to 9:30 P.M. for dinner, and Friday and Saturday 5:30 to 10:30 P.M. for dinner. Closed Sunday.

Honker's. 211 East Day Road; (574) 259–3000. For family dining, selections are virtually unlimited. Honker's, with another location in South Bend, is a popular choice.

Famous Dave's. 6402 North Grape Road; (574) 277–1888. Offers great barbecue and lots of fun.

Where to Stay

Fairfield Inn. 425 University Drive; (574) 273–2202. **Free** continental breakfast, indoor pool and spa; kids 18 and under stay **free.**

Hampton Inn. 455 University Drive; (574) 273–2309. One of the area's newer hotels, the Hampton Inn features a **free** deluxe continental breakfast and is just minutes from Notre Dame.

Courtyard by Marriott. 4825 Main Street; (574) 273–9900.

For More Information

South Bend/Mishawaka Convention and Visitors Bureau. 401 East Colfax Avenue, Suite 310; (800) 828–7881; www.livethelegends.org.

Wakarusa

You can feast on Amish cooking and have a ride on a train pulled by a steam engine before or after your meal at Come & Dine Restaurant and the Old Wakarusa Railroad (all ages). You'll find this unique combination of restaurant and railroad on State Road 19 in Wakarusa. The railroad runs from 11:00 A.M. to after dark on Monday through Saturday starting in April and continuing through October. Then in October, there are pumpkin trains that will take you to a pumpkin patch to select your pumpkin. In December there is a Winter Wonderland train. Before boarding the train, you can look at the antique tractor collection dating back to the early 1900s or visit the gift shop. For more information about the railroad and restaurant, phone (574) 862–2714. You can have even more fun in Wakarusa if you visit in late March for the **Maple Syrup Festival** or in September for the **Harvest Festival.** Call the Chamber of Commerce at (574) 862–4344 for more festival information or visit its Web site at www.wakarusachamber.com.

Where to Eat

Cook's Pizza. 101 South Elkhart Street; (574) 862–4425. Family restaurant pizza, sandwiches, ice cream, homemade soups, and salads. Carry-out pizza available. Open Monday 11:00 A.M. to 6:00 P.M., Tuesday through Thursday 11:00 A.M. to 10:00 P.M., Friday and Saturday 11:00 A.M. to 11:00 P.M., Sunday 4:00 to 10:00 P.M.

Deenene's. 106 South Elkhart Street; (574) 862–2765. Family restaurant lunch menu, appetizers, sandwiches, breakfast menu, beverages, and desserts. Open Monday through Thursday and Saturday 5:00 A.M. to 2:00 P.M., Friday 5:00 A.M. to 8:00 P.M., closed on Sunday.

Happy Days Cafe. 920 East Waterford Street; (574) 862–1952. Serving specialty sandwiches, daily lunch and dinner specials. Open Monday through Saturday 5:00 A.M. to 2:00 P.M., Thursday and Friday 4:30 to 8:30 P.M.

Where to Stay

Shamrock Inn. 1501 East Market Street; (574) 773–3193. Direct-dial phones. **Free** HBO and ESPN. Nearby restaurants. Located 1½ miles from Amish Acres.

The Homespun Country Inn. State Road 19; (800) 311–2996; www.homespun inn.com. Historic Queen Anne–style home. Offers special occasion packages. Enjoy Homespun hospitality.

The Nappanee Inn. Highway 6 West; (800) 800–4942. Sixty-six rooms, patterned quilts, oak furniture, continental breakfast buffet included. Breathtaking countryside views from guest rooms. Outdoor pool in private courtyard. Packages available with activities. AAA 3-Diamond rated. Located ¼ mile west of Amish Acres.

Goshen

Goshen, the Elkhart county seat, is a picturesque city that your whole family will enjoy visiting. The Goshen Chamber of Commerce is located at 232 South Main Street; (800) 307–4204; www.goshen.org; e-mail: goshence@tln.net.

Did you know why Goshen is called the "Maple City"? Because there are so many leafy maple trees along the Elkhart River. Remember to bring everyone's bicycle or good hiking shoes so you will be able to enjoy the new network of bicycle and hiking trails that have recently been built to connect residential neighborhoods, schools, parks, the library, and the downtown area. A pedestrian/bicycle bridge lets you cross the Elkhart River without using the busy automobile bridge. The trails cover 13½ miles in the heart of Goshen. This project earned Goshen the name "Bicycle Friendly Community," a title awarded to the city by the Indiana Bicycle Coalition.

The Old Bag Factory (all ages)

1100 Chicago Avenue; (574) 534–2502; www.oldbagfactory.com. Open Monday through Friday 9:00 A.M. to 5:00 P.M., Saturday 9:00 A.M. to 4:00 P.M. Free.

A collection of interesting stores, The Old Bag Factory is housed in a building that started out as a place for making soap and then became a bag manufacturing plant. The building was constructed to house the Cosmo Buttermilk Soap company in 1895. It was purchased by Larion and Nancy Swartzendruber in 1984 and the change has been remarkable, although its historical character has been preserved. The Old Bag Factory is filled with stores that will intrigue the entire family. There are shops featuring stained-glass windows, handcrafted furniture, pottery, everlasting flowers, quilts, posters, prints, and artwork.

Where to Eat

Goshen Inn and Conference Center.
1375 Lincolnway East; (574) 533–9551.
Delicious breakfast, lunch, and dinner.
Weekend buffets and Sunday brunch.

Town Haus Family Restaurant. U.S. 33;
(574) 534–1004. Reasonably priced casual
dining, senior meals, famous breakfast
buffet. Open Sunday through Thursday
5:30 A.M. to 11:00 P.M., Friday and Saturday open twenty-four hours. Closed
Thanksgiving and Christmas and usually
closed the first week in August, so be sure
to call ahead.

Bread & Chocolate. 119 South Main
Street; (574) 534–3053. Unique European-
style cafe. Variety of entrees, salads,
soups; specialty desserts and gourmet coffee made fresh daily. Open Monday
through Saturday 8:00 A.M. to 2:00 P.M.
Closed Sunday.

Where to Stay

Goshen Inn and Conference Center.
1375 Lincolnway East (U.S. 33); (888)
2GOSHEN; www.gosheninn.com. Staying
here will be a family vacation in itself. Everyone will be able to enjoy the Family Fun

Dome, which is the center of fun and
games, with an Olympic-sized indoor swimming pool. After swimming, adults can
enjoy the whirlpool and sauna or even get
some sun under the sunlamps. If you would
like to work on your golf game, you can use
the putting green or even challenge a family
member to a game of Ping-Pong. There are
211 beautifully appointed guest rooms and
delicious restaurant dining.

Best Western Inn. 900 Lincoln Way, on U.S.
33; (574) 533–0408; www.bestwestern.com.
Here your family will be able to experience
heartland hospitality fifteen minutes south
of I–80/90. There are 77 rooms; complimentary coffee and Danish.

Courtyard by Marriott. 1930 Lincoln
Way East on U.S. 33; (574) 534–3133;
www.marriott.com. Courtyard guests
enjoy clean, comfortable guest rooms in a
home-style atmosphere. The Courtyard
Cafe serves a hot breakfast buffet daily.
Spa suites, exercise room, indoor/outdoor
pool, in-room coffee.

For More Information

**Elkhart County Convention and Visi-
tors Bureau.** (800) 250–4827; www.amish
country.org.

Indiana **Trivia**

What NBA team did Vince Boryla play on between 1950 and 1954?

Where was Major League Baseball's pitcher Don Larsen born?

New York Knicks, Michigan City

Middlebury

Das Dutchman Essenhaus (all ages) 🏨 🍴 ⊖
240 U.S. 20; (574) 825–9471; www.essenhaus.com. **Summer shop hours 9:00 A.M. to 7:00 P.M. Monday through Thursday and to 8:00 P.M. on Friday and Saturday. Shops closed Sunday; winter hours vary. Restaurant hours are Monday through Thursday 6:00 A.M. to 8:00 P.M., Friday and Saturday 6:00 A.M. to 9:00 P.M. Closed Sunday.**

Here your family will be able to enjoy the total Amish heritage and tradition because visiting Das Dutchman Essenhaus is an opportunity to experience Amish country living. You can try the home-style cooking at the Amish Country Kitchen, where you'll sample such robust food as roast beef, roasted chicken, bread dressing, and real mashed potatoes with brown gravy. Stroll around the more than one hundred beautiful acres, take a buggy ride along the trails, visit the bakery, try your hand at making a craft you can keep, watch a weaver at work, and visit one of the many shops. If you want to spend the evening, you can elect to stay at the Essenhaus Country Inn (800–455–9471), a step back to a time when life's pace was slower. Or you may stay at the smaller Dawdy Haus Inn (800–455–9471), which is the name used for a grandparent house on Amish farms. Reservations are recommended three to six months in advance, especially in the summertime when the Shipshewana flea market is occurring.

Where to Eat

Village Inn. 107 Main Street; (574) 825–2043. "Where local people meet and eat." Home cooking, fresh-baked pies, breakfast and lunch specials. Open Monday through Friday 5:00 A.M. to 8:00 P.M., Saturday 5:00 A.M. to 2:00 P.M. Closed Sunday.

Where to Stay

Country Victorian Bed & Breakfast. 435 South Main Street; (800) 262–7829. Beautifully restored Victorian home with elegant decor. Five rooms with private baths. Master suite with whirlpool. Air-conditioned. AAA approved.

Camping

Middlebury KOA Campgrounds. 52867 State Road 13; (574) 825–5932. Heated pool, hiking trails, putt-putt, and Kamping Kabins.

Shipshewana

Menno-Hof Mennonite Visitors Center (all ages)

510 South Van Buren Street (State Road 5), north of the intersection of U.S. 20; (260) 768–4117; www.mennohof.org; e-mail: timlichti@tln.net. Open 10:00 A.M. to 5:00 P.M. Monday and Wednesday through Saturday; 10:00 A.M. to 7:00 P.M. Tuesday. Admission $.

When you step inside Menno-Hof, a barn erected by Amish builders, you will begin a journey that will teach you about the history and practices of the Mennonites and the Amish. You will learn the reasons behind the Amish lifestyle. You will get the experience of being locked in a dungeon just like the ones where thousands of men and women were imprisoned for their beliefs, and squeezed into the cramped bowels of a sailing ship that brought Mennonites and Amish to North America. Children are invited to play in a loft stocked with toys that Amish and Mennonite children would have played with. The museum is divided into twenty-four display areas that chronicle the history. The tour begins with a fifteen-minute multiprojector introduction to the Anabaptists. Throughout the entire museum, interactive displays, videos, multimedia presentations, and moving testimonies will help history come alive for you, and then you can conclude your visit in the hush of a meeting-house and witness the quiet faith that still sustains these people of peace.

Riegsecker Marketplace (all ages)

State Road 5 North at the four-way stop in Shipshewana; (260) 768–4725; www.riegsecker .com. Open 9:00 A.M. to 8:00 P.M. Monday through Saturday, closed Sunday. Free.

The Amish have a reputation for a high standard of craftsmanship. You can visit a variety of shops: furniture, country decor, toys, dolls, crafts, baked goods, glass, clothes, brass and copper, and eighty different craft booths. Also, while you are at the marketplace, you can take a buggy or carriage ride through the streets of Shipshewana. Put your name in at the Blue Gate Restaurant in the Riegsecker Marketplace and you'll be paged when your table is ready, or you can stop for just a cup of coffee and a luscious homemade pastry or dessert.

Where to Stay

Shipshewana Amish Log Cabin Lodging. State Road 5 at State Road 120; (260) 768–7770; www.amish.org. Every family will enjoy a peaceful stay in a hand-built Amish cabin nestled in the whispering pines. The full-service cabins are decorated with quilted comforters, lacy curtains, and handmade furniture; on the porch you'll find an old-fashioned porch swing. Modern amenities include private bath, color television, air-conditioning, and continental breakfast. The cabins are perfect for family getaways. Pets are not allowed.

Remember to stroll the grounds and visit the **Shipshewana Custard Company,** where you can enjoy a frozen custard, ice cream, or banana split under the shade or twinkling night lights of the gazebo.

Also part of the Log Cabin Lodging is the **Shipshewana Campground,** which is adjacent to Amish Log Cabins and rounds out this blend of lodging options. Featuring clean, modern facilities with water, sewer, and electric service, the campground is home away from home to visitors from all over the world. The native oak pavilion and Florida Room provide guests with nice places to mix and mingle.

Country Inn & Suites. 3440 North State Road 5; (260) 768–7780. Beautifully Victorian, elegantly decorated, and tastefully furnished suites welcome you to Shipshewana. Close to shopping/flea market. Forty-four rooms. Complimentary fresh-baked pastries for breakfast. Indoor pool. Children under 18 stay free with adult.

The Farmstead Inn. 370 South Van Buren Street, across from Shipshewana Flea Market/Auction; (260) 768–4595. Beautiful, new, charming country inn. Three-story atrium with six fireplaces. Eighty-five spacious rooms and suites, indoor pool, kiddie pool, playland, game room, continental breakfast. No pets allowed.

For More Information

LaGrange County Convention and Visitors Bureau. 4401/2 Van Buren Street; (800) 254–8090; www.backroads.org.

Nappanee

Amish Acres (all ages) 🏛 🍽 ⊖ 🎵

1600 West Market Street; (574) 773–4188 or (800) 800–4942; www.amishacres.com. Hours vary with the seasons. Call for times. Fees vary with attraction.

Amish Acres is a truly fantastic place for the family to spend a whole day or have an overnight stay. Here you can see a way of life that the rest of the United States has left behind, as you become acquainted with the simple world of the Amish. By the time your visit to this eighty-acre farm with eighteen restored buildings is complete, you and your family will appreciate the ways of the Amish.

Step inside the farmhouse to see original family furnishings; then visit the barn and outbuildings. While walking around the grounds, you can explore the tools and the trappings of yesterday. Depending on the time of year, you may see tapping for maple syrup, a horse-pulled plow turning the soil, fruit being dried, or the making of apple butter. You can watch demonstrations of traditional crafts, such as making lye soap and brooms, rug weaving, quilting, and candle dipping. After all this walking around, you can take an old-time buggy ride down the lane and see the woods and people working in the fields. Or you can hop aboard a tour bus and see the Amish farms in the community. Before your day is over, you will want to browse in the shops, which are filled with local foods and country crafts. For a meal beyond belief, dine at the Restaurant Barn, where you can enjoy the Threshers' Dinner, a family-style feast of Amish country favorite foods. You may also want to include in your day a performance of the play *Plain and Fancy,* which showcases the values of the Amish and originally played on Broadway. You can lengthen your stay at Amish Acres by spending the night in the inn. It is also possible to stay in the home of a nearby farm family, to experience more closely the plain and simple life—usually without television.

Borkholder Dutch Village (all ages)

County Road 101, just north of U.S. 6; (574) 773–2828; www.borkholder.com. Tuesday auction at 8:00 A.M. all year. Summer hours are Monday through Saturday 9:00 A.M. to 5:00 P.M.; winter hours (October through April) are Monday, Wednesday, and Friday 10:00 A.M. to 5:00 P.M., Tuesday and Saturday 9:00 A.M. to 5:00 P.M., closed Sunday. Free.

A shoppers' paradise awaits you in Nappanee. On Tuesday, try attending the indoor antiques auction. There is also an indoor flea market all year. More shopping yet is available at the Arts and Crafts Mall, with more than 400 artists and craftspersons selling what they and others have created. Right alongside the Arts and Crafts Mall is the Antiques Mall, for even more opportunities to shop. There are also specialty shops in the mall area. In addition, you can get food at the Dutch Kitchen.

Victorian Guest House (ages 5 and up)

302 East Market; (574) 773–4383.

Also in Nappanee, you can see and even stay at this one-hundred-year-old Victorian mansion, nestled in the Amish countryside and listed on the National Register of Historic Places. Groups of ten people of more can get a free tour if they call ahead.

Where to Eat

Barn Loft Grill. 1600 West Market Street; (800) 800–4942; www.amishacres.com. Feast on its famous family-style thresher's dinner; dine on antique tables surrounded by the hand-hewn beams of the century-old restaurant barn. Hours are seasonal.

Where to Stay

Nappanee Inn. 2004 West Market Street (U.S. 6W); (574) 773–5999. A rural setting a half mile from Amish Acres has all the amenities including sixty-six large rooms, outdoor pool, and complimentary breakfast.

Shamrock Inn. 1501 East Market Street; (574) 773–3193. Located 1½ miles from Amish Acres and adjacent to a good family restaurant. Twenty-four rooms. Pets are allowed.

Plymouth

When you visit the town of Plymouth, you can get a glimpse of the past as you stroll through the downtown area on Michigan Street. The exteriors of the buildings reflect their turn-of-the-century heritage. Throughout the town, there are historic spots to view, including the **Marshall County Courthouse,** the **firehouse,** and the **LaPorte Street Iron Foot Bridge**—all are registered National Historical Landmarks. Spending time in Plymouth will let you experience the fun of being in a small town. Josh Logan, the famous Broadway writer of *South Pacific,* was raised here. You will want to stop at the **Marshall County Historical Society Museum** at 123 North Michigan Street to learn more about early pioneers and Indians who lived in this area. Since the area around Plymouth is known for its great berries, you may want to stop at one of the numerous road stands in the summer. Or the annual **Blueberry Festival** held during the Labor Day holiday may be appealing to you. It is one of the largest in the state. Call the Marshall County Convention and Visitors Bureau at (800) 626–5353 or visit its Web site at www.blueberrycountry.org.

Centennial Park (all ages)
North Michigan Street; (219) 936–2876. **Free.**

When you are looking for a park that can be enjoyed during any season, make plans to visit Centennial Park. Located in Plymouth, the park has more than one hundred acres of beautiful recreation area. It is on the Yellow River and has a covered bridge, playground, and a swimming pool. It is an excellent place to enjoy a family picnic in the summer. After the picnic, you can have fun on the baseball and soccer fields, basketball and tennis courts, the 2 miles of exercise trail, or the shuffleboard court. During the winter, the family can enjoy cross-country skiing and the sledding hill.

Culver

Culver Military Academy (all ages)
1300 Academy Road; (574) 842–7000; www.culver.org. **Free.**

Culver Academy is a coed military school that has become world renowned for its instructional programs since it opened in 1894. You can walk around the 300-acre campus and enjoy the numerous historic structures. If your family is looking for something educational and historical, visit the campus during the summer. You will be able to see the "Black Horse Troop" perform. This group has served as escorts during presidential inauguration parades since 1896.

Lake Maxinkuckee (all ages)
State Road 10 and State Road 17, on the campus of the Culver Military Academy.

Indiana's second-largest natural lake is not only part of the campus of the military academy, it is also an excellent area for recreation. There is a public beach with a sandy, sunny shoreline, plus a wooded park with benches and picnic tables. Your family can rent floats, canoes, and boats to take out on the lake. There are also a couple of challenging golf courses that are near the lake.

Rochester

Fulton County Museum, Round Barn Museum, and Living History Village (all ages) 🏛
37 East 375 North; (574) 223–4436. Museum and Round Barn Museum open all year Monday through Saturday 9:00 A.M. to 5:00 P.M. Free.

Take a look at the past on thirty-five acres of land at Fulton County, the round barn capital of the world. You can inspect one of these interesting structures and view a display of farm machinery and antique tools. Then in the Living History Village, which is open in summer, you can see the Rochester Depot, Pioneer Woman's Log Cabin, blacksmith shop, 1832 William Polke house, print shop, and Rochester Bridge Company footbridge and enjoy reenactments during festivals. The museum has seventeen displays including an old-time general store, circus, first Tarzan, Indians, and military displays.

Besides seeing the museums, you may want to attend one of the two festivals held there. The **Trail of Courage Festival** is a living history festival held on the third weekend in September. Here is a chance to go back in time to pre-1840 America. You can visit historic encampments of the French and Indian War, Revolutionary War, Voyageur, Western Fur Trade, Plains Indians, and Woodland Indians. You will also see muzzle loading and tomahawk contests, blanket trading, and a historic canoe landing and fur-trading skit. In the Woodlands Indian Village, you can see Potawatomi and Miami history, crafts, wigwams, and lifeways. The Chippeway Village portrays frontier Northern Indiana of 1832 and has pioneer and Indian crafts, stage shows, a general store, and a post office. There is also a storyteller, a Frontier Blab School, an eighteenth-century puppet show, and pioneer food. Here's your chance to eat buffalo burgers and Indian fry bread. You will also see traditional crafts like basketry, blacksmithing, pewter casting, candle dipping, gun making, the fashioning of cornhusk dolls, and wheat weaving. Your family can also enjoy canoe rides, a frontier fashion show, Indian lore, and a log cabin trading post. On the last weekend of April, there is the smaller Redbud Trail Rendezvous, which has some of the activities of the Trail of Courage Festival. (There is a moderate admission charge for both festivals.)

Indiana **Trivia**

What state flower did the Peony replace?

How many people from Indiana served in the armed forces during World War I?

Zinnia, 130,670

Southern Indiana

The southern part of Indiana has the most beautiful scenery in the state. The glaciers extended approximately 45 miles south of Indianapolis, thus sparing southern Indiana from the leveling effects that accompanied them. You'll see beautiful valleys, hills, caves, and the beginning of the Cumberland Mountains. This area was the home of Native American tribes and some of the earliest French and American settlements in the West. In southern Indiana, you have many historical places, exciting state parks, and scenic spots to explore. Heading south out of Indianapolis on Route 37 you will arrive in Bloomington. The town is located in the rolling hills of south central Indiana and has long been known for its big-city offerings while retaining a quaint Midwestern atmosphere. Indiana University is located here, along with plenty of outdoor activities such as hiking, biking, canoeing, and caving at Monroe County's three lakes and two forests.

TopPicks for fun in Southern Indiana

1. Indiana University, Bloomington

2. Nashville Town and Brown County State Park, Nashville

3. French Lick

4. New Harmony State Historic Site, New Harmony

5. Holiday World and Splashin' Safari, Santa Claus

6. Lincoln Boyhood National Memorial, Lincoln City

7. Fourwinds Resort, Bloomington

8. Mesker Park Zoo, Evansville

9. Squire Boone Caverns and Village, Corydon

SOUTHERN INDIANA

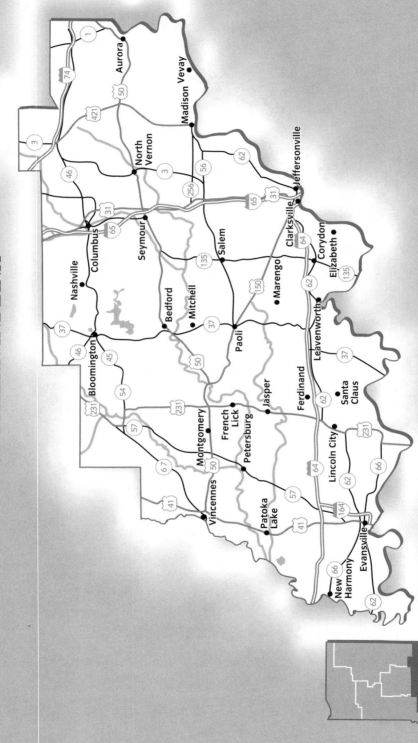

Bloomington

As you approach the city, you will be able to observe large limestone quarries—some are open for visitors. When you arrive in the charming downtown square, you will see the Monroe County Courthouse. Look up at the top of the structure. You will notice a golden fish weather vane more than 5 feet in length. The fish was hammered out of copper in 1826 by Austin Seward and has become the city's logo. Also, outside the courthouse are several war memorials and a drinking fountain that is over eighty years old. On the courthouse grounds you will see the William T. Dahman's Four Freedoms Monument and a limestone statue of the Mother of Mankind. Be sure to enter the courthouse so you can see the beautiful marble staircase and stained-glass window.

Indiana University (all ages) 🏛️ 🎒 🌸
East Seventh Street; (812) 855–0661 (tour information); www.indiana.edu. Free.

Many of the activities in Bloomington center around Indiana University. When you visit the campus you will see many limestone buildings—some covered with ivy. You'll need to spend considerable time on the campus to explore all its offerings. What is especially great is that there is no admission charge for the many places you will visit. If you don't want to conduct your own tour, call the Office of Admissions to make arrangements for a guided tour. Here are some places you should visit on the campus: Go inside the auditorium to see the **Hall of Murals,** which is bordered by two marble staircases and has paintings by Thomas Hart Benton depicting the stages of Indiana's economic growth. The **Indiana Memorial Union** at Seventh and Woodlawn is one of the largest student unions in the country, and its contents will absolutely amaze you. There is an inn, restaurants, cafeteria, bakery, and a huge bookstore. There are even a billiards room, bowling alley,

Costume **Collection**

The Elizabeth Sage Costume Collection in Wylie Hall is a must for that fashion designer in the family. This museum shows children how styles have changed and repeated over the years. You can see the dress and work clothing worn by men, women, and children from 1820 until today. For more information call (812) 855–5497. The Lilly Library at Seventh Street has a collection of Abraham Lincoln works and a copy of the 1454 Gutenberg New Testament. This is an interesting place for the history buff in the family.

and barber shop. Southwest of the union is the **Dunn Family Cemetery.** The cemetery is shaped like a kite, supposedly to help people on their flight to heaven. To this day, the Dunn family owns the cemetery and only its descendants can be buried there. In a corner of the cemetery is the Beck Chapel.

Be sure to stroll through the **Jordan Hall Greenhouse** on East Third Street, where you can see a tropical jungle and plants from around the world. The greenhouse phone number is (812) 855–7717. If you are ever in Bloomington on a Wednesday night when school is in session, try to visit the **Kirkwood Observatory** on Indiana Avenue, which has a 12-inch refractor telescope, a solar telescope, and an optics lab. For more information call (812) 855–6911. On the corner of East Second and Lincoln Streets you will be able to see the Wylie House, home of the university's first president, Andrew Wylie. The home was built in 1835 and is now a historic house museum. At Seventh and Woodlawn Streets is **Ernie Pyle Hall.** This building is named after Ernest Taylor Pyle, the famous World War II correspondent for the *Indianapolis Times*. The lounge on the second floor contains Pyle's memorabilia. Stop by **The Gables** at 114 South Indiana, which has been serving fast food to university students since 1919. The Gables was called the Book Nook when songwriter Hoagy Carmichael composed his famous song "Stardust" there. In the **Hoagy Carmichael Room** in Morrison Hall you can see his memorabilia including a piano, juke-box, and records.

Learn more about IU football by visiting the **Memorial Stadium** on Seventeenth Street, the team's home. Here you can see the weight room and view the trophy cabinets. Your visit to this college football stadium is made special when you are allowed to take snapshots of everyone on the field.

Lilly Library is Indiana University's principal repository for rare books, manuscripts, and special collections. Based on its holdings, which range from a Gutenberg Bible to the

A Gisler **Adventure**

Even before two of our children were old enough to attend IU, our family would take day trips down to the lovely campus grounds. When the children were small, we traveled to IU for swim meets, and during school breaks we would take the family over to the Indiana Memorial Union for meals. They enjoyed walking through the country's largest student union, which houses a 190-room hotel, seven dining areas, bowling, billiards, a game room, a hair salon, and the Indiana Memorial Union Gallery. Of course, we could never leave the union without stopping to see Assembly Hall, the home of the Indiana University Hoosiers basketball team, and Memorial Stadium to learn more about IU football. As we walked across the gorgeous campus, we would visit the Art Museum, Showalter Fountain, and Metz Carillon Tower.

letters of Sylvia Plath, the museum hosts exhibitions throughout the year. Although browsing in the stacks is not allowed, visitors can use the Reading Room to enjoy the collection of more than 400,000 books, 100,000 pieces of sheet music, and more than 6 million manuscripts. Hours: Monday through Friday 9:00 a.m. to 6:00 P.M. and Saturday 9:00 A.M. to 1:00 P.M.; no admission fee. For more information you can call (812) 855–2452.

Indiana University Art Museum is one of the top university art museums in the country, with more than 30,000 objects representing nearly every art-producing culture throughout history. The collections range from ancient gold jewelry and African masks to paintings by Claude Monet. The museum building, dedicated in 1982, was designed by I. M. Pei and Partners. The museum is open Tuesday through Saturday 10:00 A.M. to 5:00 P.M., Sunday noon to 5:00 P.M. **Free.** For information call (812) 855–5445.

Mathers Museum (ages 5 and up)

416 North Indiana Avenue; (812) 855–6873. Open Tuesday through Friday 9:00 A.M. to 4:30 P.M., Saturday and Sunday 1:00 to 4:30 P.M. Closed major holidays and during semester breaks. Free.

Here your children can explore world cultures. This museum is a training ground for students interested in museum-related careers. The museum's more than 20,000 artifacts and 10,000 photographs are constantly being studied for different scholarly publications. The museum has programs to help you explore its exhibits, and there are guided tours that give an in-depth look at the artifacts and where they came from.

If you are not tired of walking after touring the university, then stroll over to the **Bloomington Antique Mall** (all ages) at 311 West Seventh Street. There are more than a hundred booths with every kind of memorabilia (from books to furniture) you can think of. The mall hours are Monday through Thursday 10:00 A.M. to 5:00 P.M., Friday and Saturday 10:00 A.M. to 6:00 P.M., Sunday noon to 5:00 P.M. Call (812) 332–2290 for more information.

Griffey Lake (all ages)

Matlock Road, 5 miles north of downtown Bloomington; (812) 349–3700. Bloomington Parks and Recreation; 410 North Morton Street; (812) 349–3700. Open daily, no fees.

While you are in the Bloomington area, you might like to visit one of the many nearby lakes that are perfect for family fun. Griffey Lake has scenic woodlands and two self-guided hiking trails. You can enjoy a day here hiking, renting a canoe, or doing a little fishing.

Indiana **Trivia**

What Indiana city had the largest population in 1850?

What is the oldest Indiana town?

Madison, Vincennes

Lake Lemon (all ages) ⚠ 🏊

7599 North Tunnel Road; (812) 334–0233 for lake and fishing conditions or (812) 331–9115. Open twenty-four hours. Annual permit $76; daily permit $18, plus a $4 ramp fee.

The Bloomington Yacht Club is located on this 1,650-acre human-made lake that was created in 1953. Here is a good place to learn and practice sailing. Relax with your family for a day at Riddle Point Park overlooking the lake. There are picnic tables and grills in the park, and children will enjoy all the modern playground equipment. A canoe and boat rental is located next to the swimming beach. Boats can be rented by the hour or by the day so that you can enjoy one of the more popular fishing lakes in Indiana. Everyone can have fun on the 300-foot-long sand beach that is open from Memorial Day weekend through Labor Day. Lifeguards are on duty for swimming safety. There are water volleyball courts and a swim platform. Call ahead to find out about beach "fun days" that are scheduled throughout the summer.

Little Africa Wildlife Area (all ages) ⚠ 🎣 🛶 🍁

At the southeast part of Lake Lemon in the headwaters; (812) 334–0233. Free.

Little Africa Wildlife Area provides a ¾-mile loop of open grass area teeming with birds looking for food along the shores of the lake. Take a camera and get some great impromptu pictures of the birds skimming the water for fish from the observation deck or rent a boat or canoe and paddle along the stream of Salt Creek, which feeds Lake Monroe. Boat rentals, wet slips, and camping gear are available from North Shore Marina, (812) 988–4663. If you have your own boat, you can rent a boat slip from I and S Marine, (812) 333–7377. Located in the northern portion is the Northfork Waterfowl Resting Area. Open only April through October, this area boasts beautiful scenery and abundant wildlife. Bring your fishing pole and compete with the blue herons for dinner or just paddle around. The area is very fragile, so remember to take out whatever you brought in.

Lake Monroe (all ages) ⚠ 🎣 ⛺

10 miles southeast of Bloomington. No charge for public facilities, open all the time.

This is the state's largest lake, surrounded by the Hoosier National Forest. It's a great place for boating, fishing, camping, waterskiing, and sailing. And there are lakeside accommodations in three resorts.

Fourwinds Resort (all ages) ⚠ 🎾 🏊 🏈

On Lake Monroe, 9301 Fairfax Road, a year-round resort with fees for certain activities; (800) 824–2628.

This is the perfect choice any season of the year for lunch or a family vacation. Of course, if you visit during the summer months, there is lots of activity at the lake, especially at the 800 boat slips at the Fourwinds Marina. You can also enjoy golf, volleyball, a jogging/fitness trail, hiking, and tennis. Every member of the family will find something to do here. Next to the Fourwinds Hotel is Fairfax Beach, the largest human-made white-sand beach in Indiana. It is free to the public.

Where to Eat

Tradewinds at the Fourwinds. Fourwinds Resort, 9301 Fairfax Road; (812) 824–9904.

The Tudor Room. At Indiana Memorial Union (IMU), Indiana University, 900 East Seventh Street; (812) 855–1620. Collegiate elegance is abundant in the IMU restaurant. The IMU is the largest student union in the country and The Tudor Room has to have the largest selection of freshly made desserts in the country! Try the luncheon buffet and taste a little of everything. Be sure to grab a couple of fried biscuits and apple butter (a Hoosier favorite) at the bread station. In fact, the person who said "Man does not live by bread alone," evidently didn't visit this bread station.

Encore Cafe. 316 West Sixth Street; (812) 333–7312. Daily 11:00 A.M. to 11:00 P.M., Friday and Saturday open to 1:00 A.M., Sunday 10:00 A.M. to 11:00 P.M. "Cool!" describes this New Age cafeteria. Booths, upper levels, and window seats are surrounded by art galore. This place bustles with a full-service cappuccino bar in the middle and a list of daily specials that are out of this world. Grab a tray and peruse the options before you even consider making a selection. They start you off at the desserts first, and you'll see why when you decide it might be best to try a little of everything. Sandwiches and main entree portions are big and there's jazz on Sunday evenings. Be sure to get some gourmet spreads to share.

The Scholar Inn Bakehouse. 125 North College Avenue; (812) 331–6029. This downtown establishment features breads developed by Michael London, one of America's premier bakers. New owners have added a new French flavor to the restaurant. Freshly baked loaves of farm bread, raisin pecan, sourdough, and many others grace the back shelves, while Danish, tarts, and many other delectables are on show in the glass cases. Check out the deli, where you can have a number of unusual meats and cheeses put on your favorite bread, or select one of their fifteen different sandwiches. You and your family can also enjoy homemade soup or select one of the seven different salads. Children also love the pizza that has been added to the menu. Your family can enjoy a home-cooked breakfast, lunch, or dinner here. The kids will definitely want to try French toast circles for breakfast.

Scholars Inn Gourmet Cafe. 717 North College Avenue; (812) 382–1892. Just a few blocks down the street, you can enjoy a meal at a gourmet cafe and wine bar. Lunch served Tuesday through Friday 11:30 A.M. to 2:00 P.M. Dinner served Tuesday through Sunday 5:00 P.M. until closing. Champagne brunch Sunday 10:00 A.M. to 2:00 P.M.

Nick's English Hut. 423 East Kirkwood Avenue; (812) 332–4040. This establishment is an IU tradition beyond all others! Open since 1927, the building has a historical character much like the taverns of that day. Walk in the door and you'll find booths lining the walls, in the back room you'll find tables for groups, and upstairs you'll find the "hump" room, perfect for large groups. The menu offers a variety of sandwiches, burgers, pizza, and strombolis (stroms). They have specialty dinners that include steak, chicken, and a pizza special for two.

Ladyman's Cafe. 122 East Kirkwood Avenue; (812) 336–5557. You'll walk in the door and feel like you've stepped into your favorite hometown diner. This food is home cooking at its best, featuring a variety of traditional Hoosier favorites such as biscuits and gravy, eggs any way you want 'em, chicken and noodles, beef Manhattan, and several other favorites that only your mom could make.

Where to Stay

Century Suites. 300 South State Road 446; (812) 336–7777, (800) 766–5446. Bloomington's only all-suite hotel featuring one- and two-bedroom suites in a Williamsburg setting. Each is furnished with a fully equipped kitchenette and a queen-size sofa sleeper. Large whirlpool tubs and fireplaces available. Upscale accommodations at hotel prices. Dining available at Chapman's restaurant. Close to College Mall, Lake Monroe, and Indiana University.

Best Western–Fireside Inn. 4501 East Third Street; (812) 332–2141, (800) 528–1234; www.bestwestern.com. Prime location minutes from IU, Lake Monroe, and Brown County. Relax in newly remodeled rooms with cable TV. Continental breakfast served daily; swimming pool with country setting. Dine at the Fisherman's Dock restaurant on the premises. Ideal for family vacations.

Courtyard by Marriott. 310 South College Avenue; (812) 335–8000, (800) 321–2211; www.courtyard.com. Bloomington's premier hotel, the Courtyard by Marriott is located downtown, adjacent to the Convention Center and within walking distance of fine dining and shopping. Experience a relaxing and enjoyable atmosphere, oversized rooms, in-room coffee and tea, remote-control color TVs, data ports on room phones, guest voice mail, indoor pool and whirlpool, exercise room, and breakfast restaurant. Suites are available.

Eagle Pointe Golf & Tennis Resort. 2250 East Point Road; (812) 824–4040, ext. 117; www.eaglepointe.com. Experience the beauty of southern Indiana and enjoy Lake Monroe, the state's largest lake. Eagle Point offers 120 luxurious one- to four-bedroom condominiums, which are available for nightly, monthly, or yearly rental. The condos are equipped with full kitchens and washer/dryers and have spectacular lake, golf course, or wooded views. Most of the units have fireplaces, decks, and patios. Eagle Pointe is a full-service resort and is open all year.

Indiana Memorial Union. 900 East Seventh Street; (812) 856–6381, (800) 209–8145; www.indiana.edu/~imupromo. One-hundred-eighty-six-room, full-service luxury facility nestled in the heart of the scenic woodland campus of Indiana University. Enjoy the many attractions on the IU campus along with several restaurants, exercise room, and **free** parking.

Pointe Connection Rentals & Sales. 9394 South Strain Ridge Road; (812) 824–2050, (800) 467–2050; www.pointeconnection .com. Enjoy a family vacation at the Pointe in a condominium of your choice. One-, two-, three-, and four-bedroom units available with all the comforts of home. Stay three nights for the price of two! Close to restaurants, pool, golf, and tennis. Pets not allowed.

Camping

Monroe Lake Park. 4850 South State Road 446. State owned, located on the southeast side of the lake; situated on a peninsula of 380 acres. **Free** primitive camping, access by walking or boat. Ramp and overnight mooring available.

Hardin Ridge Recreation Area. 6464 Hardin Ridge Road; office: Rural Route 1, Heltonville; (812) 837–9453 (April–October), (800) 280–2267 (reservations only); www.reserveusa.com. Operated by the U.S. Forest Service. Includes 1,000 acres of land, full-service camping area, picnic areas, shelters, ramp, beach, hiking, and showers.

Lake Monroe Village. 8107 South Fairfax Road; (812) 824–2267. A-frame home, RV rentals, and fully furnished vacation villas for rent and sale. Log cabins in wooded setting. Cabins include air-conditioning,

Fried Biscuits **with Apple Butter, Please**

Children and adults of all ages enjoy stepping back into an era when many proprietors made their own wares. Throughout southern Indiana's Brown County, you can view potters, glassblowers, and weavers; watch candle, basket, toy, and candy makers at work; or treasure hunt through craft and specialty shops—each with its own unique theme. Whether your interest is original paintings, sculpture, stained glass, solid wood furniture, wood carving, metal sculpture, pewter, toys from yesterday and today, handmade jewelry, select clothing, perfume, wind chimes, or birdhouses—to name a few—the selection and quality are always exceptional.

When you're ready for a snack or a full-course meal, Brown County has the perfect spot to please your appetite. Many rustic restaurants boast original recipes—such as fried biscuits with apple butter, country ham, turkey with all the fixin's, and even wild game entrees—while others specialize in a variety of traditional, ethnic, and gourmet dishes. There is an old-fashioned soda and ice-cream shop, and other shops selling aromatic coffee are available for snacks or light lunches, as well as many cafes, pubs, and bars offering sandwiches or full-course meals. If you are staying in one of the county's several bed-and-breakfast inns, you will be sure to find a delicious breakfast awaiting you every morning.

heater, beds, and refrigerator. You bring bedding and cooking utensils; no indoor water in cabins; public rest rooms and showers. Facilities include pool, kiddie pool, hot tub, recreation hall, picnic pavilion, playground, and hiking trails. Overnight accommodations for campers.

Monroe Lake Park. 4850 State Road 446; (812) 837–9546. State owned; centrally located on the north side of the lake. Has 440 acres with primitive and modern camping sites. Boat ramp, beach, hiking trails,

showers, and wheelchair-accessible fishing dock. Overnight mooring for campers. Visitors center located at entrance. Entrance fee or state park pass required.

For More Information

Bloomington/Monroe County Convention and Visitors Bureau. (866) 333–0088; www.visitbloomington.com.

Bloomington Visitors Bureau. 2855 North Walnut; (800) 678–9828.

Something for **Everyone**

Some of the unique attractions to be found in Brown County include country festivals, musical shows and jamborees, historical sites and museums, horse-drawn carriage rides, a marionette theater, panning for gold and gemstones, replica steam engine train rides and tours, strolling carolers in Victorian costume at Christmas, and much, much more! Exciting high-energy entertainment overflows in Brown County, in theaters such as the Little Nashville Opry, the Country Time Jamboree, the Nashville Follies Theatre, the Pine Box Theatre, and the Brown County Playhouse. Nashville and Brown County have plenty of entertainment for your whole family to enjoy.

Nashville

Travel east out of Bloomington on State Road 45 or south from Indianapolis on State Road 135 and you will arrive in Nashville.

Stop in at the Brown County Convention and Visitors Bureau office at the corner of Main and Van Buren Streets to browse the brochure rack and have any of your questions answered; or you can write, call, or browse its Web site—P.O. Box 840, Nashville 47448; (800) 753–3255; www.browncounty.com.

Nashville is the county seat of Brown County, an area of beauty, serenity, homecooking, and a place that first gained fame in 1870 as a mecca for artists and craftspeople who were inspired by the peace and beauty of these hills. Today Nashville is the hub of activity in Brown County. Nashville and Brown County offer more to do, see, indulge in, and enjoy than most people can imagine. **Brown County State Park** offers more than 15,000 acres available for biking, horseback riding, cross-country skiing, fishing, backpacking, jogging, and inspirational nature-trail exploring. Brown County's more than 350 shops feature such varied wares as original painting, sculpture, stained glass, solid wood furniture, pewter, handmade jewelry, toys, select clothing, and perfume; plus demonstrations by candy makers, potters, weavers, candle makers, glassblowers, and much, much more. You will visit this picturesque town many times to see the latest work of artists and craftspeople as well as browse in the stores and museums and to savor the food in the many restaurants. The well-known **Nashville House** at Main and Van Buren has a country store as well as a fine family restaurant. If a cool drink is what you want after a long walk, then drop in at the **Hobnob Corner Restaurant** ice-cream bar for an old-fashioned chocolate soda.

A Gisler **Adventure**

While Nashville is fun to visit any time of the year, we especially enjoy a day trip during the fall when the leaves are beginning to turn colors. We love to spend a few hours walking the streets of the town seeing the latest work of artists and craftspeople as well as browsing the 300-plus fascinating stores and museums. After walking through the town and shopping, we always drop in at the Hobnob Corner Restaurant for an old-fashioned chocolate soda.

While there are many restaurants to choose from, we always head toward the Nashville House for fried chicken, rolls, and apple butter. Just east of Nashville is Brown County State Park. We have spent many autumn afternoons picnicking, hiking, and bike riding through the park. We have also gone on the horseback riding tours that the park offers. Always before leaving the park, we stop by the Brown County Inn for a light snack for the road.

Northeast of the courthouse is a collection of nineteenth-century buildings known as the **Brown County Historical Society Museum.** One of the buildings is an unusual log jail. This structure has the distinction of being the only jail where a prisoner was allowed to be his own keeper. While serving a sentence for bootlegging, one prisoner went wherever he wanted during the day and locked himself up at night. He was known to have assisted the sheriff in an arrest and acted as a guide to tourists.

Nashville Walking Tour of Historic Sites and Homes

This tour was provided by the Brown County Convention and Visitors Bureau. Remember to stop in and meet Mary G. Fredericksen, Visitors Center Manager, and the whole staff when you are in town.

This walking tour throughout the streets of historic Nashville should take about an hour and will bring you within a block of the original starting point. As you walk, be sure to take in all of the sights and enjoy yourself in this relaxing community. You will no doubt make many interesting discoveries on your own. Don't forget to visit the Brown County Convention and Visitors Bureau office at the corner of Main and Van Buren Streets to browse the brochure rack and have any of your questions answered.

The tour begins at Gould Street and Old School Way, northeast of the courthouse.

1. Brown County Historical Society Museum. The museum complex includes a pioneer cabin, built around 1844 with handhewn logs reconstructed here using only pioneer tools; the old log jail, built in 1879—men were kept on the bottom level and the women were kept on the upper level (the last prisoner was kept there in 1919); Dr. Alfred J. Ralphy's office, complete with the original tools and furniture, built in 1898 in New Bellesville, Indiana, in southeastern Brown County (Dr. Ralphy made all of his house calls by horse and buggy since he never owned an automobile); the blacksmith shop, a replica of the one from the nineteenth century, with authentic tools of the trade donated by interested local citizens; and the Loom Room where weaving and spinning took place.

Go West on Gould Street, turn south onto Van Buren Street.

2. Brown County Courthouse. The original courthouse was built in 1853. The current courthouse was built in 1874 and still houses some of the county offices and the current jail. The famous "Liar's Bench" that once stood on the grounds was destroyed in a Halloween prank years ago. The Brown County Lions Club recently placed a newer version of the "Liars Bench" in front of the Courthouse. The courthouse and grounds were totally renovated in 1922–23.

Indiana **Trivia**

Where was the first Indiana prison built?

Where are the headquarters for the Hoosier National Forest?

In what Indiana city was some of the film *Breaking Away* shot?

Jeffersonville, Bedford, Bloomington

Head east on Main Street across from the Courthouse.
3. Gustave Baumann home. Now the Carousel Café, this was the location of his home. Gustave Baumann (1881–1971) was a world-renowned woodblock printer who came to the United States in 1891 from Germany. He printed his famous series of woodcuts, Hills of Brown, while living in Nashville from 1909 to 1916. In 1915 he won the Gold Medal at the Pan American International Exhibition in San Francisco.

Backtrack on Main Street to the intersection of Main and Van Buren Streets; then head south on Van Buren.
4. Nashville House. Made from a combination of stone and weathered wood, this one-story building houses a charming restaurant with down-home country cooking, a general store specializing in culinary utensils, fresh bread, jellies and jams, teas, and its famous apple butter. Rocking chairs on the front porch invite you to take a rest. A plaque in front states that since 1867 a "public hostelry has occupied the corner, first serving the logging industry and later a gathering place for artists." The original building burned in 1927, and again in 1943; the present structure was completed in 1948.

Go back to the corner and cross Van Buren Street.
5. Hobnob Corner Restaurant. Built in 1873, this is the oldest place of business in town. The building originally housed Taggart's General Store and Grocery. Meat hooks still remain in the back room. The building later housed Miller's Drug Store.

Head south on Van Buren Street.
6. The Brown County Art Guild. The Art Guild is located in the Old Minor House and is home to the collection of Marie Goth's works. Step inside to see the wonderful masterpieces inspired by the hills of Brown County and see the works of famous local artists.

7. The Olde Bartley House. Located on the corner of Franklin and Van Buren Streets, this two-story, yellow-and-red house was built in 1886. The house was the home of then-famous photographer Frank Hohenberger until his death in 1963. The house was also home to Georges "Jack" LaChance (1888–1964). Born in Utica, New York, he attended the A. Louiss School of Fine Art. He lived in Brown County with his wife, Sally, during the

Depression years, when he could exchange paintings for groceries. He painted murals on the walls inside the Nashville House for meals before a fire destroyed the building.

Cross Van Buren Street, heading east.
8. House of the Weaver. The building that now houses Quintessence Gallery is one of three houses constructed of locally made bricks in the 1840s. The building was previously a teachers' boardinghouse, a Methodist parsonage, and the home of the town weaver, Mary Bissel.

Backtrack to the corner of Franklin and Van Buren and continue south on Van Buren.
9. Anthony Buchta home. Now home of Crows Nest in Possum Trot Square. A native of Cedar Rapids, Iowa, Anthony Buchta (1896–1967) first came to Brown County with three fellow artists in 1929. He began exhibiting in Chicago in 1928 and exhibited at the 1933 World's Fair.

10. Lester Nagley Sr. home. Now home of Dislefink gift shop and the local T-shirt shop. Born in Greenfield, Indiana, Lester Nagley Sr. (1891–1967) began his career at the H. Lieber Co. picture frame department, learning the trade of silver gilting. He came to Brown County in 1936 to try his hand at painting and wrote the Hoosier Vignettes column for the *Greenfield Daily Reporter* and the *Brown County Democrat*.

Cross Van Buren at Washington Street and head north on the other side of Van Buren.
11. Calvin House. This blue, two-story Victorian house was built in 1875 by T. D. Calvin Jr., who was originally a schoolteacher, then opened the Main Street Dry Goods Store. Note the five-sided "bay" and fan window, typical Victorian trim, and front gazebo. The Calvin House is now the home of the Thomas Kinkade Brown County Gallery.

Go west on the south side of Franklin Street.
12. Honeysuckle Place. Across Honeysuckle Alley, notice the white, two-story house with architectural details painted green. The house was built in 1875 and the side room was added on later. **Acorn Cottage Gallery** now occupies the house.

13. Old Ferguson home. Directly across the street from Honeysuckle Place, now the home of Reflections Fine Arts and Crafts. This two-story yellow house has a full-length porch. Until the house was remodeled and turned into Reflections, it was renowned for its dust-covered, cobwebbed collection of antiques and miscellaneous things filling the yard, porch, outbuildings, and entire house, leaving only a narrow path for visitors. Built in 1873, it was a well-known tourist boarding home in the early 1900s, where Allie Ferguson was famous for her cooking. It is rumored that she kept a skeleton in the house to play tricks on people and scare them.

At Jefferson Street, look north across the street.
14. Allison House. This attractive, two-story yellow house was built in 1870 and restored inside for the current-day bed-and-breakfast now located here. The original owner began the *Jacksonian* here, the local newspaper until 1883, now the *Brown County Democrat*.

Head south on Jefferson Street toward Washington Street.
15. Brown County Presbyterian Fellowship/Remax Realty. This building was originally the Bond Funeral Home, until 1992 when Bob and Tomilda Hamontre bought it and turned it into the Pine Box Theater. Bob and Tomilda now perform in the theater at Ski World.

Cross Washington Street and continue south on Jefferson.
16. Old Magnolia House. This two-story, white Victorian house was built in 1912 and is now a bed-and-breakfast.

17. At 240 South Jefferson, across the street and south of the Old Magnolia House, notice the **gray-painted log cottage.** This was the typical style of the late 1800s and early 1900s in Brown County.

Go west on Washington Street to Johnson Street.
18. Abe's Cabin. This small log cottage with lean-to was built in the 1940s.

Head north on Johnson Street and cross Main Street.
19. "Here's Home." This interesting log home was built in the 1860s. Note the veranda posts and railing.

20. The Banner Brummett House. This log cottage, surrounded by shrubs and trees, was the first house built in Brown County by Banner Brummett in 1839. Gunports, originally installed because of Indians, were found inside when the house was restored.

Go east on Gould Street until you get to Jefferson Street; head south on Jefferson Street to the corner of Jefferson and Main Street.
21. Glen Cooper Henshaw home. Now the Harvest Moon Pizzeria. Painter Glen Cooper Henshaw (1884–1946) studied extensively abroad and was well known in New York City around the turn of the century. He came to Brown County late in his life for the serenity the area offered. Many of his paintings are exhibited in the permanent collection of the Brown County Art Gallery in the Memorial Room.

Now backtrack north on Jefferson Street toward Mound Street.
22. Notice the two-story yellow house on the left, with the interesting front treatment. It was built in 1853 by **Judge Hester,** who helped recruit soldiers for the Civil War. It is now The Hester House Bed-and-Breakfast.

23. Toll House. The lower level of this white-painted brick house, built in 1879, was a toll-house when Jefferson Street was the main north–south road through Nashville.

Head east on Mound Street past Hotel Nashville, to Van Buren Street and then head south on Van Buren.
24. The *Brown County Democrat*. The office of the local newspaper, which consolidated with the *Jacksonian* in 1883, is located in one of the older cabin structures in town.

Don't limit your visit to Nashville to the town itself. The winding roads in the area can lead to adventure. Travel down old country roads with unusual names such as Gnaw Bone, Bear Wallow Hill, Bean Blossom, and Booger Holler, as they can lead to unusual places.

Ski World (all ages)

2887 State Road 46 West; 49 miles south of Indianapolis, 4.5 miles west of Nashville, 12 miles east of Bloomington, and 20 miles west of Columbus. Snow report and summer activities: (812) 988–6693; office: (812) 988–6638; show and camping reservations: (812) 988–6630. Hours for skiing: Monday through Friday 10:00 A.M. to 10:00 P.M., Saturday and Sunday 9:00 A.M. to 10:00 P.M. Fee on weekdays $18; weekends $28; children 12 and under $10; prices may vary with time of day. Country Western show Friday and Saturday evenings mid-April through mid-November; Christmas show December, New Year's show December 31.

Snowmaking and grooming are an ongoing process, and constantly changing weather conditions can obviously affect snow conditions. Call for current conditions. With the Small World Bumpsters program on Saturday and Sunday and holidays 10:00 A.M. till 1:00 P.M., parents can enjoy a few hours of skiing while their four- to ten-year-olds learn to ski and have fun under the supervision of one of the instructors. The price, which includes lift ticket, instruction, and lunch is $40.00; second child in family is $30.00; equipment $5.00 extra. Call about specials: Learn to Ski free, Sixth Grade Program, Night Owl Special, Winter Carnival Days, Tubing. In the summer there are water slides, batting cages, go-carts, and bumper boats.

Entertainment

Red Barn Jamboree 🎵

One mile east of Nashville on the south side of Highway 46; (812) 323–7125 or (317) 791–7067.

The new home for real country music featuring The Country Plus Band with special performances by guest artists throughout the season from May to December. Shows on Friday and Saturday nights at 7:00 P.M.

Melchior Marionette Theatre 🎵

West side of South Van Buren Street; (800) 849–4853; weekend shows at 1:00 and 3:00 P.M. July through October.

A small outdoor theater for all ages, featuring a twenty-minute show with handcrafted marionettes. During October enjoy "The Slightly Haunted Puppet Theatre." Call for admission charge and updated schedule.

Brown County Playhouse 🎵

70 Van Buren Street South; (812) 988–2123. Open between 10:00 A.M. and 4:00 P.M. daily June through August and September 15 through mid-October. Other times of the year, call the Indiana University Box Office at (812) 855–1103 or your local TicketMaster.

This is Indiana's oldest professional stock theater, with performers from the Indiana University drama department.

National Follies Musical Theatre 🎵

P.O. Box 1124, Nashville, 47448; (812) 988–9007 or (800) 449–SHOW; www.nashvillefollies.com. $$$; children under 12 free.

This show for all ages is full of singing, dancing, and comedy. The company is dedicated to bringing you the very best of family entertainment, with professional, top-quality, fast-paced, high-energy shows. Shows on Friday and Saturday evenings at 8:00 P.M. June through mid-December. There are some weeknight, morning, and afternoon shows; however, you will need to call to get the schedule.

Pine Box Theatre at Ski World 🎵

168 South Jefferson Street; (812) 988–6827 or (800) 685–9624; www.pineboxtheatre.com. $$$.

Great local talent perform songs from the twenties through the sixties in an energetic family show that is full of music, dance, and comedy. This is one of the best shows that I have seen in years. This is a great night of entertainment that everyone will enjoy. Shows run from February through December on Wednesday, Friday, and Saturday evenings at 8:00 P.M., and there is an afternoon show on Sunday at 2:00 P.M. When the show is over, you have the opportunity to shake hands and talk with all the performers as you leave.

Mike's Music and Dance Barn 🎵

2277 West State Road 46; (812) 988–8636; www.mikesmusicdancebarn.com. Call for schedule. $$.

An all-ages place where no alcohol is served and no smoking is allowed. You can take country dance lessons on Monday and Tuesday evenings from 7:00 to 9:00 P.M. On Friday and Saturday from 6:00 to 11:30 P.M., everyone will enjoy listening to a live country band and ordering soft drinks, sandwiches, or other items from the menu. The entry fee is $6.00 for adults and $3.00 for children ages 3 to 12.

Little Nashville Opry 🎵

State Road 46 West; (812) 988–2235; www.thelittlenashvilleopry.com.

Local talent every Friday. Features well-known stars and local artists every weekend March through November. Call for schedule.

The Artists Colony Inn 🍴 ⊖ 🍁

Corner of Franklin and Van Buren Streets; (812) 988–0600 or (800) 737–0255. P.O. Box 1099, Nashville, IN 47448; www.artistscolonyinn.com.

A hotel and restaurant located right in the heart of downtown Nashville just off Main Street, surrounded by beautiful gardens. This is definitely a place worth staying at if you are looking for something a little bit different. Its nineteenth-century architectural style will let you enjoy stepping back in time. The inn is owned by Ellen and Jay Carter, a delightful couple who will make you feel right at home whether you are staying with them overnight or just having dinner in the restaurant. Ellen's father is Frederick Rigley, a well-known Brown County artist who was captivated by the landscape years ago. He usually has a paint box, an easel, and canvases with him, and you might even be lucky enough to meet Fred, since he usually enjoys his breakfast at the Artists Colony and sometimes even does some painting on the porch. In the restaurant you can see some of his original pieces of artwork, along with that of other Brown County artists, and enjoy some fantastic food. In fact, I would recommend this restaurant to everyone for breakfast, lunch, or dinner. The theme of the inn is Brown County artists past and present, and it's furnished with early American and Shaker-style furniture crafted by local artisans. The name of a different Brown County artist is given to each of the twenty guest rooms, and some of that artist's work can be found hanging in the room. Pets not allowed.

Brown County State Park (all ages) 🏕 👫 🍁

Just east of Nashville on State Road 46 East; (812) 988–6406; www.browncountystatepark.com.

Here's a great opportunity for you and your family to spend the day at one of Indiana's greatest parks. Entering the park, you will cross a two-lane covered bridge built around

1838. You can hike through the woods, picnic in one of the many picnic areas throughout the park, or horseback ride on one of the many trails. A nature trail leads through Ogle Hollow State Nature Preserve, where you can see rare yellowwood trees. The most beautiful thing you will ever see is Brown County in the fall. All the leaves changing color is an unforgettable sight. Once you come here in the fall, you'll never tire of coming back. People journey here from all over the world. Accommodations include the Abe Martin Lodge, housekeeping cabins, and camping. For lodge information call (877) 265–6343. For camping information call (812) 988–6406.

T. C. Steele State Historic Site (all ages)

4220 South T. C. Steele Road, off State Road 46; 9 miles west of Nashville; 10 miles east of Bloomington; and 1½ miles south of Belmont; (812) 988–2785. Open Sunday 1:00 to 5:00 P.M. and Tuesday through Saturday 9:00 A.M. to 5:00 P.M. Closed Monday and holidays. Hours may vary according to season. Open mid-March through late December. Free.

The site includes four hiking trails, the Dewar Log Cabin, and the ninety-acre Selma Steele Nature Preserve. Guided tours are offered through The House of the Singing Winds and the Large Studio, where changing exhibits display paintings done throughout Steele's life. Mrs. Steele's gardens display a festival of flowers from spring to autumn. Many seasonal activities and events are offered here, and educational outreach programs and a teacher packet are available on request. T. C. Steele State Historic Site is part of the State Museum and Historic Sites Division of the Department of Natural Resources, with fifteen sites around the state.

Brown County Art Guild, Inc.

48 South Van Buren Street; (812) 988–6185. Open March through December, Monday through Saturday 10:00 A.M. to 5:00 P.M., Sunday 11:00 A.M. to 5:00 P.M. Open weekends only January and February. Donations accepted.

The work of more than fifty artists displayed, including permanent collections of Marie Goth, V. J. Cariani, and other renowned early artists of the Brown County area.

Christmas in Brown County

21 Main at Van Buren Street; (800) 753–3255. Beginning after Thanksgiving in November through December. Hours vary.

Strolling carolers in Victorian costumes, a winter arts and crafts fair, art exhibitions, and holiday performances downtown and in the county.

Is your family really adventurous? Then head over to the **Hoosier National Forest** for some great hiking. Two areas stand out the most for parking and marked trails, **Grubb Ridge** and **Hickory Ridge.** Hickory has a fire tower that you can climb that was used until the 1970s to look for forest fires. Be prepared though; this is serious hiking, so bring plenty of water, some snacks, and a compass. Trails are long but not too difficult and be sure whatever you take in you take out!

The House of the **Singing Winds**

Theodore Clement Steele (1847–1926), well-known Indiana artist and member of the Hoosier Group of American regional impressionist painters, was inspired by the picturesque scenes he encountered in Brown County. In 1907, Steele and his second wife, Selma Neubacher Steele, purchased 211 acres in Brown County and built their home, The House of the Singing Winds. They built the Large Studio to accommodate Steele's work and landscaped the surrounding hillsides to enhance the beauty of their property. Selma created several acres of gardens around the home. From 1907 to 1921 the Steeles wintered in Indianapolis. They established a home in Bloomington when Steele became artist-in-residence at Indiana University in 1922. Each spring they returned to their Brown County property. As Steele's reputation grew, an increasing number of visitors were attracted to Brown County to meet the artist and to see his work and estate. Steele was at the forefront of the state's art movement and is still one of Indiana's most honored artists. His appreciation of nature, combined with his intelligence and his capacity for concentrated study, raised his works to an extraordinary level. The T. C. Steele State Historic Site, bequeathed to the state of Indiana by Selma Steele at her death in 1945, is a fitting tribute to this Indiana artist.

Where to Eat

Story Inn. See below.

Artists Colony Inn and Restaurant. Corner of Franklin and Van Buren Streets; (800) 737–0255. Reservations required.

Nashville House. Corner of Main and Van Buren Streets; (812) 988–4554. Here you'll find a world-famous restaurant that is located on a historic site dating back to 1859, where you can enjoy fried biscuits and baked apple butter served with baked ham and fried chicken. Open 11:30 A.M. to 8:00 P.M. and on Friday and Saturday until 9:00 P.M. Closed Tuesday except in October and December 23 to January 7. Entrees range from $10.95 to $19.95.

The Ordinary. Van Buren Street; (812) 988–6166. A step back in time to when America was young and the gathering places for local folk and travelers to partake of food and drink were called Ordinaries. This tradition lives on here. Open Tuesday, Wednesday, and Thursday from 11:30 A.M. to 8:00 P.M. and on Friday and Saturday until 10:00 P.M. Open Monday in October.

Where to Stay

The Artists Colony Inn. Corner of Franklin and Van Buren Streets; (812) 988–0600; (800) 370–4703; www.artists colonyinn.com. P.O. Box 1099, Nashville, IN 47448. See description in text.

The Brown County Inn. (800) 772–5249; www.browncountyinn.com. A rustic hotel with a great park and indoor/outdoor swimming pool. The large pool has garage doors that open up for getting some sunshine; however, the pool is covered so that children are able to swim in shade. The hotel has a dining room and is within walking distance of downtown Nashville.

Comfort Inn. 75 West Chestnut; (812) 988–6118; www.comfortinn.com. Deluxe whirlpool rooms, big-screen cable TV with HBO, kitchenette efficiencies, exercise room, heated indoor pool, and free breakfast bar.

Abe Martin Lodge. Brown County State Park, State Road 46 East; (812) 988–4418; www.browncountystatepark.com/lodge .html. Located on 15,000 acres of rolling hills. You have your choice of comfortable hotel rooms, family cabins, and hideaway cabins in the woods.

Story Inn. 6404 South State Road 135, 13 miles south of Nashville; (812) 988–2273; (800) 881–1183; www.storyinn.com. Take a step back in time at one of the quaint cottages or in one of the suites located on this rural property. The site of the original 1850s Story General Store. The food is excellent and you and your family will enjoy the relaxed atmosphere.

Lee's Retreat Log Cabins. 1352 Oak Grove Road; (812) 988–4117; www.nashvillein.com. Log cabins on private wooded acreage. Deluxe accommodations with full kitchens, air-conditioning, and electric heat. Daffodil Hill cabin has one bedroom, bath, fireplace, and cable TV. Curly Shingles has two bedrooms, two baths, wood-burning stove, TV, and VCR.

McGinley's Vacation Cabins. (877) 229–6637. Eight unique furnished cabins, each on private, wooded acreage in different parts of the county. Kitchens and fireplaces. One cabin has secluded accommodations for twelve. Brown County at its best.

Hotel Nashville Resort. 245 North Jefferson Street; (812) 988–8400; (800) 848–6274; www.hotelnashville.com. All-suite resort hotel, each with one bedroom, two baths, living/dining rooms, and kitchen. Also available are indoor pool, sauna, spa, restaurant, and lounge.

Camping

Brown County State Park Campground. State Road 46 East; (812) 988–4228 or (812) 988–6406. There are 429 family sites, 179 horseman sites, and tent sites available. Open all year. Electrical hookups, shower facilities, dumping station for campers only.

Yellowwood State Forest. 772 South Yellowwood Road; (812) 988–7945; www .browncountystatepark.com/yellowwood /forest.html. Primitive camping along beautiful Yellowwood Lake; eighty sites on 23,246 acres. No showers. Boat rental, visitors center.

Last Resort RV Park and Campground. 2248 State Road 46 East; (812) 988–4675. Campground with full-hookup sites, clean tiled rest rooms, laundry, game room, swimming pool, groceries, RV supplies, LP gas, and ice.

Bedford

Take State Road 37 south out of Bloomington and you will arrive in Bedford, or take State Road 446 south out of Bloomington if you are going directly to the Hoosier National Forest.

When you drive through the rolling hills of southern Indiana to Bedford and the surrounding area, you are in the limestone capital of the world. The limestone mills and quarries here have supplied stone for buildings throughout the country. The limestone used in the Empire State Building came from Bedford's Empire Quarry and proved the use of limestone in skyscrapers in 1930. Other notable buildings that have Indiana limestone are the Pentagon, the National Cathedral in Washington, D.C., the Merchandise Mart in Chicago, and Rockefeller Center in New York City. Stone carvers have practiced their art here for more than a century. ABC's *Good Morning, America* has featured carvings from area cemeteries; make it a point to see these intricate stone carvings. You will also want to see the longest covered bridge still open to traffic in Indiana, the Williams Covered Bridge. A century old and 376 feet long, it spans the White River west of Bedford.

Elliott Stone Quarry (all ages) 🏛

P.O. Box 1267, 3326 Mitchell Road, Bedford, IN 47421-9562; (800) 234-6227. Open June through December, weekdays 8:00 A.M. to 5:00 P.M., Saturday by appointment only. Closed on Sunday. Free.

Here you can learn more about Indiana's prized limestone from a maker of handcrafted limestone gifts. A fifteen-minute videotape of this working quarry highlights the history and the future of the limestone industry. Old pictures and related articles are also on view in the showroom. A self-guided walking path takes visitors past the stacking yard of a working quarry and an abandoned quarry.

Antique Auto and Race Car Museum (all ages) 🚗

Highways 37 and 50; 3348 Sixteenth Street; (812) 275-0556; www.autoracemuseum.com. Open April through December, noon to 6:00 P.M. $.

More than a hundred antique and race cars; vintage and current movies. Gift shop.

Bluespring Caverns (ages 3 and up; not recommended to bring your infants here) 🔺

County Road 450 South, ½ mile north of U.S. 50 near State Road 37; (812) 279-9471; www.bluespringcaverns.com. Open daily May 1 through September 30, 9:00 A.M. to 5:00 P.M.; open weekends in April and October. Last tour begins an hour before closing. $$$.

Most caves are explored by hiking through them, but here you can also explore by boat, as this is America's longest navigable underground river. The boat trip lasts an hour and lets you see rare blind fish and crayfish in their natural habitat and learn about the formation of the cave. With more than 20 miles of known passageways, this is the longest cave in Indiana. The temperature is fifty-two degrees year-round, so bring a light jacket for this adventure.

Where to Eat

Mamma's Mexican-Italian Restaurant. 1707 M Street; (812) 275–0684. Open Monday through Thursday and Sunday 11:00 A.M. to 10:00 P.M., Friday and Saturday to 11:00 P.M. Mamma's serves Mexican, Italian, and American food.

Early Bird Cafe. 1529 L Street or 1516 Sixteenth Street; (812) 275–8215.

Pappa's. 2810 Washington Avenue; (812) 275–6225. Open Sunday through Thursday 11:00 A.M. to midnight and on Friday and Saturday until 1:00 A.M. Casual dining. Kids' menu available.

Where to Stay

Plaza Motel. U.S. 50 East; (812) 834–5522. Thirteen rooms, some kitchenettes available, outdoor pool. Pets allowed with advance notice.

Rose Mount Motel. 1923 Main Street; (812) 275–5953. Twenty-four rooms. Pets allowed.

Stone City Motel. 2816 Mitchell Road (Highway 50 West Business); (812) 275–7515.

Stonehenge Lodge. 911 Constitution Avenue; (812) 279–8111; www.stonehenge lodge.com. Ninety rooms. Pets not allowed.

Columbus

The city of Columbus has been described as "America's Architectural Showcase." It is the gateway to central and southern Indiana. It all began back in the 1950s when a local philanthropic foundation provided the architectural fees for twenty-five of the buildings. The idea quickly snowballed as other institutions also offered to pay for the design of buildings. Such architectural "stars" as I. M. Pei, Eero and Eliel Saarinen, Robert Trent Jones, and Harry Weese have designed projects in Columbus.

Today there are more than fifty architecturally significant public and private buildings including banks, churches, a library, schools, storefronts, and golf courses. Each reflects the creativity and ingenuity of its individual architect. Together this is the most concentrated collection of contemporary architecture in the world. Your family deserves to see the work of these great architects.

It is easy to see this architecture. All you have to do is to go to the **Visitors/Architectural Center** at 506 Fifth Street; e-mail: visitcol@kiva.net; (812) 378–2622, (800) 468–6564. Begin with the free slide presentation, and then decide if you want to take a self-guided walking or driving tour. There are also regularly scheduled guided bus tours of the architecture. The center is typically open 9:00 A.M. to 5:00 P.M. Monday through Saturday, and Sunday 10:00 A.M. to 4:00 P.M. March through November. Hours are subject to change so it is wise to call ahead.

People Trail (all ages)
For information call Columbus Parks and Recreation at (812) 376–2680.

The People Trail is 9.4 miles of paved trail available to walkers, runners, and bikers in Columbus. If your family enjoys the outdoors this is a must. The Mill Race/Noblitt segment is the most scenic.

Zaharako's (all ages)
329 Washington Street; (812) 379–9329.

Zaharaoplastion is the Greek work for confectionery, and there is a lot to see at this confectionery shop, which was opened in Columbus in 1900 by the Zaharakos brothers. In 1905 they purchased the soda fountains they still use today. A full concert German pipe organ from 1908 still rings the tunes of the 1890s. Along the back bar is a 40-foot counter made of Mexican and Italian marble. Zaharako's specializes in homemade ice cream, fountain treats, sandwiches, and candies.

Indianapolis Museum of Art–Columbus Gallery (all ages)
390 The Commons; (812) 376–2597. Open Tuesday through Saturday 10:00 A.M. to 5:00 P.M. and Sunday noon to 4:00 P.M.

Features four exhibitions during the year. Handcrafted artifacts are available in the museum shop.

Festivals

Columbus Scottish Festival. Mill Race Park; (800) 468–6564; www.scottishfestival.org. Held annually second weekend in September. Enjoy bagpipe demonstrations, clan exhibits, GTE athletic competitions, the Columbus Midwest Open Sheepdog Trials, highland dancing, British cars, Celidh, Kirkin O'the Tartan, Scottish vendors, and food.

Festival of Lights. Mill Race Park; (800) 468–6564; www.columbusin.com. November through January 1, Sunday through Thursday 6:00 to 10:00 P.M. Admission charge. Winter park featuring more than 200 displays lighted with over a million lights. In November and December there are music and choral events, community displays, and a parade.

Where to Eat

American Cafe–Ramada Inn. I–65, Junction 46; (812) 376–3051. American Cafe restaurant at the Ramada Inn.

Holiday Inn–Old Columbus Restaurant. 2480 Jonathan Moore Pike; (812) 372–1541. Award-winning chef. Friday and Saturday prime rib dinner buffet, best Sunday brunch in town.

Papa's Downtown Deli. 412 Washington Street; (812) 376–8705.

Where to Stay

Holiday Inn. 2480 Jonathan Moore Pike; (812) 372–1541.

Ramada Inn. 2485 Jonathan Moore Pike, I–65 at State Road 46; (812) 376–3051; www.ramada.com. There are 166 rooms, three floors, handicapped accessible, indoor and outdoor pools.

Courtyard by Marriott. 3888 Mimosa Drive; (812) 342–8888; www.courtyard.com.

For More Information

Columbus Area Visitors Center. www.columbus.in.us.

Aurora

U.S. Route 50 runs east and west; on the east you will be in Aurora and the west in Vincennes.

Hillforest (all ages)
213 Fifth Street; (812) 926–0087; www.hillforest.org. $.

Imagine a mansion that looks a little bit like a steamboat, and you are envisioning Hillforest. The appearance of the mansion is no accident because its original owner, Gaff, was a prominent river shipper who owned several steamboats. He liked to watch his boats on the river from his hilltop home. Today you can watch boats on the river and see a faithful re-creation of Gaff's lifestyle. Hillforest is listed as a National Historic Landmark and is open Tuesday through Sunday 1:00 to 5:00 P.M. April 1 through December 30.

Where to Eat

Applewood on the River. 215 Judiciary Street; (812) 926–1166. Casual, fine dining, entertainment, and river view.

Combs Pizza. 329 Second Street; (812) 926–3273. Open Tuesday through Friday 11:00 A.M. to 9:00 P.M., Saturday 11:00 A.M. to 3:00 P.M.. Closed Sunday and Monday. Be sure to ask your server about daily specials and other notable menu selections.

Coach Light Inn. 223 Third Street; (812) 926–4006.

Where to Stay

Hill Crest Motel. 7535 U.S. 50 West; (812) 926–1991. Twenty-five rooms. No pets.

Colony Inn. 7644 U.S. 50 West; (812) 926–2550. Ten rooms. Pets may be allowed; call ahead.

Indiana **Trivia**

What Indiana city was designed using Thomas Jefferson's plans?

Where is Indiana's largest state park?

When did Indiana University first admit female students?

Jeffersonville, Nashville, Brown County, 1867

Vincennes

As Indiana's oldest community, Vincennes has a wealth of historical sites from its colorful past. Founded in 1732 as a French fur-trading post, Vincennes played an important role in the American Revolution. It is here that Colonel George Rogers Clark secured the West from the British. From 1800 to 1813 Vincennes was capital of the Indiana Territory. Instead of reading about history, visitors can see it here. Get a walking tour map from the Chamber of Commerce and embark on a historical adventure in old Vincennes. The chamber is located at the corner of Third and Busseron Streets at 102 North Third Street; (812) 882–6440.

George Rogers Clark National Historical Park (all ages) 🚶 🏛

401 South Second Street, on the banks of the Wabash River; (812) 882–1776; www.nps.gov/gero. Open daily 9:00 A.M. to 5:00 P.M.

This twenty-four-acre park commemorates Clark's heroism in the American Revolution. There is an imposing memorial and a visitor center, and you can see a twenty-three-minute film that will quickly acquaint you with Clark's victorious campaign against the British.

Grouseland (all ages) 🏛

3 West Scott Street; (800) 886–6443. Open daily 9:00 A.M. to 5:00 P.M. (January and February 11:00 A.M. to 4:00 P.M.) except Thanksgiving, Christmas, and New Year's Day. $.

William Henry Harrison and his family of eight children lived in this house while he served as first governor of the Indiana Territory. A visit to Grouseland is a chance for history buffs to learn a lot more about Harrison, who became the ninth president of the United States and was only in office for thirty-one days. You'll see furniture used by Harrison and some of the original brick floors. A tour of the house will give you an idea of how this future president actually lived. You'll feel like a part of history as you learn about Harrison's life here. The great Indian chief Tecumseh was invited to this home by Harrison to discuss their differences. Tecumseh refused to come into the house, preferring to sit on the ground in a walnut grove on the front lawn.

Vincennes State Historic Site (all ages) 🏛

First and Harrison Streets, adjacent to Grouseland; (812) 882–7472. Open mid-March through mid-December. Hours are Tuesday through Saturday 9:00 A.M. to 5:00 P.M., Sunday 1:00 to 5:00 P.M. $.

Here you can see the two-room frame building that served as Indiana Territory's first capitol. It is considered the oldest major government building in the Midwest. Also on the grounds is the Western Sun Print Shop, a replica of the building in which the territory's first newspaper was printed in 1804. The entire site is on the edge of the campus of Vincennes University, which was founded in 1801 and is the oldest university west of the Alleghenies.

The Old Cathedral Complex (all ages) 🏛

207 Church Street; (800) 886–6443. Open daily 8:00 A.M. to 4:00 P.M. $.

Here is an interesting complex to visit. St. Francis Xavier Cathedral is the oldest Catholic church in Indiana, dating back to 1702. For those of you who are interested in old books, the Brute Library in this complex is a must-see. It is the oldest library in Indiana and has many rare books and documents. One document dates back to 1319 and is written on heavy parchment. Also at this complex you'll find a French and Indian cemetery.

Sonotabac Prehistoric Indian Mound (all ages) 🏛

2401 Wabash Avenue; (812) 882–7679. Open May 1 to September 30, noon to 5:00 P.M. Admission: adults 50 cents, children 25 cents.

The history of the Vincennes area goes back to prehistory, and here's a chance to step back into the Stone Age. Named after an Indian chief who aided George Rogers Clark, the mound was built around 2,000 years ago as a ceremonial temple. Begin your tour here by visiting the center museum to see tools made by Stone Age people and actually used in Vincennes in 8000 B.C.

Spirit of Vincennes Rendezvous (all ages)

On the French Commons, next to George Rogers Clark National Historic Park; (800) 886–6443.

Every Memorial Day weekend, you can relive the battlefield activities of George Rogers Clark. Hear the sounds of battle, from bagpipes to artillery fire, and see demonstrations of early American skills such as rope making, spinning, moccasin sewing, and chair caning. There is also entertainment and food.

Indiana Military Museum (all ages) 🎖

4305 Old Bruceville Road; (800) 886–6443. $.

One of the best overall collections of military memorabilia in the country, spanning the Civil War to Desert Storm. You will be able to see armored vehicles from World War II and cannons from both World Wars I and II.

The Old French House and Indiana Museum (all ages) 🎖

First and Seminary Streets; (800) 886–6443. Open Wednesday through Sunday in season. Call for details. $.

This 1806 home of French fur trader Michael Brouillet is an excellent example of a French Creole cottage.

Where to Eat

Market Street Restaurant. 102 Saint Honore Place; (812) 886–5201. Open Monday through Thursday 11:30 A.M. to 9:00 P.M., Friday and Saturday 10:00 A.M. to 11:00 P.M. Closed Sunday.

Aunt Helen's Old-Fashioned Family Cooking. 1925 Hart Street; (812) 882–6288. Open 4:00 A.M. to 11:00 P.M. daily.

Bakery. (See Executive Inn, below.) (812) 886–5000. Open 7 days a week from 6:00 A.M. to 2:00 P.M. Evening hours Monday through Thursday 5:00 to 9:00 P.M., Friday and Saturday 5:00 to 10:00 P.M. Breakfast is served 6:00 to 10:00 A.M.

Where to Stay

Executive Inn. One Executive Boulevard; (812) 886–5000. One hundred seventy rooms. Pets allowed.

Super 8 Motel. 600 Shirlee Street; (812) 882–5101; (812) 882–5101. Thirty-nine rooms, two floors, handicapped accessible, indoor pool. Pets allowed with permission.

For More Information

City of Vincennes. www.vincennes.org.

Take U.S. 41 south out of Vincennes and you are on your way to I–64 and New Harmony, Lincoln City, Ferdinand, and Santa Claus land. However, on the way you can visit Petersburg, Patoka Lake, and Jasper.

Petersburg

Do you like spending time camping with your family? Then there's no place better to do that than **Prides Creek Park.** This park has 200 acres with a ninety-acre lake and a nine-hole golf course. The many hills give the park a peaceful setting. The park gives you the opportunity to do so much in one day with your family that you'll always want to come back. There's golf, tennis, picnic areas, swimming, and jogging, just to mention a few of the things that can be done here. There are also pleasant walks, boating, and volleyball. All the camping sites are in wooded areas and have hot showers and a laundry room. For more information on Prides Creek Park, call (812) 354–6798.

Patoka Lake

Lick Fork Marina (all ages) ⛰️ 🌊
10306 East Lick Fork Marina Road; (812) 678–4991.

Families who love the water will love the 26,000-acre Patoka Lake Reservoir, which is the second-largest lake in Indiana; you can ride jet skis, water-ski, or just wade or swim in the water. There are also houseboats that you can rent so that you are always close to the water.

Patoka Lake Village (all ages) ⛺ 🏊

Pines Lake Village Drive; (812) 936–9854; www.patoka-lake.net or www.patokalake.com.

If your family loves the woods but finds roughing it too challenging, Patoka Lake Village may be the answer, offering twelve two-bedroom log cabins fully equipped with kitchen and bathrooms. This is a perfect way to retreat into the woods because there are 8,800 forest acres here. You are also just a short walk away from Patoka Lake, where you can enjoy all the water activities.

Jasper

The Dubois County Tourism Commission, 610 Main Street, assists in showcasing A Southern Indiana Adventure (Dubois and Spencer Counties) for customized tours for visitors. Hours: Monday through Friday 9:00 A.M. to 4:00 P.M.; (800) 968–4578.

Let your family experience what a celebration would be like if you were in Germany by attending the **Strassenfest.** Jasper was settled by many German immigrants, who celebrate their heritage annually from Thursday through Sunday on the first weekend in August. There are rides, music, dancing, all kinds of delicious food, entertainment, athletic events, a parade, and a big fireworks show.

The **Holy Family Catholic Church,** 950 Church Avenue, has the second-largest stained-glass window in the world, and the longest unsupported wood beam in its ceiling. Open daily until 8:00 P.M.; (812) 482–3076.

St. Joseph's Church, at U.S. 231 and Thirteenth Street, is an Old World church completed in 1880 that is listed on the National Register of Historic Places; German stained-glass windows. Open Monday through Friday until 9:00 P.M.; (812) 482–9115.

Indiana Baseball Hall of Fame (all ages)

Highway 231 and College Avenue; (800) ADVENTURE. Open Monday through Friday all year from 9:00 A.M. to 6:00 P.M. and on Saturday and Sunday from 10:00 A.M. to 4:00 P.M. No admission charge.

Do you have some baseball fans in your family? If so then the Indiana Baseball Hall of Fame, located on Vincennes University's Jasper campus, is the answer. Here you can see Indiana baseball memorabilia from high school to the professional level. This is an exciting opportunity to learn just a little bit more about baseball. Once you go through the hall, you'll come out a baseball fan even if you weren't one before.

Where to Eat

Schnitzebank Restaurant. 393 Third Avenue on State Road 162; (812) 482–2640; www.schnitzebank.com. From southern German dishes to seafood and steaks, dining at the "Schnitz" is Wunderbar! Hours: Monday through Thursday 8:00 A.M. to 10:00 P.M., Friday and Saturday to 11:00 P.M.

Where to Stay

Days Inn. State Road 162 and State Road 164; (812) 482–6000. Eighty-four rooms, two floors, handicapped accessible rooms, outdoor pool. Pets allowed.

Holiday Inn. U.S. Highway 231 South; (812) 482–5555; www.holiday-inn.com.

Sleep-Inn. 75 Indiana Street and Highway 231; (812) 481–2008.

Evansville

Angel Mounds State Historic Site (all ages)

8215 Pollack Avenue; (812) 853–3956; www.angelmounds.org. Free. Open Tuesday through Saturday 9:00 A.M. to 5:00 P.M. and Sunday 1:00 to 5:00 P.M.

Between A.D. 1200 and 1400, about 3,000 Mississippi Indians lived here. Today you can see eleven platform mounds and a re-creation of the town. There are an interpretive center and trails, picnic areas, and a nature preserve. This archaeological site is named after the Angel family who owned the land before it was purchased by the state. (It is traditional to name archaeological finds after landowners.)

Mesker Park Zoo (all ages)

2421 Bement Avenue; (812) 435–6143. Open year-round, daily 9:00 A.M. to 5:00 P.M. $$.

More than 700 animals and seventy acres of beautiful hills. Many animals roam in open-terrain settings surrounded by moats. There is a Discovery Center focusing on the rain forest that has monkeys and parrots. Tram, paddleboats, gift shop, and petting zoo.

Reitz Home Museum (all ages)

224 South East First Street; (812) 426–1871. Open Tuesday through Saturday 11:00 A.M. to 3:30 P.M. and Sunday 1:00 to 3:30 P.M. Closed Monday and major holidays. $.

Built in 1871, this Victorian home offers elaborate architectural features and is filled with original period furniture.

Indiana **Trivia**

What Indiana City is named for George Rogers Clark?

What Indiana City is named after a U.S. President?

Clarksville, Madison

Wesselman Wood Nature Preserve (all ages)

551 North Boeke Road; (812) 479–0771; www.wesselman.evansville.net. Open Tuesday through Sunday 8:00 A.M. to 4:00 P.M.

This is a national Natural Landmark and state nature preserve with 190 acres of virgin forest, fifty acres of younger forest, a field, and a pond.

Willard Library (ages 5 and up)

21 First Avenue; (812) 425–4309; www.willard.lib.in.us. Open Monday and Tuesday 9:00 A.M. to 8:00 P.M., Wednesday through Friday 9:00 A.M. to 5:30 P.M., Saturday 9:00 A.M. to 5:00 P.M., and Sunday 1:00 to 5:00 P.M.

Built in 1885, this is Indiana's oldest public library, featuring one of the state's best genealogical libraries. An example of high-Gothic architecture.

Burdette Park and Aquatic Center (all ages)

5301 Nurreburn Road; (812) 435–5602. Admission charge for Aquatic Center. Open Memorial Day to Labor Day, Monday through Thursday 10:00 A.M. to 6:00 P.M., Friday 10:00 A.M. to 10:00 P.M., Saturday and Sunday 10:00 A.M. to 7:00 P.M. From Labor Day to Memorial Day, open Monday through Friday 8:00 A.M. to 4:00 P.M.

Water slides, bumper boats, camping, hiking, rental chalets, party houses, BMX course, batting cages, and pavilions.

Festival

Evansville Riverfest. Riverside Drive, downtown; (812) 424–2986; www.downtownevansville.org. Held at the end of July, Wednesday and Thursday 11:00 A.M. to 11:00 P.M.; Friday and Saturday 11:00 A.M. to 1:00 A.M. Call for exact dates. Carnival rides, games, food booth, three stages of entertainment, children's activities, car show, and more.

Where to Eat

GD Ritzy's. 601 North Green River Road; (812) 474–6259. Grilled hamburgers, grilled chicken, new chicken strips, kids' meals, hot dogs, peanut butter and jelly sandwiches, ultrathin shoestring-style french fries, old-fashioned ice cream and milk shakes. Voted 2003 Best Hamburger in Evansville.

The Old Mill Restaurant. 5031 New Harmony Road; (812) 963–6000. Unique shrine for Saint Christopher, patron saint of travelers. Loft/outside dining, fireplace, 14-foot waterwheel, entertainment (hayrides, dancing), annual Germanfest (June), and its own "friendly ghost"! Open Monday through Thursday 4:00 to 9:00 P.M., Sunday 11:00 A.M. to 8:30 P.M.

Where to Stay

Evansville Conference Center. 4101 US 41 North; (812) 424–6400; fax: (812) 424–6409; www.holiday-inn.com.

Signature Inn. Green River Road and Vogel Road; (812) 476–9626; www .signatureinn.com. One hundred twenty-five rooms. **Free** continental breakfast.

Super 8 Motel. 19601 Elpers Road; (812) 867–8500 or (800) 800–8000. Located on Evansville's north side, with easy access from I–64.

Marriott. 7101 US 41 North; (812) 867–7999, (800) 228–1990; www .marriott.com. Cloud's Restaurant. One hundred ninety-nine rooms, two suites, indoor pool, health club, children's play gym, whirlpool, game room, handicapped accessible rooms.

For More Information

Evansville Convention and Visitors Bureau. (800) 433–3025 or www .evansvillecvb.org.

New Harmony

New Harmony is the site of two of America's earliest and most important utopian communities. You can visit these communities on Indiana 68 just 12 miles south of I–64. It is here on the Wabash River that a group of German people called Harmonists tried to establish a utopian community. Later, Robert Owen, a British social reformer, attempted to establish another such community. The experiment failed after two years, but the impact was felt in the Midwest for three decades. Your children will be glad to know that the nation's first free kindergarten and public school were started in New Harmony. Six historic sites are operated by the Indiana State Museum System. Admission is **free** to Thrall's Opera House, Dormitory Number Two, the Fauntleroy Home, the School House, the Harmonist Labyrinth, and Harmonist Cemetery. Phone (800) 231–2168 for times, as they vary with the season.

Historic New Harmony Tour (all ages) 🏛

Atheneum, North and Arthur Streets; (800) 231–2168; www.newharmony.org. Daily tours March 15 to December 30, 9:30 A.M. to 5:00 P.M. Closed in January and February. $$.

This guided tour starting at the Atheneum covers approximately 1 mile of restored buildings and will give you a broad overview of New Harmony's historical development. Many of the Harmonists were good craftspeople; you'll see many of the utensils, furniture, and structures they built. The Atheneum is a visitors center with exhibits and a seventeen-minute film on New Harmony. Also housed here are models of the town in 1824 and of the second Harmonist church. A biographical exhibit of the Owenite community will introduce you to leading nineteenth-century intellectuals and scientists who lived here. The museum gift shop offers a wide range of historical souvenirs, gifts, and books related to the town's history.

Harmonie State Park (all ages) 🏕 🚶 🌊 🍂

State Road 269 off State Road 69; (812) 682–4821. Open from 7:00 A.M. to 11:00 P.M. all year. $.

Harmonie State Park is located "on the banks of the Wabash," near historic New Harmony. A beautiful swimming pool, shady picnic areas, ravines, and pristine landscapes await you here. This is a trail lover's paradise! Trails for walking, biking, and nature hikes will lure you for a visit.

Where to Eat

Red Geranium Restaurant. 508 North Street; (812) 682–4431. One of the Midwest's most popular restaurants, the Red Geranium offers an exceptional dining experience in a comfortable atmosphere. Open Tuesday through Thursday 11:00 A.M. to 10:00 P.M., Friday and Saturday 11:00 A.M. to 11:00 P.M., Sunday 11:00 A.M. to 8:00 P.M. Closed Monday.

Country Cottage Restaurant. 317 Church Street; (812) 682–4291. Family dining at affordable prices. Plate lunches, sandwiches, pizza, homemade fudge, ice cream, salads, and much more. Open seven days a week. Winter hours 11:00 A.M. to 8:00 P.M. Summer hours 11:00 A.M. to 9:00 P.M.

Aunt Sallie's Soda Shoppe. 514 South Main Street; (812) 682–3383. Take a walk in the past through the forties and fifties. Everyone will love getting a soda, shake, banana split, phosphate, or just a plain ice-cream cone at this step-back-in-time soda shoppe.

Bayou Grill. 504 North Street; (812) 682–4431. Enjoy breakfast, lunch, or dinner in the pleasant surroundings of the Bayou Grill. The diverse menu selections range from delicious omelettes to hearty sandwiches to fried chicken and daily specials. The exciting Sunday brunch offers a wide variety of breakfast and lunch entrees highlighted by displays of fresh fruit and cheeses, magnificent ice carvings, and homemade desserts. Open 7:00 A.M. to 8:00 P.M. seven days a week.

Where to Stay

The New Harmony Inn. 508 North Street; (800) 782–8605. Located in the peaceful countryside of southwestern Indiana, New Harmony offers both intellectual stimulation as well as relaxation for your whole family. The New Harmony Inn reflects the cultural tradition of the area allowing guests a unique experience in a resort atmosphere. Features ninety guest rooms, eighteen with fireplaces; many have balconies overlooking the peaceful landscape and gardens. Enclosed swimming pool, tennis courts, and a distinctive art collection throughout. Also the famous Red Geranium Restaurant, The Bayou Grill, and the Dutch Biscuit Bakery. Pets not allowed.

Lincoln City

Lincoln Boyhood National Memorial (all ages) 🏛

State Road 162; (812) 937–4541; www.nps.gov/libo.com. Visitor center open daily from 8:00 A.M. to 5:00 P.M. March through November and 8:00 A.M. to 4:30 P.M. December through February. $.

See what the early life of one of America's greatest presidents, Abraham Lincoln, was like. At this historic site you can see his boyhood home. Lincoln moved here when he was seven and stayed until he was twenty-one. This is the farm where he worked with his father—splitting rails, plowing, and planting. Everything on this farm is historically accurate. Between mid-April and the end of September, costumed "pioneers" will show you everyday farming and home activities of the time. As you wander through the farm, your children will see these pioneers milking cows, kneading bread, and performing other chores, and a thirty-minute film, *Here I Grew Up,* is shown in the visitors center.

While you are visiting the memorial, you can enjoy a nice picnic at one of the many picnic tables located there, or head across the street to Lincoln State Park. The park is 1,747 acres of pure fun. You can enjoy the hiking areas, picnic spots, swimming, boating, camping, and fishing. Everybody will love all the outdoor activities at the park. If you'd like more information, call (812) 937–4541.

In the evening during summer, the whole family can attend the all-ages musical adventure *Young Abe Lincoln* in Lincoln State Park and hear about how Lincoln developed his honesty, character, love for family, and respect for others. The show, which has humor and drama, starts at 7:30 P.M. Tuesday through Saturday and at 2:30 P.M. Sunday. All seats are reserved. Seats are $10.00 for adults and $6.00 for children twelve and under. Reservations are recommended. Call (800) 264–4ABE to reserve tickets. Before the show, you can enjoy a catered picnic supper in the park and ask questions of President Abraham Lincoln as he mingles with guests. Reservations must be made for the supper.

Ferdinand

Ferdinand is rich in German heritage. Saint Meinrad Archabbey is nearby, as are many local landmarks. Heimatfest is a community festival, held in the end of June at the Eighteenth Street Park. It is a community festival celebrating the town's German heritage. Tractor pull, food concessions, games, special performances on Saturday evening.

Ferdinand State Forest (all ages) Ⓐ ⊜ ⚠ 🌰

6583 East State Road 264; (812) 367–1524. Open daily 7:00 A.M. to 11:00 P.M. $.

Ferdinand was established in 1934 as a Civilian Conservation Corps (CCC) camp. CCC workers built roads, service buildings, and one of the most beautiful forest lakes in the state.

For camping families, this is one of the best spots in all of Indiana. The 7,000-acre forest is open year-round. There are seventy primitive campsites, swimming, boating, fishing, and hunting. This will be one of the most relaxing trips you've been on in a while, as you'll spend most of your time outdoors.

Monastery of the Immaculate Conception (all ages)

802 East Tenth Street; (812) 367–1411; www.thedome.org. Information center open daily except Monday, 8:30 A.M. to 4:30 P.M. Guided tours daily. Call for times. Donations welcome.

The "Castle on the Hill" houses one of the largest communities of Benedictine women in the United States.

Santa Claus

Whether you have been naughty or nice, the only post office with a Santa Claus postmark is here in Santa Claus, Indiana. This tiny post office handles a flood of mail each Christmas.

Holiday World (all ages) 🎠

Highways 162 and 245, in Santa Claus; (877) 463–2645; www .holidayworld.com. Open daily June and July, most days in August, and on certain days in April, May, September, and October. Park opens at 11:00 A.M.; closing time varies. Admission charge. Visit its Web site or call for ticket prices and exact hours.

Everyone in your family will enjoy Holiday World. There's something for everyone at this magical place that celebrates Christmas, the Fourth of July, and Halloween and has twenty-one rides from mild to wild, games, and other attractions. Young children experience the joy of seeing where Santa lives and can visit with Santa, and there is a kiddyland for them, too. Teenagers will like the amusements and thrill rides. And there is much more. You can visit the wax museum and view fifty figures who have helped shape this country. Holiday World also has two musical shows, one high-dive show, and a costume character review.

Splashin' Safari (all ages)
Part of Holiday World.

Does your family like water parks and rides? Then look no further than this park to experience the thrill of white-water rafting, a wave pool, and water rides. Or you can just relax in the pool or in a lounge chair and take it easy. Splashin' Safari and Holiday World have combined to make two theme parks for one price.

Where to Eat

St. Nick's Restaurant. Highway 162; (812) 937–4359. Everything from sandwiches to steaks. Open Monday through Friday 10:00 A.M. to 9:00 P.M., Saturday and Sunday 7:00 A.M. to 9:00 P.M.

Where to Stay

Holiday Inn. U.S. 231, Jasper; (800) 872–3176.

Santa Lodge. Highway 162; (812) 937–1902; (800) 640–7895. Forty-six rooms. Indoor pool, hot tub, pond with paddleboats, and children's playground. Pets not allowed.

Camping

Lake Rudolph Outdoor Resort. 78 North Holiday Boulevard, junction of Highways 162 and 245; (812) 937–4458. You and your family can enjoy camping at Lake Rudolph Outdoor Resort, located adjacent to Holiday World. Featuring full hookups, fishing, beach area, playground, miniature golf, swimming pool, game room, and country store.

Leavenworth

The Crawford County Board of Tourism Commissioners is open year-round. To get more information call (888) 846–5397. Enjoy a nature getaway and discover the pot of gold at rainbow's end.

You and your family can go canoeing—rent canoes at Cave Country Canoes, (812) 365–2705, Highway 66. West of Jeffersonville near Leavenworth are the **Wyandotte Caves** on Wyandotte Cave Road off State Road 62. Big Wyandotte Cave and Little Wyandotte Cave were used by prehistoric Indians for shelter and as a source of materials for tools. You can take a brief thirty- to forty-five-minute tour of Little Wyandotte or a longer two-hour tour of Big Wyandotte. There is also a longer all-day tour for the truly adventurous. On this tour, you'll spend 25 percent of your time crawling and some of the going may be muddy. A very rugged tour that features 40 percent crawling is also offered. You must meet age and size requirements for these demanding tours. Admission to the visitor center is free, but there is a fee for cave tours. Call (812) 738–2782 to get more tour information.

Visit **Stephenson and Co. General Store and Museum,** 618 West Plaza Drive, an eighty-year-old, family-operated working general store. Crafts, antiques, historical photographs, and paraphernalia. Open year-round, Monday through Saturday 10:30 A.M. to 5:30 P.M.; open Sunday May through November 1:00 to 5:00 P.M.; (812) 739–4242.

For annual weekends in the fall, remember to call Sharon Wilson (888–846–5397) for more information. The Leavenworth River Fest is the last weekend in September. The Sorghum Festival, Crawford County High School, Highway 66, is the third weekend in October. Rain or shine.

Where to Eat

Overlook Restaurant. 1153 West Highway 52; (812) 739–4264. Everything to eat with a specialty in chicken.

Dock Restaurant. 764 South Nelson; (812) 739–4449. Specializes in fish. Fun eating outdoors with paper plates.

Where to Stay

Carefree Days Inn. Highway 66, Carefree; (812) 739–4805.

Leavenworth Inn. Highway 62; (812) 739–2120; www.leavenworthinn.com. Eleven rooms.

Corydon

Corydon was the state capital from 1816 until 1825, when the government was moved to Indianapolis. Focus on the past by taking a walking tour of this historic town. Brochures are available at the visitors center at 310 Elm Street. The **restored capitol building, Governor Hendricks's Headquarters,** and **Constitution Elm** can be seen for no charge on Sunday and Tuesday between 1:00 and 5:00 P.M. and on Wednesday through Saturday between 9:00 A.M. and 5:00 P.M. The square, Federal-style limestone building, which became Indiana's first capitol, was originally to be built as the courthouse for Harrison County. Between 1814 and 1816, the need for a building to house the legislature finally prompted construction. Blue limestone was hauled from nearby quarries to erect the walls. In June of 1816, in the midst of construction, all attention was focused on Corydon, as delegates from throughout the territory gathered to forge the state's first constitution. In the heat of a southern Indiana summer, several unofficial deliberations were held under the shade of a large elm tree that has since been dubbed the "Constitution Elm." For more information, call (888) 738–2137: www.tourindiana.com.

Battle of Corydon Memorial Park (all ages) 🏛 🏕

Old State Road 135; (812) 738–8236. Open daily 8:00 A.M. until dark. **Free.**

Indiana's only Civil War battle, the Battle of Corydon, took place on July 9, 1863, when members of the Harrison County Home Guard attempted to delay General John Hunt Morgan's Confederate soldiers in hopes that Union reinforcements would arrive in time to stop Morgan's march through southern Indiana. The site of the Battle of Corydon is now a memorial park. A small log cabin sits in the park, giving visitors an idea of the houses of that period. A trail meanders through this almost completely wooded five-acre park.

Squire Boone Caverns and Village (all ages) 🏛

Highway 135 South; (812) 732–4382; www.squireboonecaverns.com.

Daniel Boone and his younger brother Squire discovered these caverns in 1790. They have massive stalactites and underground waterfalls. The village features log cabins, a gristmill, a hayride, a farm animal petting zoo, Indian artifacts, and craft demonstrations. You can visit the caverns throughout the year and the village in the summer.

Where to Eat

Magdalena's. 103 East Chestnut Street; (812) 738–8075. Open daily 10:30 A.M. to 9:30 P.M.

The Chestnut Street Cafe. 100 East Chestnut; (812) 738–2655.

Where to Stay

Holiday Inn Express. 249 Federal Drive NW; (800) 465–4329. Fifty-seven rooms, wheelchair accessible, Jacuzzi rooms with fireplace, indoor heated pool, and hot tub; restaurants nearby include Cracker Barrel and Ryans. AAA discounts available.

Kintner House Inn. 101 South Capitol Avenue at Chestnut Street; (812) 738–2020. Fifteen rooms. Children under 12 stay **free.** Breakfast included. No pets. No smoking.

Baymont Inns. 2495 Landmark Avenue; (812) 738–1500; (877) 229–6668.

Elizabeth

Needmore Buffalo Farm (all ages) 🐘 🍴 🚪
4100 Buffalo Lane; (812) 968–3473. Open 9:00 A.M. to 6:00 P.M. daily except Tuesday and holidays. Free.

Thousands of buffalo once roamed Indiana, and you can see the largest buffalo herd in North America at Needmore Buffalo Farm. Following the custom of early Native Americans, the staff here respectfully converts every part of the buffalo into useful and artistic items. The Thundering Buffalo Trading Post sells antiques and historical artifacts, along with buffalo leather, yarn spun from bison hair, hides, bleached skulls, scrimshaw, and other bison-related crafts; it also sells bison meat. For different fare, try the buffalo burgers and buffalo chili at Nana Jane's Restaurant. You can also stay at the lodge and spend more time observing the buffalo; call to find out about buffalo roundups, annual festivals, and accommodations.

For More Information

Harrison County Convention and Visitors Bureau. 310 North Elm Street, Corydon, (888) 738–2137.

Jeffersonville

The Clark–Floyd Counties Convention and Tourism Bureau, 315 Southern Indiana Avenue (812–282–6654), www.sunnysideoflouisville.org, has a new visitors information center featuring information on attractions, hotel rooms, festivals, maps, and shopping. Community tours and Indiana souvenirs are available.

Hillerich and Bradsby Co. (all ages) 🏛
1525 Charleson–New Albany Pike; (502) 588–7228. Free tours weekdays from 9:00 A.M. to 5:00 P.M.

Have you ever wondered where the famous Louisville Slugger baseball bats were made? If you said "Louisville," you are incorrect. Every year, more than 50,000 visitors watch bats being made here at Hillerich and Bradsby in Jeffersonville, much as they were when the first Louisville Slugger was made in 1884. The Louisville Slugger has been called "one of the greatest original American products ever made." If you're lucky, you might see your favorite major-leaguer's bat being hand-turned right in front of your eyes during your tour.

Howard Steamboat Museum (all ages)

1101 East Market Street; (888) 472–0606; www.steamboatmuseum.org. Museum tours Tuesday through Saturday 10:00 A.M. to 4:00 P.M. and Sunday 1:00 to 4:00 P.M. Under age 6 are free. $.

You can get a glimpse of the steamboat era here in the mansion of the Howard steamboat-building family. You'll see many models, tools, photos, and other artifacts. The mansion is quite elegant, with a grand staircase and leaded and stained-glass windows.

Where to Eat

Ann's by the River Cafeteria. 149 Spring Street; (812) 284–2667.

Schimpff's Confectionery. 347 Spring Street; (812) 283–8367. A century-old confectionery in the historic district. Complete with tin ceiling, soda fountain, and candy store. Open Monday through Friday 10:00 A.M. to 5:00 P.M., Saturday 10:00 A.M. to 3:00 P.M. Closed Sunday and major holidays.

Holiday Inn Lakeview. Address and phone number below.

Where to Stay

Ramada Inn Riverside. 700 West Riverside Drive; (812) 284–6711; www.ramada.com.

Holiday Inn Lakeview. 505 Marriott Drive, Clarksville; (812) 283–4411; www.holidayinn.com. The hotel has a restaurant and an indoor pool.

Super 8. 2102 Highway 31 East; (812) 282–8000; www.super8.com.

Clarksville

Derby Dinner Playhouse (all ages)

525 Marriott Drive; (812) 288–8281; www.derbydiner.com. Performances nightly except Monday. Doors open at 6:00 P.M. Buffet dinner 6:15 to 7:15 P.M. Show at 8:00 P.M. Matinees on Wednesday and Sunday; doors open at 11:45 A.M., show at 1:30 P.M. $$$$.

Would your family like some good entertainment along with some good food at the same time? Then head on down to the Derby Dinner Playhouse, where you can enjoy both. The playhouse offers top-notch performances of Broadway productions and an excellent buffet dinner. The seating is arranged so that everyone has a great view of the stage. This exciting place will be one your family will remember.

Falls of the Ohio State Park (all ages)

201 West Riverside Drive; (812) 280–9970; www.fallsoftheohio.org. Hours are 9:00 A.M. to 5:00 P.M. Monday through Saturday, 1:00 to 5:00 P.M. Sunday. Closed Thanksgiving and Christmas. Guided tours May 1 through October 31. $.

If you want to look back 375 million years, this is the place to do it. The fossilized coral reef here is the largest Devonian fossil bed in the world. While you can't collect fossils, you can certainly explore the thousands of fossils in the park. The best time to visit is between August and October, when the river is lowest and the fossil beds are most accessible. There is also an interpretive center overlooking the Ohio River, where you can take a "walking tour through time." You will especially want to see the laser video, which dramatically takes you back to the area's geologic past. You'll also find extensive wildlife in the park. You can launch a boat for river fishing or just for enjoying the river.

Where to Eat

All restaurants are on Highway 131 at I–65 exit 4.

Hometown Buffet. (812) 285–1893.

Red Lobster. (812) 285–0444.

O'Charlie's. (812) 284–9646.

Applebee's. (812) 283–3594.

Where to Stay

Best Western Green Tree Inn. 1425 Broadway, I–65 exit 4; (812) 288–9281; www.bestwestern.com.

Holiday Inn Lakeview. 505 Marriott Drive; (800) 544–7075; www.holiday inn.com.

Hampton Inn Clarksville. 1501 Broadway; (812) 280–1901. Continental breakfast, outdoor pool.

Minutes away from Clarksville in Jeffersonville, New Albany, or Louisville, Kentucky, you can find accommodations in large chain hotels.

Madison

Sit on the bank of the Ohio River in Madison, and you may hear the toot of a whistle and see a steamboat on the river. Stroll through town and you may think that you have gone back 150 years in time, because this town has so many preserved homes. Stop at the visitors center at 601 West First Street to pick up brochures and tourist information and watch a video. Then walk around the town visiting historic homes and offices and specialty shops. Plan on spending a day in Madison—there is so much to see.

Tour the **mansion of James F. D. Lanier,** a frontier banker who saved the state of Indiana from bankruptcy during the Civil War. You will be fascinated by the three-story spiral staircase in this stately mansion at Elm and West First Streets. Admission is **free.** Make it a point to visit Dr. William Hutchings Office and Hospital at 120 West Third Street, the **Fair Play Fire Company** at 403 East Main, the **Schofield House** at 217 West Second, the **Shrewsbury House** at 301 West First Street, the Sullivan House at 304 West Second Street, and the **Madison Railroad Depot** at 615 West First Street, which has permanent and special exhibits on the history of southeastern Indiana with an emphasis on steamboating and railroading; there's also a gift shop. To learn about hours and days of operation and admission fees for these historic places, call (800) 559–2956.

Don't expect to be satisfied with just one visit to Madison. Come back to the town frequently for the many festivals held here. Watching the **Madison Regatta** in July can be a real treat, as it is an opportunity to see unusual events, including an unlimited hydroplane race and a balloon race. In the nights before Christmas in November and December, **candlelight tours** of public and private homes can be a special holiday treat. For all festival information call the visitors center at (800) 559–2956.

Riverfront Park (all ages)
Vaughn Drive, at the river; (800) 559–2956.

Scenic walkways and a picnic area, floating restaurant, boat ramp and docks, watercraft rentals, and a trolley. Watch the paddle wheelers of the past and speedy modern crafts on the Ohio River.

Scenic Bicycle Trails (ages 5 and up)
(800) 559–2956.

Bicycle Indiana's most beautiful county. Exhilarating routes for road or mountain biking. **Free** brochures.

Clifty Falls Park and Clifty Inn (all ages)
1501 Green Road; park, (812) 273–8885; inn, (812) 265–4135. Park is open 7:00 A.M. to 11:00 P.M. $.

The name paints a beautiful picture in your mind. See breathtaking waterfalls and a deep boulder canyon as you hike along the trails through this scenic park. The park overlooks the Ohio River and is perfect for a day's visit or an overnight stay at the Clifty Inn.

Where to Eat

Hinkles. 204 West Main Street; (812) 265–3919. Open Monday and Tuesday 6:00 A.M. to 10:00 P.M., Wednesday through Saturday 6:00 A.M. to 4:00 A.M. Hamburgers, home fries, homemade chili, hand-breaded fish, and sandwiches.

The Wharf Restaurant. 326 Vaughn Drive, on the river at Broadway; (812) 265–2688. Riverfront restaurant serving sandwiches, steaks, and seafood. Open Wednesday and Friday 4:00 to 9:00 P.M., Saturday and Sunday 11:00 A.M. to 9:00 P.M.

Where to Stay

Best Western. 700 Clifty Drive; (812) 273–5151. Indoor pool, free continental breakfast. Children under 12 stay free.

Clifty Inn. Clifty Falls State Park; P.O. Box 387, Madison, IN 47250; (812) 265–4135. Seventy-two rooms. Outdoor pool. Pets not allowed.

President Madison Motel. 906 East First Street, off Highway 421; (800) 456–6835. Twenty-five rooms. Outdoor pool. Pets allowed.

For More Information

Madison Area Convention and Visitors Bureau. 301 East Main; (800) 559–2956; www.visitmadison.org.

A Gisler **Adventure**

One of our most memorable family trips was to French Lick Springs Resort. Here our family had the opportunity to turn back the clock and see how the rich and famous used to live during the early twentieth century. Between swimming, golfing, riding horseback, taking horse-drawn carriage rides, enjoying a health and fitness spa, bowling, or bicycling, everyone in our family found his or her favorite activity. After a few hours of outdoor fun, we jumped in the car for a short drive to the French Lick West Baden & Southern train station. The family thoroughly enjoyed the two-hour ride through 20 miles of Hoosier National Forest, the longest railroad tunnel in the state, and the stories recounted by the crew as we traveled. After the exciting train ride, our family headed back to the resort to one of the restaurants.

French Lick

French Lick Springs Resort (all ages)
8670 West State Road 56; (800) 960–3577; www.frenchlick.com.

Travel back to yesteryear and see how the rich and famous enjoyed life at the start of the twentieth century. Here is a complete four-season resort. You can swim in the indoor pool or the outdoor Olympic-size pool, golf on two eighteen-hole courses, ride horseback, take horse-drawn carriage rides, enjoy a health and fitness spa, bowl, bicycle, or take part in daily events. There are four restaurants to meet every dining need from casual to formal.

French Lick West Baden & Southern Railroad (all ages)
Highway 56; (812) 936–2405; www.indianarailwaymuseum.org. Trips leave at 10:00 A.M., 1:00 P.M., and 4:00 P.M. Saturday, Sunday, and holidays, April through October; 1:00 P.M. Tuesday, June through October; and weekends in November. $$. Children under 3 are free.

Does your family love trains? Then hop aboard the French Lick West Baden & Southern at the depot for an almost two-hour ride through 20 miles of the Hoosier National Forest. This trip lets you experience a train ride through the longest railroad tunnel in the state. The crew will tell you special stories as you travel along.

French Lick Spring Villas (all ages)
8718 West State Road 56; (800) 522–9210.

Here's another spot to relax. These villas are fully equipped condos with living room, fireplace, two bedrooms, two baths, whirlpool, sauna, full kitchen, inside grill, and washer/dryer. Each villa sleeps eight. The children will love doing all the activities here while you relax.

Where to Eat

There are four restaurants at the French Lick Springs Resort: **Le Bistro, Jack's Steakhouse,** the **Ice Cream Parlor,** and the **Country Club Restaurant** (at the golf course clubhouse).

Where to Stay

French Lick Springs Resort. 8670 West State Road 56; (800) 960–3577. The resort offers many weekend specials and babysitting.

Patoka Lake Village Log Cabin Rentals. Rural Route 2, Box 255 E; (812) 936–9854; www.patokalakevillage.webjump.com.

Wilstem Guest Ranch. Highway 56 East; (812) 936–4484. Eleven cabins, one lodge. This is a 1,100-acre working ranch with a historic lodge and two- and three-bedroom condo-style furnished cabins. The cabins have hot tubs, covered porches, fireplaces, and grills. Pool on-site.

Paoli

Ski Paoli Peaks (ages 5 and up) ⊘

State Road 150 West; (812) 723–4696; www.paolipeaks.com. Midnight Madness midnight to 6:00 A.M. Friday and Saturday. Weekdays from 10:00 A.M. to 9:30 P.M. and from 9:00 A.M. on weekends.

Do you love to ski? Well, here's the place to go for experts and beginners alike. There are fourteen trails for skiing and a lodge with breathtaking views. Getting up to the top of the ski runs is not difficult, since there are one quad and three triple chairlifts and four surface tows. If you haven't been on the slopes before, taking lessons is easy as there are seventy instructors available. Children as young as five can take lessons and soon join you on the slopes after attending the Children's Ski School. You don't need to own equipment to ski here because the Ski Pro Shop has rental equipment, including a large selection of snowboards. So conquer the winter doldrums at Ski Paoli Peaks by skiing or snowboarding.

Patoka River Cabins (all ages) ⊖ ⊗ ⊜ ⊘

7355 South County Road 50 West; (812) 723–5544; www.patokarivercabins.com. Open year-round.

Here is another vacation idea that will have your whole family excited and ready to go. In the heart of the Hoosier National Forest you can rent one of many beautiful cabins to stay in. Once you get here you will be awestruck by how beautiful the woods are. Patoka River Cabins offers year-round vacation cabins so you can be there in the fall when all the leaves change color or in the winter when everything is covered with a blanket of snow. Whenever you decide to visit, it will be perfect. You have the freedom to do whatever you want, from swimming to hiking to skiing, depending on the season; then you can return to a cozy cabin. Rates from $72.50 to $180.00. Pets are allowed for a fee.

Marengo

Marengo Cave (all ages) ⊜ ⊕ ⊘

Marengo Cave Road, ten minutes from I-64; (812) 365–2705; canoeing information, (812) 633–4993; www.marengocave.com. Open all year except Thanksgiving and Christmas. Hours are seasonal. Call for details.

Does your family love caving, horseback riding, swimming, camping, and canoeing? If so, visit Marengo Cave, a U.S. National Landmark. Two tours are offered. On the Crystal Palace tour, you see a beautiful cave room that is dramatically lighted. On the longer Dripstone Trail tour, you go by totem pole stalagmites and delicate soda-straw formations as well as the "Penny Ceiling." There are also a large gift shop, several shaded picnic areas, cave arcade, and a signed nature trail; trail rides and canoe outings are offered, too. Canoeing is rapidly becoming a very popular outdoor activity here, and you can take scenic float trips on the Blue River for an outdoor adventure.

Mitchell

Spring Mill State Park is another park that offers endless opportunities for recreation. The restored pioneer village is a delight as you travel through time to the early 1800s. There's truly a lot to see in the village—all in excellent condition. Besides the pioneer log houses, village store, hatmaker's shop, post office, sawmill, shoemakers, weavers, and apothecary shop, you can see up close a fully functioning, water-powered gristmill. (Seeing in this case is so much better than reading about gristmills.) Plan to take a boat ride into Twin Cave or a walk into Donaldson Cave. The Grissom Memorial in the park honors Hoosier astronaut Virgil "Gus" Grissom, one of the seven Mercury astronauts and America's second man in space. You can see a space capsule and a video. The park is open daily throughout the year. Park admission is a modest cost for private vehicles. Phone (812) 849–4129 for park information, and (812) 849–4081 if you want to stay at the inn in the park. Visit the Web site at www.in.gov/dnr/parklake/parks/springmill.

Festival

Annual Mitchell Persimmon Festival. Open Monday through Friday 5:00 to 10:00 P.M. and Saturday 10:00 A.M. to midnight. For exact dates call (800) 798–0769. Held for one week during the end of September. Persimmon pudding and novelty contests, parade, carnival, arts and crafts, fine arts and photography shows, antique autos and machinery, pioneer village candlelight tour, free nightly entertainment, food, and more.

Where to Eat/ Where to Stay

Spring Mill Inn. Highway 60 East; (812) 849–4081. Located within the state park. Seventy-four rooms. Indoor and outdoor pools. Dining room. Open year-round. No pets allowed. (See park listing for more information.)

For More Information

Lawrence County Tourism Commission. (800) 798–0769; www.limestonecountry.com.

Montgomery

In Southern Indiana you can experience the Amish way of life at **The Gasthof,** a two-story bank barn created by Amish carpenters on County Road 650 East. The Gasthof has an immense restaurant, a craft shop, and a bakery. The restaurant features "made from scratch" cooking, and meals are served family style. There is a year-round Village Market that has seasonal produce as well as Amish baked goods. If you want to see the Amish way of life, schedule a personally guided tour (fun for all ages), offered Monday through Saturday. Call (812) 486–2600 for more information; www.gasthofamishvillage.com.

North Vernon

If your family loves to camp and have fun in the outdoors, then there's no better place to go than **Muscatatuck County Park** on State Road 3. This 260-acre park offers something for kids of all ages, so much you won't have time to do everything. There are bird trails, picnic grounds, the remnants of a gristmill to explore, shelter houses, a wildlife marsh, a fenced kiddie playground, and an old school. For you athletes there is also softball, basketball, soccer, volleyball, archery, and horseshoes. You can also hike to scenic overlooks, take the Marsh Walk, or walk along river trails. For more information call (812) 346–2953.

Salem

Salem is one of the oldest cities in Indiana, and you can go to the **John Hay Center** at 307 East Market Street to relive its past. You may remember the name of John Hay, personal secretary to Abraham Lincoln and secretary of state under presidents McKinley and Theodore Roosevelt, as well as a native of Salem. At the **Stevens Memorial Museum** in the town center, you can see old-time law and dentist offices as well as Civil War mementos, tools, furniture, and other displays of the past. Then you can visit the **pioneer village** to see how the early settlers lived. The admission cost is modest, and children under thirteen are admitted **free.** Village tours are given 9:00 A.M. to 5:00 P.M.; the center is closed Monday and holidays.

Another reason to visit the center is to attend the **Old Settlers' Days Festival** on the second weekend in September. Many of the craftspeople will be showing how they have created their wares. There are hourly demonstrations of weaving, spinning, rug braiding, and other domestic crafts, as well as story telling and good food. All these festivities are designed to honor the stalwart and brave people who settled this area. For information about the John Hay Center and festival, call (812) 883–6495.

Seymour

Escape into the peace and quiet of southern Indiana for a week or just a weekend at **Red-brush Park.** This family resort is located on 750 acres of woodlands on Highway 258. You can explore hiking trails and experience excellent fishing. But more than that, there are a tremendous number of kid-pleasing attractions. They'll enjoy a giant water slide, miniature golf, pedal boats, kiddie rides, and even a petting zoo, along with swimming in the lake. Accommodations range from campsites to cozy villas or rooms, and fully furnished tree-house cottages. For information and reservations, call (812) 497–2480.

Your family may wish to visit Seymour in October to enjoy the **Oktoberfest.** Each year the first weekend in October (Thursday, Friday, and Saturday) you can enjoy the festivities. Family fun comes from the dancing, good food, **free** entertainment, arts and crafts, a parade, flea market, and carnival. For the athletes, there is a 5K run. You can call (888) 524–1914 to find out more about the Oktoberfest.

Where to Eat

Cracker Barrel. 211 Sandy Creek Drive; (812) 522–3122. Pasta, chicken, steak, and seafood entrees. Open Monday through Thursday 6:00 A.M. to 10:00 P.M., Friday through Sunday 6:00 A.M. to 11:00 P.M.

Ryan's. 203 North Sandy Creek Drive; (812) 523–1626. Children under 3 eat **free.**

Sonic Drive-In. 811 West Tipton Street; (812) 522–6984.

Where to Stay

Holiday Inn. 2025 East Tipton Street; (812) 522–6767; www.holiday-inn.com.

Lees Inn. 2075 East Tipton Street; (812) 523–1850; www.leesinn.com.

Hometown Inn. 207 North Sandy Creek Drive; (812) 522–3523. One hundred seventeen rooms. Outdoor pool. Pets are welcome.

For More Information

Jackson County Visitors Center. 351 Tanger Boulevard, Suite 231, Seymour; (888) 524–1914; www.jacksoncountyin .com or www.seymour.com.

The Ohio River in **Southern Indiana**

The 981-mile Ohio River winds its way through six states and has had an enormous impact on our nation's history. You can enjoy a leisurely and scenic drive along State Roads 62 and 66; along the way you will discover many small southern Indiana towns. The landscape provides your family with a pleasant escape from the sameness of today's suburban growth, while the historic architecture has a charm and grace missing from modern city life. You will enjoy agricultural countryside with well-kept barns, vineyards, and orchards; vistas of rural villages dominated by church spires and historic courthouses; and thriving cities with imposing architecture. Tucked away in the very toe of southwestern Indiana is something you would expect to find only in our southern states: cypress swamps, complete with water lilies and rare birds. You can fish or just drift along lazily in a boat at **Hovey Lake State Fish and Wildlife Area,** a 4,300-acre wetland, and adjoining the lake is **Twin Swamps Nature Preserve,** a cypress swamp in Indiana.

Vevay

Swiss immigrants from Vevay, Switzerland, settled in this small river town in 1802. You can learn about modern Vevay by visiting the **Switzerland County Welcome Center** at 209 Ferry Street. Get a copy of the walking tour so you can visit some of the forty-nine historic spots on this tour. Plan to stay at a local bed-and-breakfast so you can shop, watch the river, enjoy river activities, and look at the historic homes. You may see a paddle wheeler on the Ohio River, find vintage clothing or native clay pottery at a store, or take part in one of the many events like the **Legend of Sleepy Hollow Celebration.** Be sure to drive north along the Ohio River on Highway 156 to visit **Markland Dam Park.** You won't have to wait long here before boats arrive to go through the locks—an exciting event for everyone to watch.

For More Information

Switzerland County Welcome Center.
209 Ferry Street; (800) HELLO–VV.

Central Indiana

A great place to start your family adventures in Indiana is Indianapolis, the state capital. You won't have any trouble getting to Indianapolis because more rail lines and interstate highways go through this city than any other metropolis in the country. That's why it is called the Crossroads of America. Right in the Indianapolis area your family will be able to enjoy a day or several days' worth of family fun. The capital is full of many different attractions that all of you will enjoy visiting.

TopPicks for fun in Central Indiana

1. Children's Museum, Indianapolis

2. Indianapolis Motor Speedway, Indianapolis

3. Eagle Creek Park, Indianapolis

4. Conner Prairie, Fishers

5. Indiana State Museum, Indianapolis

6. Eiteljorg Museum of American Indian and Western Art, Indianapolis

7. IMAX 3-D Theater, Indianapolis

8. Victory Field, Indianapolis Indians Baseball, Indianapolis

9. The Quaint Victorian Village, Zionsville

CENTRAL INDIANA

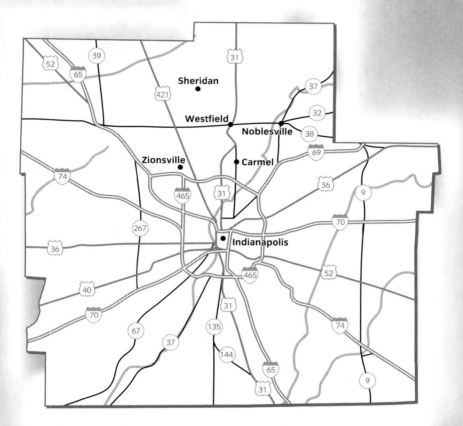

Sheridan

Westfield

Noblesville

Zionsville

Carmel

Indianapolis

Today Indianapolis is the twelfth-largest city in the United States and is also known as a city that has hosted more than 250 national and international sporting events. The best part about all of this is that your family will be able to enjoy many facilities used by the world's best athletes because they are open to the public. Within the city, which is one of the biggest state capitals in land area (403 square miles), you'll find historic landmarks, museums, and recreation areas to capture the interest of every member of your family. You will especially want to see the largest children's museum in the world. To the delight of sports lovers, the city is the home of the Indianapolis Colts, the Indiana Pacers, the Indianapolis Indians, and the Indianapolis Ice. There is also the exciting Indianapolis 500 race, the largest one-day sporting event in the world. The city considers itself the amateur sports capital of the world and hosts many national and international events. The past is preserved in Indianapolis for you to see at museums and restored homes, especially those of James Whitcomb Riley and President Benjamin Harrison. You also will want to step into the city's proud past at the Indiana Soldiers' and Sailors' Monument and Crown Hill Cemetery. For relaxation and all kinds of activities, a marvelous parks system awaits you and your family in Indianapolis.

Calderfest is a citywide celebration of creativity inspired by the works of Alexander Calder, the famous mobile sculptor. A Calder exhibit at the Children's Museum, a Calderfest artboat flotilla, and a Dance Kaleidoscope performance around one of Calder's sculptures will be included in the festivities May through December.

When you visit a new city, the first thing to do is to find a tour like the **Gray Line of Indianapolis** that will give you a quick overview of the city. This orients you to the locations of all the places on the tour that your family will probably want to visit and helps you plan future excursions. The Gray Line City Tour will show you the following places:

- Indianapolis Motor Speedway and Museum
- Indiana War Memorial and Plaza
- Governor's Residence
- Soldiers' and Sailors' Monument
- Children's Museum
- Indianapolis Museum of Art
- RCA (Hoosier) Dome
- Indiana State Museum
- Circle Center
- President Benjamin Harrison's Home
- Lockerbie Square
- Pan American Plaza and City Center
- Butler University Campus
- State Capitol Building

- Eiteljorg Museum
- Victory Field
- Scottish Rite Cathedral
- Conseco Field House

All tours depart from the Hyatt Regency Hotel–Downtown. The City Tour runs on Wednesday from April 1 through October 31 from 1:00 to 4:00 P.M. Call (800) 447–4526 for more information. Prices are $20.00 adults, $15.50 seniors 62 and over, $11.00 children 3 to 11. Reservations should be made the Monday before the Wednesday tour.

If you have a family of hikers you definitely need to take a walking tour of the city. **Landmarks on Foot** is a walking tour of the historic downtown by Historic Landmarks Foundation of Indiana (317) 639–4534 or (800) 450–4534. Walking is a great way to see some of the unique things about Indianapolis. This is a one-and-a-half-hour guided walking tour of the old Wholesale District and Monument Circle. You will hear the story of Indianapolis, old and new, as you walk through its restored historic places and modern landmarks. Tours are offered weekly on Friday, Saturday, and Sunday at 1:00 P.M. May through October. Call for prices.

Indiana Soldiers' and Sailors' Monument (ages 5 and up, unless toddlers are carried) 🏛

Monument Circle, Meridian at Market; (317) 232–7615. Observation deck open year-round, Wednesday through Sunday 10:00 A.M. to 4:30 P.M. $.

To get a bird's-eye view of downtown Indianapolis, you will want to visit this monument. Do you have energetic children? A family outing to the top is a challenging 336-stair climb—the monument is only 15 feet shorter than the Statue of Liberty. Parents can always let older children start the climb and then skip quite a few stairs by riding the elevator; however, everyone must climb the last forty-five stairs to reach the glass-enclosed balcony at the top. This is where your family will be able to get a panoramic view of Indianapolis. When you are at the monument, you are in the center of Indianapolis. The city got the name "Circle City" from nineteenth-century architect Alexander Ralston, who designed Indianapolis in concentric circles, starting at the century-old Soldiers' and Sailors' Monument. You should also stop by the City Center to see how the city was designed.

When you visit the Soldiers' and Sailors' Monument, you are seeing what is considered one of the world's outstanding monuments. John Philip Sousa wrote the march "Messiah of the Nations" for its dedication in 1902, at which time James Whitcomb Riley read his poem "The Soldier." Before entering the monument, have everyone take a minute to look at *Victory*, the 38-foot-tall bronze statue at the top, nicknamed "Miss Indiana." Since

Amazing
Indiana Facts

Did you know that Indianapolis was once an early-nineteenth-century fur traders' outpost? Today Indianapolis is the twelfth-largest city in the United States.

the glassed-in viewing area can be quite warm in the summer, you may decide to visit the monument during the holiday season, when it is decorated with 4,600 lights and draws carloads of spectators each evening. No matter when you visit, don't forget to visit the newly remodeled display of a world-class Civil War museum that can be found in the basement at the **Colonel Eli Lilly Civil War Museum** at the Soldiers' and Sailors' Monument, Monument Circle; (317) 232–7615. Admission is **free**. Open Wednesday through Sunday 9:00 A.M. to 6:00 P.M. Closed Monday and Tuesday and major holidays. Visitors can experience the Civil War from the battlefield to the home front. Located on the lower level of the Soldiers' and Sailors' Monument, the museum houses artifacts, letters, and personal diaries written by Hoosiers during the War. The museum preserves the rich history of the Soldiers' and Sailors' Monument.

Horse-Drawn Carriage Rides (all ages)

Circle City Carriages Inc., (317) 387–1516; Blue Ribbon Carriage Company, (317) 631–4169; Yellow Rose Carriage, (317) 634–3400.

After you have climbed down the 336 stairs of the monument, continue your exploration of downtown Indianapolis with a carriage ride. For approximately $30, four people can enjoy a thirty-minute ride during the week, but prices do vary and are slightly higher on the weekend and over the holidays. Carriages can usually be found at Adams Mark Hotel, Circle Centre Mall, The Circle, or at the Hyatt Regency Hotel–Downtown. To make sure that your family is not disappointed, call ahead to book a ride.

City Center (all ages)

Pan American Plaza, 201 South Capitol; (317) 237–5200. Open Monday through Friday 10:00 A.M. to 5:30 P.M., Saturday 10:00 A.M. to 5:00 P.M., and Sunday noon to 5:00 P.M. Free.

This is the place to discover everything you should know about Indianapolis. As you walk through the front door, you will see "Light Up Indianapolis," a hands-on model that lets everyone locate places of interest by just touching a button. The display includes more than 4,000 buildings and took more than 6,000 hours to complete. You will be able to locate museums, theaters, highways, hotels, the state's third-largest university, the state capitol and government complex, sports facilities, and landmarks in the downtown area. You can pick up **free** brochures at the City Center that will help you plan your visit in the Indianapolis area and throughout Indiana. This is also a great place to pick up souvenirs of your trip. During the month of May, a video of the Indy "500" race can be viewed as you select brochures or gifts. There is always an authentic "500" race car that children and adults can see.

United Artists Movie Complex (all ages) 🎟️

Circle Centre, 49 West Maryland Street, fourth floor; (317) 237–6356. $–$$.

Tired of shopping? This large complex includes a nine-screen movie theater, as well as the entertainment center Gameworks (see below).

Gameworks (all ages)

Fourth floor Circle Centre Mall; (317) 226–9267. Open Monday through Thursday 11:00 A.M. to 10:00 P.M., Friday 11:00 A.M. to midnight, Saturday 10:00 A.M. to midnight, Sunday 10:00 A.M. to 8:00 P.M. The ultimate group or individual entertainment experience.

This is a magical, state-of-the art virtual theme park with the latest in computer-simulated virtual reality experiences. It includes Max Flight, a virtual roller coaster; virtual full-size Indy Cars, where you can race around the "500" track. Gameworks Studio also offers more than 150 of the latest arcade attractions.

Pan American Plaza Skating Rink (children old enough to ice skate)

Call for schedule; (317) 237–5565.

Enjoy an ice-skating session on this fantastic ice rink. You don't have to worry about bringing your own skates; you can rent them.

Racers Indoor Karting at Union Station (adults and older children)

302 South Meridian Street; (317) 972–6666. Call for hours and group, individual, public, and private rates.

State-of-the-art indoor go-cart racing facility located in historic Union Station.

Union Station Crowne Plaza Hotel (all ages)

123 West Louisiana Street; (317) 631–2221.

If your family is planning to spend a night in Indianapolis, consider staying at this hotel, which is part of and connected to the railroad station on the second floor. The hotel lobby was once the pick-up and delivery area of a freight shipping company. The ceiling of the lobby atrium is made of massive steel girders that supported 200 trains a day at the turn of the twentieth century. Besides traditional hotel rooms, your family can stay in one of thirteen Pullman sleeper cars dating back to the 1920s. Each car houses two suites. The individual suites have been named after well-known celebrities from the past and are decorated with a unique blend of traditional and contemporary decor related to the lives of these individuals. The train station is still active, with as many as twenty trains passing through each day. Stay at this hotel and the gentle rumbling of the trains will give you the feeling that you are actually aboard a train.

RCA Dome (all ages) ⬤

100 South Capitol, directly west of Union Station Crown Plaza Hotel; (317) 262–3400. Tours Monday through Saturday 11:00 A.M., 1:00 P.M., and 3:00 P.M. and on Sunday at 1:00 and 3:00 P.M. $. No tours on event days and some holidays. Event hotline: (317) 262–3452.

Are there any sports fans in your family? If so, they will want to visit the home of the Indianapolis Colts. A tour of the RCA Dome, formerly known as the Hoosier Dome, begins with a multimedia presentation followed by a forty-five-minute walk through the interior of the stadium. You will be able to see the press box and the visitors' locker rooms and even have a look at the VIP suites. During the tour, you will hear lots of facts about the RCA Dome.

City-County Building (all ages)

200 East Washington Street; (317) 236–4345. Open Monday through Friday 9:30 A.M. to 5:30 P.M. Free.

On a clear day, you can have a fantastic view of Indianapolis from the observation platform on the twenty-eighth floor of the City–County Building. After looking at the city through the binoculars available, you can enjoy exhibits and scale models of different points of interest in the city. Everyone also should read the information card that tells more about the City–County Building.

If you have older children who are studying local government, they will be able to see the City–County Council in action—usually on the first and third Monday of each month. The council meets at 7:00 P.M. in the Public Assembly room on the second floor. If you know what district you live in, you will be able to identify and see your own representative. The agenda for the meeting is available on the afternoon of the meeting. You should call ahead to find out what is going to be discussed at a meeting.

Eiteljorg Museum of American Indian and Western Art (all ages)

White River State Park, 500 West Washington Street; (317) 636–9378; www.eiteljorg.org. $$. Children under 4, free. Open Tuesday through Saturday 10:00 A.M. to 5:00 P.M. and Sunday noon to 5:00 P.M. Closed Monday except for June, July, and August and on certain holidays. Public tour at 1:00 P.M. every day. Closed Thanksgiving, after noon on Christmas Eve, Christmas, and New Year's Day.

By just going approximately 5 blocks west on Washington Street from the City–County Building, you will be at this fascinating museum. Its Native American collection consists of art and artifacts from throughout North America and includes pottery, basketry, and clothing. The American Western culture collection spans the early nineteenth century to the present. This collection has paintings, drawings, graphics, and sculptures. Before you start your tour of the museum, stop at the literature rack and get guides for each gallery so you will have interesting information about the artists and Western Native American culture exhibits you see.

Before visiting the museum, you may want to call ahead to find out when the museum will be bringing in an artist to demonstrate Native American crafts. During these visits, children can learn to rope a cow by throwing a lariat or how to make a saddle. The museum has also brought in cowboys and poets who specialize in reading Western and Native American poems.

This museum is reaching audiences who would otherwise be unable to enjoy it. A program for the blind or visually impaired, called "Touch of the West," provides a hands-on tour. After talking about a particular painting or sculpture, the guide goes to a special cart that contains items that are in the painting or

sculpture. Visitors are then able to explore by touch items such as beaded objects, drums, rawhide, ivory, Native American dolls, and a reproduction of the original sculpture *Bronco-Buster* by Frederic Remington. This program is **free** and open to individuals and families.

Indianapolis Zoo (all ages) 🐘 🦆

1200 West Washington Street, 1 mile west of downtown Indianapolis; (317) 630–2001; www.indianapoliszoo.com; tours@indyzoo.com. Open all year 9:00 A.M. to 4:00 P.M., closing at 5:00 P.M. in spring and fall. Call for hours and special events. $$$. Community Tuesdays, first Tuesday of each month March through December. Admission $5.00, free parking. Closed Monday and Tuesday January and February.

This is a fun place for the whole family to spend many hours. The zoo is located on sixty-four acres in White River State Park and opened in 1988. You never know which of the 3,400 different kinds of animals will be the "star" of your visit. Your children will view animals in their natural habitat. They will be able to see lions and elephants roaming the "African Plains" and sharks swimming in the zoo's aquarium. A stroll through the desert biome will truly give all of you the feeling that you are in the desert. You will be going through areas with desert palms and giant cacti that set the stage for the lizards and other slithering creatures that call the burning desert sands their home. The plants and animals thrive in this area because of the 80-foot transparent dome, which keeps the temperature at a constant eighty degrees in daytime and sixty degrees at night. Another fascinating area is Neptune's Gallery, where the dolphins and whales live. If you and your family visit during the summer months, you will enjoy sea lion feedings, keeper chats, and the only dolphin show in Indiana. It is also a great experience to ride an elephant or touch a baby alligator. Whenever your feet get tired, you can catch the train or enjoy a ride in a horse-drawn streetcar. Another way to rest your feet is to enjoy a ride on the carousel, a camel, a pony, or an elephant. Year-round the zoo has three dolphin shows daily at 11:00 A.M., 1:00 P.M., and 3:00 P.M.

The zoo has a large selection of educational programs, classes, workshops, and special summer programs for children. Most of these programs give children a look behind the scenes as well as hands-on encounters with some of the zoo animals. Christmas is a fun time to visit the zoo. It is open evenings from 5:00 to 9:00 P.M. from the end of November to the end of December; however, it is closed on December 24 and 25.

Indiana **Trivia**

Where was Vice President Dan Quayle born?

What U.S. Army facility was built in Marion County in 1903 that today is Indiana's newest state park?

Where was President Benjamin Harrison's sixteen-room home built?

Indianapolis, Fort Benjamin Harrison, Indianapolis

How to get to the Indianapolis Zoo:

From the north *Take I–65 south to exit 114; turn south on Dr. Martin Luther King Street/West Street to Washington Street; turn west and go 1 mile.*

From the south *Take I–65 north to I–70 west; go to West Street (exit 79A); turn north on West Street/Missouri Street to Washington Street; turn west and go 1 mile.*

From the east *Take I–70 west to I–65 north; go to West Street (exit 114); turn south on West Street to Washington Street; turn west and go 1 mile.*

From the west *Take I–70 east to West Street (exit 79A); turn north on West Street/Missouri Street to Washington Street; turn west and go 1 mile.*

Canal Walk (all ages)

This area located between West and Tenth Streets has been extended into White River State Park in the downtown area through a multi-million-dollar improvement campaign. A majority of the area has been completely renovated with such amenities as beautiful landscaping, several walkways, jogging paths, antique-style street lamps, huge fountains, a pedestrian bridge, and gorgeous murals presenting different aspects of life in Indiana. Pedal boats can be enjoyed by everyone during the spring and summer months. Several commercial and residential complexes along with headquarters of the Historic Landmarks Foundation of Indiana all enjoy the Central Canals' fabulous design. In 1995 a memorial to the USS *Indianapolis* was dedicated honoring the legendary WWII flagship that went down by Japanese torpedo. Finally, on Ohio and West Streets is where the headquarters for the Indiana Historic Society was recently built.

Circle Centre (all ages)

49 West Maryland Street; (317) 681–8000. Open Monday through Saturday 10:00 A.M. to 6:00 P.M., Sunday noon to 6:00 P.M. Extended restaurant hours.

Circle Centre is a downtown development with a retail component of more than 800,000 square feet. It occupies 2 full city blocks and rises four levels above a multilevel underground parking garage. Enclosed walkways span city streets to connect the center with hotels, the Convention Center, and the RCA Dome. Best of all, these walkways make Circle Centre convenient: It's easy to shop at large department stores such as Nordstrom and Parisian, along with a large variety of others, Indianapolis's best shopping! The food court on the third level offers a wide variety of dishes to select from and there are also many other restaurants scattered throughout the mall. Then on the fourth level of Circle Centre is where the fun begins. There is a huge arcade featuring virtual reality games. In addition to nine movie screens, United Artists offers Starport, five interactive attractions that take visitors into the future.

City Market (all ages) 🍴

222 East Market; (317) 634–9266. Open Monday through Saturday 6:00 A.M. to 6:00 P.M. Free. The building is open during the mentioned hours; however, the vendors often leave between 3:00 and 4:00 P.M.

If your family is ready for a snack, this is the place you should go. Built in 1886, City Market is a great place to have lunch, especially if you are enjoying an adventure in downtown Indianapolis. In the past, the market provided a central place for farmers to sell their fresh meat, fish, and produce in the city. Today you are still able to buy these items, along with hard-to-find foreign foods, health foods, and quick food for snacks and meals. Once family members catch the aroma of all the different foods being prepared at the market, it will be difficult to make a unanimous decision on what to eat. In fact, each family member may make a different selection, from hot dogs to exotic Greek fare. Once choices have been made, you can enjoy eating outside in the plaza on a nice day or inside on the mezzanine level. Even if you are not hungry, everyone will still enjoy a walk through the market. Children are always amazed by all the foods that are being sold here. From June through the end of October, there is a farmer's market outside the City Market building every Wednesday, weather permitting.

Indiana State Museum (all ages) 🖼️

Located in the White River State Park in the heart of Indiana's capital city; (317) 232–1637; www.in.gov/ism/. Museum hours are Monday through Saturday 9:00 A.M. to 5:00 P.M. and Sunday 11:00 A.M. to 5:00 P.M. $$.

The new museum opened in early 2002. Constructed of building materials from Indiana, including limestone, steel, brick, and glass, the building not only houses the museum's vast collections, exhibits, and office space, but is an exhibit itself. First-floor exhibits include The Birth of Earth (the history of Indiana from a geological perspective), Ancient Seas (ancient life that shaped the state and its resources explored through diverse fossil collections), The Age of Ice (depicting the glaciers' effects on Indiana—wear a sweater), The Native Americans (history of Native American culture as far back as 12,000 years), and Indiana's Natural Regions (explore the naturalist world by looking, touching, listening, and smelling).

The second-floor exhibits include The Nineteenth State (film, artifacts, video, and interactive elements trace the story of Indiana's pioneers during the period of 1790 to 1830). Enterprising Indiana showcases Indian industry from 1920 to 1950. The Hoosier Way examines who the original Hoosiers were and is set around the Civil Way period. Crossroads of America focuses on Indiana's Golden Age (1880–1920), a time of national leadership in art, literature, and politics. Global Indiana traces Indiana's effect on the world and world's effect on Indiana. Included in this gallery is the Pop Culture wall, with floor-to-ceiling displays of everyday artifacts of the 1950s, 1960s, and 1970s.

The museum also features the Hoosier Heritage Trail, an interactive database within the permanent exhibits that gives visitors information about other interesting places to explore in Indiana. Don't forget to see what is playing at the IMAX theater. Check the museum's Web site for current movie information and show times.

When the family gets hungry, enjoy lunch at the L. S. Ayers Tea Room, a full-service restaurant featuring both contemporary fare and classics from the original menu, such as Chicken Velvet Soup and the children's Hobo Lunch. The Tea Room is open seven days a week 11:00 A.M. to 2:30 P.M. Reservations suggested. Walk-ins welcome. Call (317) 234–2469 for reservations. For a more casual setting, try the Crossroads Café, which features food with an Indiana flair.

National Comedy Theatre (all ages) 🎵
721 Massachusetts Avenue; (317) 951–8499. Open Monday through Saturday 8:00 p.m. to midnight. $$.

Your family can enjoy a comedy venue while visiting the city. The National Comedy Theatre is the home of Comedy Sports Indianapolis, a competitive team that provides improv fun for the entire family. All shows are audience participation, which will be interesting because your family will be part of the show and you will never see the same show twice.

Madame Walker Urban Life Center (all ages) 🏛
617 Indiana Avenue; (317) 236–2088. Monday through Friday 8:30 A.M. to 5:00 P.M. Free.

This unique place is a cultural showcase for the city's black community, a National Historic Landmark, and is listed on the National Register of Historic Places. The Madame Walker Building/Theater was built in the 1920s as a symbol of the historic achievements and contributions of Madame C. J. Walker, American's first African-American female millionaire. The center is a symbol of the historic achievements and contributions of a successful entrepreneur, philanthropist, and social activist whose fortune came from her cosmetics and hair products company. It was the first building in Indianapolis to be built, owned, and operated by African Americans. It became a major stop on the black entertainment circuit.

In 1979 the Madame Walker Urban Life Center, Inc. purchased and restored the facility, and it became a cultural center for the black community. The center has a jazz festival each Friday evening from 6:00 to 9:00 P.M. and offers classes in the cultural and performing arts. When you tour the center, you will be able to see the Madame Walker Theater, which has played host to many of America's great jazz musicians.

Indiana Medical History Museum (all ages) 🔬
3045 West Vermont Street; (317) 635–7329; www.imhm.org; Edenharter@aol.com. Open Thursday through Saturday, 10:00 A.M. to 4:00 P.M., other times by appointment. Groups under 100 can be accommodated. $.

Does anyone in your family want to be a doctor? For people interested in medicine, this museum, located on the grounds of the former Central State Hospital, is a must. Opened in 1896, the building that houses the museum originally provided doctors in the late 1800s and early 1900s with state-of-the-art facilities to study medicine. Here you can see medical history in the museum's collection of more than 15,000 medical and health-care artifacts. You will be very surprised to see the diagnostic instruments and surgical and dental equipment that were used on patients in the nineteenth century. The museum offers a twelve-room guided tour to explain just how much of the equipment was used. When you step inside the amphitheater, you will see all the original oak paneling and chairs. In this room, teams of scientists studied medicine in the best lighting conditions, thanks to the skylight. In the medical library, more than 3,000 volumes are available for historical research. A great thing about visiting this museum is that all guided tours are adapted to the needs of the different ages in the group.

Indiana War Memorial (all ages) 🏛

431 North Meridian Street; (317) 232–7615. Open Wednesday through Sunday 9:00 A.M. to 6:00 P.M. Admission is free.

For history buffs interested in World War I, World War II, the Korean War, the Vietnam War, the Spanish-American War, or the French and Indian War, the Indiana War Memorial is the place to spend some time looking at many artifacts of these wars. The memorial occupies a 5-block area and is built of Indiana limestone. If you are in the city in the evening, make a point of going to War Memorial Plaza: The lights make it a very impressive sight.

Your family will be able to take a self-guided tour of the memorial because all items on display have information cards. Be sure to pick up the free brochure that tells you about the memorial before beginning your tour. There is definitely a lot to see here, and two rooms that you will not want to miss are the Helicopter Room and the Shrine Room. Seeing is believing in the Helicopter Room, where there are a helicopter, missiles, and airplane engines. As you climb the beautiful marble staircase that leads upstairs to the Shrine Room, you will get a good look at the large marble columns and the beautiful blue stained-glass windows. Once inside the room, your eyes will be drawn to the Star of Destiny. The star is lit with blue lights and is truly a breathtaking sight. In the memorial you will also find paintings of many famous generals, a large gun collection, and a tribute to World War II Hoosier journalist Ernie Pyle. This is a great place to have a picnic on a nice day; you can enjoy the park in front of the memorial and watch one of the two fountains.

Morris-Butler House (ages 5 and up) 🏛

1204 North Park Avenue; (317) 636–5409. Open Wednesday through Saturday 10:00 A.M. to 4:00 P.M. Closed the month of January. Tours begin on the half hour; last tour starts at 3:30 P.M. $.

Let your children see what Victorian decor was like by visiting this Victorian house built around 1864. Now restored by the Historic Landmarks Foundation, it's a wonderful example of how wealthy Americans of that time lived. Children are delighted by the specially designed tour where they find out about a tiny room on the fifth floor that can only be reached by a ladder. They will discover that Victorian decor is fanciest in the areas where guests were entertained. The first-floor rooms have the finest woodwork and beautiful furniture. When you reach the second floor, you will notice that the ceilings are lower, the rooms are smaller, and the furniture is plainer.

The end of May is a fun time to visit the Morris-Butler House because everyone can get in the swing when they attend "In the Good Ol' Summertime." The house is in "summer dress," so you will be able to see exactly how Victorian-era Hoosiers coped with hot Indiana summers. Also, the colors of red, white, and blue bunting brighten the patriotic holiday season. (There is an admission charge for this special event.)

James Whitcomb Riley Home (ages 5 and up) 🏛

528 Lockerbie Street; (317) 631–5885. Open Tuesday through Saturday 10:00 A.M. to 3:30 P.M. and Sunday noon to 3:30 P.M. Closed Monday and holidays. $.

"Such a dear little street it is nestled away/From the noise of the city and heat of the day," wrote the Hoosier poet James Whitcomb Riley to describe where he lived. The James Whitcomb Riley Home is a late Victorian preservation located in the charming Lockerbie Square area, where other Victorian homes are being restored. Author of more than 1,044 poems mostly about children and Indiana, the poet lived in this home for the last twenty-three years of his life. Many of Riley's friends, including Booth Tarkington, George Ade, William Fortune, and George C. Hitt, helped preserve the house after his death in 1916. The home became a National Historic Landmark in 1963. The highlight of the tour is Riley's room, which looks like he will return any minute, even having a pen on his desk for him to pick up and begin writing.

President Benjamin Harrison Home (ages 5 and up) 🏛

1230 North Delaware Street; (317) 631–1888; www.presidentbenjaminharrison.org. Open Monday through Saturday 10:00 A.M. to 3:30 P.M. Tours are given on the hour and half hour. Closed many holidays. Closed first three weeks in January; call for schedule. $.

Has your family ever visited the home of a president? Here you can see the possessions, original furnishings, and mementos of Benjamin Harrison, twenty-third president of the United States. The elegant home was built in 1875, and Harrison resided in it from 1875 to 1901. Today the home is a National Historic Landmark. If you visit the home in the middle of August, you can enjoy a celebration that is held in his honor. Each year the celebration is different. There is usually a military band, and on the weekend of the celebration there is a reenactment of a Civil War encampment. Also, when your family arrives at the house, President and Mrs. Harrison will be there to greet you and talk about life in the White House and in Indianapolis. Should you want to hear a little gossip, the household staff is there to share secrets of running the home. December is another festive time at the house—the home is decorated for the celebration of a Victorian Christmas. A small gift shop has Victorian America–related items.

Indiana **Trivia**

David Letterman is from what city in Indiana?

Indianapolis

Indianapolis City Parks (all ages) 🏕️ 🏊 👫 🍁

Indianapolis Department of Parks and Recreation, (317) 327–7275; Marion County Parks, (317) 327–7275.

Indianapolis is proud of its 113 city parks located throughout the city. This number does not even include Indianapolis's many neighborhood parks. If you live in the Indianapolis area, you will want to contact the parks department to get on the mailing list so that you receive the **free** newsletter published six times a year as well as the summer and winter fun guides. The newsletter contains monthly calendars of events and articles that highlight all the special upcoming events. The guides have more than twenty pages of great family activities. Each guide is full of important phone numbers that will help you get up-to-the-minute information about everything from swimming lessons to park programs.

Get your walking shoes out and try a volksmarch sponsored by the parks department. People of all ages enjoy volksmarches from small children in strollers to grandparents. This is not a race. Everyone can enjoy walking at his or her own pace. Most walks are 10 kilometers. When you begin your walk, you will pick up a registration card and then along the trail you will get the card stamped as you pass each checkpoint. At the end of the walk, you can turn in your card to receive credit for your walk.

White River State Park (all ages) 🏕️ 🍁

801 West Washington Street; (317) 233–2434. Pump house open Monday through Friday 8:30 A.M. to 5:00 P.M. Free. Park hours, Monday through Friday 9:00 A.M. to 5:00 P.M., weekends 10:00 A.M. to 4:00 P.M. From May through September the park is open Monday through Friday 8:30 A.M. to 7:00 P.M.

Without leaving the downtown area, your family can enjoy the fun at this 250-acre park located on the banks of the White River. The park is still in its building stage, but it contains fun places such as the Indianapolis Zoo, Victory Field, the Eiteljorg Museum, The National Institute for Fitness and Sport, Future Park, an IMAX Theater, the NCAA Hall of Champions, and the new Indiana State Museum. To find out what future plans are and to enjoy a little bit of history, you will want to go to the visitors center and park office that are housed in the historic pump house. The pump house is red brick and has a slate roof with a cupola on top. The Indianapolis Water Company built the pump house in 1870, and it was used until 1969. You can see the pumps that were used to supply water.

Eagle Creek Park (all ages)

7840 West 56th Street; (317) 327–7110. Open from dawn to dusk. Admission weekdays, $.

If your family really enjoys nature, and water sports along with hiking, then Eagle Creek Park is where you will want to spend some time. Eagle Creek is one of the largest municipal parks in the country, with more than 4,000 acres of wooded terrain and a 1,300-acre reservoir. With more than 10 miles of wooded trails as well as bike and fitness trails, it's easy to enjoy exercising in this park. When the weather gets hot, the reservoir is the place in the park where you want to be to enjoy water sports such as fishing, canoeing, and sailing.

The beach at Eagle Creek Park is a great place to relax. There are not many places in Indianapolis where you can lie on a beach and children can play in the sand. Here's a place where families can swim and play beach volleyball. If you don't want to bring a picnic, there is a concession stand nearby. The beach is open 11:00 A.M. to 7:00 P.M. daily. $.

At the marina in the park, you can rent canoes, rowboats, catamarans, sailboards, and pedal boats. You might want to sign up for a class so you can become a skilled sailor. Beginning and intermediate sailing and introductory board sailing classes are offered as well as rowing lessons. Marina hours are Monday through Friday 10:00 A.M. to 7:00 P.M. and 8:00 A.M. to 7:00 P.M. on weekends. Canoes and rowboats are available for rental at the marina. Scenic cruises on a pontoon boat are also available for a moderate price. For fishing, two great areas in the park—the reservoir and the secluded Lilly Lake—are available. However, you can only fish from a boat on the reservoir. For more information about the marina, call (317) 327–7131.

A Gisler **Adventure**

Our family loves outdoor activities. So whenever the weather is good, we grab our bikes and head out to one of the largest municipal parks in the country, Eagle Creek Park. With 10-plus miles of wooded trails as well as bike and fitness trails, we can each do the exercise that we prefer. After walking, running, or biking the trails, we meet on the reservoir's beach and lie out. If the weather is really hot, we rent canoes, rowboats, sailboats, or pedal boats from the marina. After working up an appetite, we cook hot dogs and hamburgers on the grill. If we forget to bring food, we enjoy the refreshments at a nearby concession stand. In the fall, we go into the park to get excellent family photographs.

To learn more about nature, you will want to visit the **Eagle Creek Park Nature Center.** The center consists of a thirty-acre arboretum, the nature center, Lilly Lodge, a reflecting pool, woodland trails, self-guided trails, a hummingbird and butterfly garden, two native wildflower gardens, and a scenic overlook. The Nature Center is open seven days a week all year long. For a great Sunday outing, try the bird walk, which starts at 8:00 A.M. during the summer months and at 9:00 A.M. the rest of the year. Be sure to investigate the programs, workshops, and special nature activities the center offers.

Garfield Park Conservatory (all ages) 🍁

2505 Conservatory Drive; (317) 327–7184. Open daily 10:00 A.M. to 6:00 P.M. $.

You will be able to enjoy a tropical paradise when you take a trip to the Garfield Park Conservatory, which is filled with thousands of different varieties of plants from tropical desert plants to endangered plants from around the world. Upon entering the conservatory, get a map to help in planning your self-guided tour. As you stroll leisurely, viewing more than 500 tropical plants, you will observe a 15-foot waterfall cascading through the plants and cacti in the midst of the seventy-degree "tropical desert." There are benches throughout the conservatory so that everyone is able to relax and enjoy the plants. This definitely is the place to bring your camera: The scenery is fantastic.

A great souvenir to bring home from the conservatory is a plant. You can select one that was raised in the conservatory from the plant shop. You can arrange for a family tour of the conservatory by calling ahead at least two weeks. There are soft-drink machines in the conservatory, but there is no food.

When your family visits the conservatory, make sure to leave some time for visiting **Garfield Park.** Along with a swimming pool, picnic areas, and playground equipment, the park has an outstanding sunken garden. Here you can enjoy the old-world charm of flowers, trees, urns, antique fountains, and stone walkways. Admission is **free,** and it is open from dawn to dusk. One of the special attractions of the park is **free** concerts on summer evenings by the Indianapolis Symphony Orchestra. This is a great way to expose your children to the symphony, and they don't have to sit still. Another attraction is the Shakespeare Festival held in the park every summer.

Holiday Park (all ages) 🏠 🍁

6349 Spring Mill Road; (317) 327–7180. Open daily dawn to dusk. Free.

Developed in 1936 as a botanical garden, Holiday Park is a great place to visit if you're interested in nature. You will be kept busy studying the 800 different plant species that are here. When visiting the park, you can't help but notice the three large statues kneeling on top of a pedestal. Each statue is three times life-size. They were brought to Indianapolis from New York, where they were once a part of the St. Paul Building. The statues represent three different races. Behind the statues is a reflecting pool.

If your family wants to see spring in full bloom, take a walk through Holiday Park toward the end of April or the first of May. This is when "Orchard in Bloom" is held at the park. You will have the experience of walking through gardens filled with blooming plants and shrubs and trees that thrive in Indiana. Stop at the gardener's market or one of the many other booths selling a variety of gardening items and plants. Although the emphasis in the park is on plants, there are also bike trails and picnic areas for your enjoyment.

Broad Ripple (all ages) 🏃 🚲 🍽

Sixty-second Street and College; www.mybroadripple.com.

Broad Ripple is a unique village within Indianapolis that offers several different activities. When you visit the Broad Ripple area, bring along some bread and crackers to feed the many friendly ducks along the canal. Or you could relax on the canal banks under the shade trees and watch the ducks swim by. If you have a fishing license, perhaps you'll be able to catch your evening meal. Art lovers will want to make sure that they attend the Indianapolis Art League's Broad Ripple Art Fair at the end of May. At the fair there are usually more than 200 artists from all over the country exhibiting their work. You will also find cultural booths, ceramics demonstrations, a children's entertainment area, and a food court, as well as live musical entertainment on the stage. (Call 317–251–2782 for exact dates.)

A walk through Broad Ripple will give you the opportunity to explore its interesting shops and taste ethnic food at one of the village's many restaurants. When the weather is nice, you may want to select a restaurant that has outdoor dining. Traveling east on Sixty-second Street for about 3 blocks will bring you to the entrance to Broad Ripple Park, a great place to spend an afternoon. The family can have a picnic, and on a hot day a swim in the pool or a rest under one of the many large shade trees. Fitness buffs can jog around the park's fitness trail, and there are tennis courts, too.

Butler University Campus (all ages) 🏛 🌲

4600 Sunset; (800) 368–6852; www.butler.edu.

From sports events to concerts, something is always happening at Butler University. Absorb the collegiate atmosphere as you stroll the campus, noticing the interesting architecture and the earnest students hurrying to class or the library. During the school year, students present many music, theater, and dance programs for **free** or at a moderate price.

On the mall as you enter the Butler University campus is **Clowes Hall,** an outstanding performing arts center where national and international groups regularly perform. Here you could see a traveling company present a Broadway play or a ballet by a Russian dance company. Call (317) 940–6444 to reach the box office.

View the sky at the **J. I. Holcomb Observatory and Planetarium** (ages five to twelve) on the Butler campus. You can enjoy a slide presentation, a seasonal star show, or a laser-light show. Reservations are not needed; however, you will need to arrive at least fifteen to twenty minutes early for the planetarium show because seating is limited to the first sixty people. Show times are Friday and Saturday evenings at 7:30 P.M. $. If weather permits, you can look at the stars through Indiana's largest telescope. Call (317) 940–9333 to hear a recording of the current show times.

Travel to the end of Clarendon Road beyond the observatory to visit Holcomb Gardens. The gardens are perfect for kids of all ages to explore, especially for children studying leaves, because the new trees planted behind the statue of Persephone are labeled. This is really helpful to parents when leaf projects are a school requirement. At the Butler Bookstore you can purchase informative books on wildflowers and other plants so you will know more about what you are seeing in the gardens. In the center of Holcomb Gardens is a pool with the statue of the above-mentioned Persephone, the goddess of spring. The story of Persephone is inscribed on a stone resting at the statue's feet. Within sight are a canal and a path where mules used to pull barges from downtown Indianapolis to Broad Ripple Village. Walks in the gardens are especially enjoyable during the **carillon concerts,** which are held Sunday evening from 5:00 to 6:00 p.m. June through August. If you need more information about the carillon concerts, call (317) 632–1391. Admission to the gardens is free.

Rustic Gardens (ages 5 and up) 😊 🌱
1500 South Arlington Avenue; (317) 359–8183. $.

Rustic Gardens is unlike any miniature golf course you have ever seen. The course was built in 1930 and is still fantastic. It has slow-rolling, grassy holes with plenty of shade trees, and all obstacles on the course are natural. This eighteen-hole course is a different family outing that everyone will enjoy—real, old-fashioned family fun. There is not another miniature golf course like it in the country! After playing a round of golf, everyone can enjoy visiting and feeding the goats, ducks, geese, chickens, and pheasants on the grounds.

Make a **Splash**

On a hot day your family will enjoy a splash in one of the fourteen outdoor pools in city parks. On wet or cold days, one of the three indoor pools would be appealing. The pool season typically runs from Memorial Day to Labor Day. All pools offer youth swimming lessons, lap swimming, adult swimming, and parent-tot swimming. Call (317) 327–7275 to find out exactly what each pool offers: Some pools have swimming teams, free swimming, and even aqua-exercise classes. Prices are modest at all the pools. Sunday is family swim day and up to five family members can swim for one low price of $6.00.

Children's Museum (all ages) 🔈

3000 North Meridian Street; (317) 334–3322; www.childrensmuseum.org. Open seven days a week in summer from 10:00 A.M. to 5:00 P.M. Open until 8:00 P.M. Thursday. Closed Monday after Labor Day. $$. Free admission first Thursday of every month, 5:00 to 8:00 P.M.

For a family day that is full of fun and excitement, visit the world's largest children's museum. The fun begins at the entrance, where you can see the largest water clock in the world keeping time. Then it's on to five floors of exhibits with a fantastic number of hands-on exhibits. You can experience walking through a cave and panning for gold. You and your family will be able to conduct experiments, observe physical and natural science exhibits, explore a log cabin, read hieroglyphics on a 2,700-year-old mummy's case, or hop on an 1868 wood-burning locomotive for a pretend ride.

Everyone will be on the go in the museum from the minute you walk through the front doors. There are computers to challenge imaginations. Children ages two to seven put on rubber aprons in the playscape area to help keep them dry while they play in the sand and water, or they can dress up and pretend to be a firefighter or a pioneer. Older children enjoy the innovative Eli Lilly Center. No trip to the Children's Museum is complete without a ride on the hand-carved carousel that was built in the early 1900s and was originally in Broad Ripple City Park. Adults and children seem to be scared when they first come face-to-face with the life-sized replica of *Tyrannosaurus rex* (35 feet in length). But fear soon turns to fascination. Experience the future in the Space Quest Planetarium, where you can explore the stars, asteroid fields, and life in our galaxy through the Digistar projection system, a computerized star projector that simulates three-dimensional flight. See a show at the Lilly Theater. On weekends your children can swap their rocks, shells, fossils, and other collectibles at the Nature Swap Shop. The shop's staff will help identify items in its collections. Of course, you will want to look at everything in the museum store before the day is completed. When hunger strikes, the museum has a food court where a variety of fast-food restaurants and fresh food items are available for your family to select from. There is also a covered shelter and several picnic tables on the north side of the building for picnic lunches and an indoor picnic area.

At the museum you can obtain information about annual passes, group rates, and memberships available. Members get special benefits, including previews of special exhibits, admission to members-only functions, a newsletter, free rides on the carousel, and discounts on museum store items.

Crown Hill Cemetery (all ages) 🏛 🍁

700 West Thirty-eighth Street; (317) 925–8231. (For tours, call 317–920–2726.) Open 8:00 A.M. to 6:00 P.M. every day. Office closes earlier than cemetery and is closed Sunday. A history book outlining three self-guided tours can be picked up during office hours. $.

A strange but different family outing that gives you a chance to delve back in history is a visit to Crown Hill Cemetery—the third-largest private cemetery in the country. The cemetery, which is located on more than 555 acres, is listed in the National Register of Historic Places. Tours can be arranged, or you can take off on your own with a map from the

Indiana Trivia

What city did James Whitcomb Riley live in from 1892 to 1916?

Where can you visit the world's largest children's museum?

Indianapolis, Indianapolis

cemetery office that identifies 137 graves. Walk or drive through while discovering the graves of President Benjamin Harrison, three vice presidents of the United States, the famous gangster John Dillinger, and the poet James Whitcomb Riley. Be sure to look at the artwork within the cemetery grounds, such as the three statues of Greek goddesses who at one time adorned the old Marion County Courthouse. Notice the brick and wrought-iron fence that surrounds the cemetery, a work of art in itself. You should also see the chapel that was built in 1875 in a lovely wooded area. When you view the inside, you will discover a beautiful carved cherry interior that is an example of Victorian craftsmanship. Adolph Scherrer designed the chapel and Gothic-style gateway at the entrance to the cemetery on Thirty-fourth Street. The funeral procession of Vice President Hendricks was the first to pass through these gates.

Indianapolis International Airport (all ages)
2500 South High School Road; (317) 487–5039. Call for tour information.

Up, up, and away! **Free** one-hour tours for families are available at Indianapolis International Airport. This is really great fun for young children because the tour is just like taking a real trip. You will visit places in the airport as if you were really traveling. First you'll stop by the ticket desk, then you'll go to the observation deck, and finally down to the baggage-claim area. If you are planning to take the tour with older children or adults, tell the receptionist when you are arranging the tour, because the tour is different for older participants.

The Indiana State Fairgrounds (all ages)
1202 East Thirty-eighth Street; (317) 927–7500; www.state.in.us/statefair/yearinfo.html. Fair is in August. Hours vary.

This is the home of the state fair, which is held each year in August. The state fair is really a great family outing. If you have young children, however, you may wish to attend one of the smaller county fairs that are held throughout the summer in preparation for the large state fair. The Indiana State Fairgrounds is not just the home of the state fair; there are activities on the 238-acre fairgrounds throughout the year in the fifty-six permanent buildings. The Coliseum houses Indiana's oldest ice-skating rink and is also the home of the Indianapolis Ice hockey team. The Shrine Circus is also held at the Coliseum. Throughout the year, some of the buildings are used for flea markets. If you have never visited a flea market as a family outing, it is one that you should consider. Call ahead to get the flea market schedule for the year. Most flea markets are **free;** however, a few special flea markets during the year have a small admission fee.

Some of the other shows that are held on the fairgrounds are the Indiana Home Show, the Boat Show, the Car Show, and the Christmas Gift and Hobby Show, as well as other big shows that come to the fairgrounds throughout the year. You can also see car races and harness-horse training and races on the fairground's racetrack.

Indianapolis Motor Speedway (ages 4 and up)

4790 West Sixteenth Street; (317) 484–6747; www.indy500.com. Museum open daily 9:00 A.M. to 5:00 P.M. except Christmas Day. $. Children 6 and under free. In May there is an additional fee to enter the grounds. Contact the museum at (317) 492–6784.

The Indianapolis 500 is the "greatest spectacle in racing." In Indianapolis, the entire month of May is filled with activities relating to the race. There are two days of time trials and many days during the month when the track is open for practice. You can attend these events for a fee as well as the exciting carburetion tests several days before the race, when the thirty-three drivers make sure that everything on their cars is running exactly the way they want. In August 1994 the Speedway hosted the Brickyard 400 NASCAR Race. This was the first time that the Indianapolis Motor Speedway had been used other than the month of May. The NASCAR race has since become an annual event. The 500-mile race and the Brickyard 400 are the two largest single-day sporting events in the world. The U.S. Grand Prix Formula One Race is a new addition.

A Gisler **Adventure**

Not very far from downtown is the location of the greatest spectacle in racing, the Indianapolis Motor Speedway, home of the Indianapolis 500. We all enjoy going down to the speedway in May, the month of the race, and watch the drivers practice for the race. A few days before the race begins, we watch the exciting carburetion tests, wherein the thirty-three drivers ensure that everything on their car is performing up to speed. In August, the guys in our family go to the Brickyard 400 Nascar Race, which became an annual event in 1994. When we have out-of-town guests, we like to entertain them with a visit to the Indianapolis Motor Speedway Hall of Fame Museum, located in the infield of the track. There you can view a twenty-minute film presenting highlights from the track, see the Borg-Warner Trophy featuring all the faces of all the winners, and inspect one of the largest collections of racing cars in the world. Before we leave the speedway, it is always a must to take a ride on the trolley that goes around the track.

A fun way to introduce your family to racing and the track is by visiting the Indianapolis Motor Speedway Hall of Fame Museum that is located in the infield of the racetrack. Inside the museum you can view a twenty-minute film highlighting the history of the track, see the famous Borg-Warner Trophy that has the faces of all the winning drivers on it, and view one of the largest collections in the world of racing, classic, and antique passenger cars. There are more than seventy-five racing cars in the collection, including winning Indianapolis cars as well as race cars from around the world. The oldest vehicle in the collection is an 1895 Reeves motorcycle built in Columbus, Indiana. You can even have your picture taken sitting in a "500" mile race car. In addition to cars you will be able to see helmets, goggles, and other racing memorabilia. The gift shop is large and well stocked with everything from key chains to toy race cars and souvenir postcards. To complete your visit to the Speedway, you will want to take the minibus tour around the famous "500" racetrack that leaves from the museum. The bus travels all the way around the track and stops at the start/finish line where you can take pictures. You will also be able to see the entrance to Gasoline Alley and the original 3-foot section of brick—all the brick that remains from the original track. $. Children ages five and under are **free.**

If you are planning to come to town for the "500"-mile race, you won't want to miss the large "500" Festival Parade, where you will be able to see all thirty-three drivers, celebrities, and great bands. There is a charge if you want reserved seating. You will need to call Ticket-Master at (317) 239–5151 or the "500" Festival at (800) 638–4296 or (317) 636–4556.

German Park (all ages)

8600 South Meridian Street; (317) 886–8751. Open 4:00 P.M. to midnight. $.

If you have older children who are studying the German language or just want to sample German culture, a visit to German Park will be a great activity. On nine Saturday nights in the summer, you can enjoy German music and food at the park. The park is a private club; however, the gates are open during the summer and during Octoberfest, which is held the last weekend in August and the first weekend in September. Octoberfest is a very large event with a wide variety of German food as well as good old American hot dogs for the less adventurous. Children can also enjoy the playground. There is a basketball net and horseshoe pit; however, you will need to remember to bring your own basketballs or horseshoes.

Indiana Black Expo Celebrates African-American Heritage (all ages)

For more information, call (317) 925–2702 or visit IBE's Web site, www.indianablackexpo.com.

This is a real cultural event for the whole family. More than 200,000 people flock to Indianapolis to enjoy the event.

Indiana **Trivia**

Where was the nation's first belt railroad built in 1873?

Indianapolis

Indianapolis Museum of Art (all ages) 🏛️🍴🌱

38th Street and Michigan Road; (317) 923–1331; www.ima-art.org. Open Tuesday, Wednesday, Friday, and Saturday 10:00 A.M. to 5:00 P.M., Thursday 10:00 A.M. to 8:30 P.M., and Sunday noon to 5:00 P.M. Closed Monday and major holidays. Free.

A great place for a family outing is the Indianapolis Museum of Art because before and after visiting the art museum, energetic children can romp in the museum's 152-acre park. On the grounds can also be found the Botanical Garden of the Oldfields Estate, four art pavilions, a lecture hall, a theater, concert terraces, a restaurant, and shops. Because admission to the museum is free, art lovers can make many visits to see all the treasures stored here. The museum has permanent gallery displays and several galleries that feature special changing exhibits. It also offers a full schedule of programs to promote art appreciation among adults and children.

The museum cafe serves lunch Tuesday through Saturday 11:00 A.M. to 2:00 P.M. The museum also has a large snack area with several vending machines and tables. Or, after visiting the museum, you might want to enjoy lunch at the beautiful Garden Terrace Restaurant. If you are energetic, you may want to walk rather than drive from the art museum to the restaurant. The gift shop in the art museum offers books, calendars, notepaper, postcards, and other items—all with beautiful art.

Tours are given at the museum on Tuesday through Sunday at 1:00 P.M. On Thursday evening there is a tour at 7:00 P.M. Tours of the museum's grounds and gardens are given during the spring and summer (April through September). Call for exact dates and times.

Crispus Attucks Museum (ages 5 to 12) 🏛️🏛️

1140 Dr. Martin Luther King Jr. Street; (317) 226–2432. Open 10:00 A.M. to 2:00 P.M. Free.

The Indiana Public Schools Crispus Attucks Museum is a history museum established to recognize, honor, and celebrate the outstanding contributions made by African Americans and, more specifically, Crispus Attucks High School graduates. It also complements the African-American curriculum of the Indianapolis Public Schools.

Indiana State Police Youth Education and Historical Center (all ages) 🏛️

8500 East Twenty-first Street; (317) 899–8293; Admission free; donations accepted. Open Monday through Friday 8:00 to 11:00 A.M. and 1:00 to 4:00 P.M.

The Indiana State Police Historical Center houses one of the finest police exhibition museums in the nation. Inside this warehouse of history are police vehicles, firearms, photographs, displays, and souvenirs of many types. This extensive collection is a treasure that all ages can enjoy. Indiana State Police officers conduct tours and educational programs by appointment for groups of all ages. Educational programs on many topics are available.

Fort Harrison State Park (all ages) ⊗ ⊛ ⊕ ⊜
5753 Glenn Road; (317) 591–0904.

Since 1903 Fort Harrison has played an important role in Indiana history. In 1995 the U.S. Department of the Interior approved the State of Indiana's request to convert 1,700 acres of the 2,500-acre post that had been closed into a state park and nature preserve. Fort Harrison State Park includes one of the largest tracts of unbroken hardwood forest in central Indiana, several small lakes, 3½ miles of Fall Creek and its tributaries, trails, and picnic areas.

Fort Harrison State Park Facilities:
• Bicycle trail
• Cultural arts program
• Fishing
• Hiking trails/paved multi-use trail
• Fort Harrison Golf Resort and Conference Center
• Harrison House Suites and three officers' homes
• The Garrison, with dining, meeting, and conference facilities
• Golf course with eighteen holes and driving range
• Nature center
• Naturalist services
• Picnicking
• Shelter reservation
• Saddle barn
• Horse trail rides, hayrides

Post Road Recreation Center (older children) ⊛ ⊜
4700 North Post Road; (317) 897–7908. Open seven days a week.

Three go-cart tracks to choose from. Minigolf, bankshot basketball, video game room, paintball, target shoot, bumper cars, picnic area, and volleyball courts.

IMAX 3-D Theater (ages 3 and up)
650 West Washington Street; (317) 233–4629; www.imax.com/indy. Open daily 11:00 A.M. to 9:30 P.M. $$.

Your family will enjoy the 3-D experience at Indiana's only IMAX theater, located downtown in White River State Park. Using film ten times the size of normal films and a screen six stories high, these 3-D or 2-D films will present images that seem to reach out and touch you.

Indiana **Trivia**

How long did it take the first-place car to finish the first Indianapolis 500?

6 hours, 41 minutes, and 8 seconds

Indianapolis Artsgarden (all ages)

Illinois and Washington Streets; (317) 631–3301 or (317) 681–5639. Open Monday through Saturday 9:00 A.M. to 9:00 P.M., Sunday noon to 5:00 P.M. Free.

This unique $12 million structure rises seven stories from street level and holds approximately 600 people standing and 400 seated for performances. Elevated walkways link the ArtsGarden to Circle Centre, nearby hotels, offices, shops, and restaurants. The 19,000-square-foot facility serves as performance, exhibition, marketing, and ticketing space for the Indianapolis arts community. The structure is owned and operated by the Arts Council of Indianapolis.

Block Party (ages 8 and up)

4102 Claire Drive, Eighty-second Street and Dean Road; (317) 578–7941. Open Sunday through Thursday 11:00 A.M. to midnight and Friday and Saturday 11:00 A.M. to 1:00 A.M. Admission free; pay-per-play game prices vary.

Block Party offers an exciting venue for food and fun. Experience the Power Grid, an adult-oriented climbing structure. Play the latest high-tech games and be thrilled by Go-Motion Pictures simulator rides. Grab a burger or pizza along with your favorite beverage at the sports bar and grill.

Firefighters Survive Alive! (ages 5 and up)

748 Massachusetts Avenue; (317) 327–6707. Open Monday through Friday 8:00 A.M. to 4:30 P.M. by appointment. Call for arrangements. Free; donations appreciated.

The primary goal of this interactive village with state-of-the-art simulated fire and medical emergencies is to provide a permanent site of free anticipatory public fire and life safety education, with community outreach programming. The programming is designed to prevent loss of life and property due to uncontrolled fires and trauma, incorporating exciting hands-on fire and life safety experiences for everyone, from preschoolers to seniors, with special training for the handicapped.

Greatimes (ages 5 and up)

5341 Elmwood Drive; (317) 781–6365. Open Sunday through Thursday 10:00 A.M. to 10:00 P.M., Friday and Saturday 10:00 A.M. to midnight. Admission free; activity fees vary.

Miniature golf, go-carts, bumper boats, slick track, batting cages, super-collider, arcade games, redemption games, indoor children's playland.

NCAA Hall of Champions (ages 3 and up)

White River State Park, 700 West Washington Street (located in downtown Indianapolis); (800) 735–NCAA (6222); www.ncaa.org/hall_of_champions. Admission: call for pricing. Open Monday through Saturday 10:00 A.M. to 5:00 P.M. Sunday noon to 5:00 P.M.

The 35,000-square-foot, two-level Hall of Champions features six multimedia presentation exhibits for you and your family to enjoy along with many high-tech interactive displays and a turn-of-the-century gymnasium. Of course, you will need to leave time to shop at Campus Corner, where you are able to purchase NCAA-licensed merchandise.

Sports and Recreational Facilities (all ages)

Indianapolis is known as the Amateur Sports Capital of the United States. The best and most promising of rising athletes come to Indianapolis each year for various competitions. The world-class sports facilities here were built with the dreams and hopes of these young athletes in mind. That's why Indy has hosted more than 250 national and international sporting events. Most of the facilities used by the world's best athletes are also open for you and your family to enjoy.

Indiana Pacers. Conseco Fieldhouse, 125 South Pennsylvania Street; (317) 917–2500. Box office open Monday through Saturday 10:00 A.M. to 5:00 P.M. Sunday game days only noon to fifteen minutes after game. Call for ticket prices.

Indy Parks Fitness Trails. Admission free except at Eagle Creek Park. Open dawn to dusk. Enjoy biking or a fitness routine at any one of the following public parks: Bellamy Park, Broad Ripple Park, Brookside Park, Christian Park, Douglass Park, Eagle Creek Park, Garfield Park and Conservatory Municipal Gardens, Riverside Park, Sahm Park, and Southeastway Park.

Indiana State Fairgrounds Event Center. Pepsi Coliseum; 1202 East Thirty-eighth Street; (317) 927–7536.

Indiana Twisters. 11 South Meridian Street, Suite 402; (317) 951–1811. The Indiana Twisters Professional Indoor Soccer Team is Indianapolis's newest professional sports franchise. The Twisters play fourteen home games per year between the months of June and September. Compared to its outdoor soccer counterpart, indoor soccer is faster-paced, higher-scoring, and typically more exciting with its "off-the-wall" style of play.

Indiana University Natatorium. 901 West New York Street, on the IUPUI campus; (317) 274–3518. Open for swimming Monday through Friday 5:30 A.M. to 8:00 P.M. and Sunday 1:00 to 5:00 P.M. Weight room open Monday through Friday 5:30 A.M. to 10:00 P.M., Saturday noon to 3:00 P.M., and Sunday 1:00 to 5:00 P.M. No swimming on Saturday. $. Site of ten Olympic trials events since opening in 1982, the IU Natatorium hosts a variety of national and international aquatic events each year. One of the premier aquatic facilities in the world, the Natatorium has three indoor pools. Daily lap swimming, weight lifting, and fitness programs are available to the public.

IU Michael A. Carroll Track and Soccer Stadium. 1001 West New York Street, on the IUPUI campus; (317) 274–3518. Open Monday through Friday 11:00 A.M. to 7:00 P.M. Closed November 1 to March 31. The 400-meter, nine-lane, all weather track has hosted the Olympic Track and Field Trials and NCAA championships. Rated as one of the fastest tracks in the world, the IU Track Stadium is open to the public.

Indiana/World Ice Skating Academy and Research Center. 201 South Capitol Avenue, Pan Am Plaza; (317) 237–5555. $. Group rates available. Training facility featuring two indoor ice-skating rinks for hockey and figure skating. Public skating and skate rental available. Phone (317) 237–5555 for current schedule.

Indianapolis Colts. (317) 297–7000. Tickets for the NFL Indianapolis Colts games are available at all central Indiana TicketMaster outlets and the RCA Dome box office. The Colts play their home games at the RCA Dome. Call the Colts ticket office for further information.

Indianapolis Ice. 222 East Ohio Street, #810; (317) 266–1234. Tickets: (317) 239–5151 or (317) 266–1234. The Indianapolis Ice hockey team, affiliated with the Chicago Blackhawks and member of the IHL, plays forty-one home games October through April. Tickets can be purchased at any TicketMaster location. They play at the Pepsi Coliseum (1202 East Thirty-eighth Street; 317–925–4423), at the Indiana State Fairgrounds, and at Conseco Fieldhouse.

Indianapolis Indians. 501 West Maryland Street; (317) 239–3545; www.indyindians.com. AAA American Association Indians play home games at their new downtown ballpark, Victory Field, located just west of the Convention Center, from early April through early September. American Association Champions four straight years (1986–89) and title winners in 1982, 1984, 1994, and 1995, the Indians are affiliated with the Cincinnati Reds and have been Indianapolis's professional baseball team since 1887.

Indianapolis Tennis Center. 150 University Boulevard; (317) 278–2100. Open daily 6:45 A.M. to 11:00 P.M. $$$–$$$$. League play, instructional programs, and court rentals available. No membership required. Indoor and outdoor courts available as well as fully stocked pro shop. Site of the RCA Championships, voted tournament of the year for a record ten years.

Little League Baseball Central Region Headquarters. 9802 East Little League Drive; (317) 897–6127. Open Monday through Friday and for special events. Call for tours. **Free.** Headquarters for Little League Baseball's thirteen-state central region. Multimillion-dollar facility includes six playing fields (including a stadium), dormitory building, administrative building, cafeteria, junior Olympic-size swimming pool, tennis courts, and basketball court. Annual hosts of two one-week Little League Baseball camps in July and the Central Region Little League Baseball Championship each August (the winner goes on to the Little League World Series).

Major Taylor Velodrome. 3649 Cold Spring Road; (317) 327–8356 (VELO). A world-class bicycle racing track, named after one of the sport's nineteenth-century greats. The site of many national competitions and education programs that are available to the public. Next to the track is the Lake Sullivan BMX Track, an American Bicycle Association certified bicycle motocross track. Open riding, weather permitting. $. Helmets are required. Road bikes are recommended over mountain bikes. Call ahead for hours. You and your family can watch practice for **free.**

Indianapolis Raceway Park. 10267 East U.S. Highway 136; (317) 291–4090. Admission varies. One of the world's finest multipurpose motorsports facilities, IRP offers an active schedule of competitive events on its world-famous drag strip, paved oval track, and challenging road course.

National Institute for Fitness and Sport. 250 University Boulevard; (317) 274–3432; www.nifs.org. Open Monday through Thursday 5:30 A.M. to 10:00 P.M., Friday 5:30 A.M. to 9:00 P.M., Saturday and Sunday 7:00 A.M. to 6:00 P.M. Call for guest pass fees and/or membership fees; no contract required for membership. Youth and adult programs available. Indiana's world-class training center, open to the public, features a 65,000-square-foot fitness facility with state-of-the art cardiovascular and strength training equipment, 200-meter indoor track, NBA-regulation-size basketball court, volleyball, aerobics, whirlpool, sauna, and steam rooms. Staffed by degreed and certified professionals.

Royal Pin Leisure Centers. Open Sunday through Thursday 9:00 A.M. to 1:00 A.M.; Friday and Saturday 9:00 A.M. to 3:00 A.M. Admission free; bowling fees vary. Modern bowling centers offering automatic scoring, arcades, and other entertainment options.
- **Expo Bowl.** 5261 Elmwod Drive; (317) 787–3448.
- **Jubilee Bowl.** 7420 Michigan Road; (317) 291–1295.
- **Southern Bowl.** 1010 West U.S. 31 South; (317) 881–8686.

Walking Tour

Many people enjoy a walking adventure not only to sightsee but also to get in a little exercise after a car trip. Here are four walks that you could enjoy in the downtown Indianapolis area:

The American Legion Mall loop is 1¼ miles and circles the headquarters of its namesake. Start at the American Legion Mall. Go up to St. Clair Street and turn right. Go 1 block to Pennsylvania, walk down to New York Street, turn right and then right again onto Meridian Street and walk back up to the American Legion Mall.

The 2-mile canal loop is a quiet way to start your morning or end your day. Notice the USS *Indianapolis* Memorial at the north end. Centrally located, the **Monument loop** is 1¼ miles long. It runs from the Indiana State Capital over to Conseco Fieldhouse.

The 1-mile Circle Centre route takes you the full length of the shopping and entertainment complex and allows you to see the historical facades.

- **Western Bowl.** 6441 West Washington Street; (317) 247–4426.
- **Woodland Bowl.** 3421 East Ninety-sixth Street; (317) 844–4099. Smoke-free bowling.

If there are football fans in your family, you will want to visit Indianapolis during the month of October so that you can attend the Circle City Classic sponsored by Indiana Black Expo and the Indiana Sports Corporation. It is the largest and best African-American sporting event in the nation, including the Coca-Cola Circle City Classic football game and ancillary events. If you want more information about the Circle City Classic, you can call (317) 237–5222, or visit www.circlecityclassic.com.

Where to Eat

Acapulco Joe's Mexican Restaurant. 365 North Illinois Street; (317) 637–5160. The first Mexican restaurant in Indianapolis. Located on the same corner for more than thirty years. Always voted first or second for Indianapolis's most popular Mexican restaurant by readers of *Indianapolis Monthly* magazine.

Chocolate Cafe–The South Bend Chocolate Company. 30 Monument Circle; (317) 951–4816. Offers a line of fine chocolates—everything sweet from truffles to turtles, from maple walnut fudge to malted milk balls. It also serves coffees and snacks and offers unique gift items for sale.

Hard Rock Cafe. 49 South Meridian Street; (317) 636–2550. A place where the whole family can enjoy good food and a lot of fun.

Old Spaghetti Factory. 210 South Meridian Street; (317) 635–6325. Dine in the historic warehouse district at the Old Spaghetti Factory. Sit in a trolley car or canopy bed while enjoying antique decor and great food! Spaghetti is served with five taste-tempting sauces. Lasagna, fettuccini, and spinach tortellini also are favorites for family dining at family prices.

St. Elmo's Steak House. 127 South Illinois; (317) 635–0636. A famous Indianapolis tradition since 1902.

Beef & Boards Dinner Theatre. 9301 North Michigan Road; (317) 872–9664. Open Tuesday through Sunday for Broadway shows; Monday for concerts. Doors open 6:00 P.M.; buffet at 6:30 P.M.; performance at 8:00 P.M. Broadway productions by a professional equity company; excellent buffet dinner. Indiana's only year-round equity theater. Reservations suggested; best for ages 10 to 12.

Illusions. 969 Keystone Way, Carmel; (317) 575–8312. It is expensive but well worth it for a special occasion. The average dinner is between $16 and $25. Serving dinner Monday through Thursday 5:00 to 9:00 P.M., Friday 5:00 to 10:00 P.M., and Saturday 4:30 to 10:30 P.M. The chef conjures up delightful entrees and homemade pastry desserts, while a magician performs tableside sleight-of-hand. Reservations are suggested and a must on weekends. **Free** parking.

Where to Stay with Older Children

A bed-and-breakfast in the center of the city is great if you have children that are at least 10 years old.

Nestle Inn Bed and Breakfast. 637 East Street; (317) 610–5200. Children 10 and above. A stately Victorian house turned into a new five-room inn, each room with private bath and data port. Your family will love the location in Chatham Arch. You will be close to many downtown places of interest. Full breakfast daily.

The Old Northside Bed and Breakfast. 1340 North Alabama Street; (317) 635–9123, (800) 635–9127; children 12 and above. With older children you can have an adventure staying in an 1885 downtown Victorian mansion with rich European decor. You will have a private bath, whirlpool, TV/VCR, fireplace, free movies, and parking. Your family will be close to the convention center and RCA Dome.

Where to Stay with Younger Children

The Tranquil Cherub Bed & Breakfast. 2164 North Capitol Avenue; (317) 923–9036. Children of all ages are welcome here. You can enjoy this antiques-filled 1890 classical revival. A full breakfast, snacks, and beverages are also included in the nightly rate, making this an affordable choice. For longer stays of at least two nights, a week, or even a month, your family can enjoy staying in a one-bedroom fully furnished apartment that is perfect for your needs. A microwave and washer and dryer are included.

Serendipity Haus run by grandparents 1423 Hoyt Avenue; (317) 236-9844. Children of all ages are welcome here. Enjoy either of two pleasant bedrooms with private baths in an 1885 home rebuilt in 1999 in a real neighborhood. Your family will be within walking distance to many of the attractions that you want to enjoy.

Omni Severin Hotel. 40 West Jackson Place, across from Union Station; (317) 634–OMNI; www.omnihotels.com. Indianapolis's "Grand Hotel" four-diamond award–winner combines the history of the past with today's upbeat style. Located downtown, connected to the new Circle Centre Mall and Nordstrom, across from Union Station, and just 1 block from the Convention Center and RCA Dome in the heart of the business district.

Embassy Suites Hotel Downtown. 110 West Washington Street; (317) 236–1800, (800) EMBASSY; www.embassy-suites.com. A 360 all-suite hotel connected by skywalk to Circle Centre and the Indianapolis Art-Garden. Home of Boom Babys Restaurant and Lounge. Suites feature two rooms, two televisions, microwave, refrigerator.

Hampton Inn Downtown. 105 South Meridian Street; (317) 261–1200; www.hamptoninn.com. A 180-room hotel directly across from Circle Centre. An elegant historical building transformed into a beautiful hotel. Within walking distance of businesses, shopping, attractions, theater, sporting events, and the symphony.

Hyatt Regency Indianapolis. One South Capitol Avenue; (317) 632–1234; www.hyatt.com. Newly renovated 497-room hotel in the heart of downtown, across from the Indiana Convention Center and RCA Dome. This spectacular twenty-story atrium hotel features business plan rooms with full business services and in-room fax machines. The Hyatt also features a revolving rooftop restaurant, a state-of-the-art health club, and an assortment of shops and boutiques; parking available in the complex.

Radisson Hotel City Centre Indianapolis. 31 West Ohio Street; (317) 635–2000, (800) 333–3333; www.radisson.com. A 374-room hotel located in the heart of downtown on historical Monument Circle. Blocks away from the Indiana Convention Center and RCA Dome, Conseco Fieldhouse, and Circle Centre. Overlooking downtown Indianapolis.

Westin Hotel–Indianapolis. 50 South Capitol Avenue; (317) 262–8100; www.westin.com. A 573-room hotel, AAA four-diamond rating. Downtown location in the heart of the business district. Connected by skywalk to the Indiana Convention Center and RCA Dome.

Brickyard Crossing Golf Resort and Inn. 4400 West Sixteenth Street; (317) 241–2500. Adjacent to the world's most famous racecourse, the 108-room Brickyard Crossing Golf Resort and Inn provides a rare blend of history with a sense of freshness. The inn features deluxe sleeping rooms, full-service dining, a heated outdoor swimming pool, and the premier eighteen-hole championship golf course designed by Pete Dye.

Canterbury Hotel. 123 South Illinois Street; (317) 634–3000, (800) 538–8186. Tucked away within the borders of Circle Centre is Indianapolis's crown jewel of hotels. The Canterbury Hotel, a European-style boutique hotel, has a history dating back to the 1850s. As Indiana's only member of Preferred Hotels and Resorts Worldwide, its reputation has been built on quality with a style that is timeless. You will definitely be close to everything that you want to see if you stay here.

Renaissance Tower Historic Inn–Downtown. 230 East Ninth Street; (317) 261–1652, (800) 676–7786. The *New York Times*'s "Choice for downtown Indianapolis," your family can enjoy staying in one of the elegant studio suites with four-poster beds, bay windows, and Queen Anne cherry furnishings. You will also have a spacious gourmet kitchen equipped with full-sized appliances, pots and pans, dishes, linens, and silverware along with color TV and cable, complimentary adjacent parking, and best of all, you will be able to walk to many of the sights you want to visit.

Pickwick Farms Short-Term Furnished Apartments. 9300 North Ditch Road; (317) 872–6506, (800) 869–RENT. Studio, one-, two-, and three-bedroom units. Clubhouse has two racquetball courts, business center, Brunswick bowling alley, large exercise facility, outdoor swimming, outdoor tennis, and two-story party room available to guests. A forty-unit laundry facility also available. All linens, towels, bedding, and eating and cooking utensils are included. Kitchen offers all necessary appliances. Free local calls, voice mail, color cable TV; all utilities paid.

Heading north out of Indianapolis on Keystone you will come to **The Fashion Mall,** Keystone at the Crossing. Fine shopping in an elegant atmosphere, anchored by Parisian and Jacobson's. If you are hungry there is a **Dick Clark's American Bandstand Grill** at Keystone at the Crossing (3550 East 86th Street, (317–848–2002) and a **T.G.I. Friday's** (317–844–3355), along with many other restaurants. Two of the larger hotels at the shopping center are:

Sheraton Hotel Indianapolis. 8787 Keystone Crossing; (317) 846–2700, (800) 325–2525. A 393-room luxury hotel located at Keystone at the Crossing. Connected by skyway to The Fashion Mall, with more than one hundred specialty stores.

Westin Suites. 8787 Keystone Crossing; (317) 574–6770, (800) WESTIN–1. One hundred fifty-nine suites also connected by skyway to the Fashion Mall.

AmeriSuites. 9104 Keystone Crossing; (317) 843–0064, (800) 833–1516. A 126-room property featuring beautifully appointed two-room suites including refrigerator, microwave, coffeemaker, and 26-inch TV/VCR. Complimentary deluxe continental breakfast, buffet, free local calls and *USA Today.* Located within walking distance of the Keystone Fashion Mall and several fine restaurants. Convenient access to I–465.

For More Information

Airport Visitors Center, Indianapolis International Airport; (317) 487–7243.

Arts Council of Indianapolis, (317) 631–3301.

Indianapolis Black Chamber of Commerce, (317) 655–7064.

Indianapolis Chamber of Commerce, (317) 464–2200.

Indianapolis City Center, (317) 237–5200.

Indianapolis Convention and Visitors Association, (317) 639–4282; www.indy-gov.org.

Indianapolis Downtown, Inc., (317) 237–2222.

Indianapolis Hotel Reservations, (800) 556–INDY.

Indianapolis Tourism Hotline, (800) 824–INDY.

www.indianapolis.msn.com.

Noblesville

Just 20 miles from downtown Indianapolis is the quaint town of Noblesville. A stop at the Chamber of Commerce office at 54 North Ninth Street will give you up-to-date information on what is going on in the town.

Drive around the town and you will be able to see many historic sites. There is **Potter's Bridge,** built in 1870, the last bridge in the area still standing after the express highways were built. Located 1 mile north of Noblesville on Tenth Street, the bridge area is peaceful and a nice spot for small picnics, fishing, or hiking. Pioneer **William Conner's town house** still stands on Eighth Street. The home was built in 1837 and has beautiful wrought-iron balconies and porches. The house is now a gift shop and has architecture that makes a visit worthwhile. **Riverside Cemetery** is located 2 blocks from the Conner House. The first city cemetery for Noblesville is a must for anyone interested in history. In the center of the town stands the **courthouse,** built in 1879. Many famous trials have been held here, including the D. C. Stephenson Ku Klux Klan nationally headlined case in 1925. The **Craycraft Home** is 1 block east of the courthouse on Conner Street. This three-story house is a perfect example of Victorian architecture. Today the house is a gift shop. If you need something sweet to continue your travels, you can stop in at **Baier's Candy Store.** It is an old-fashioned ice-cream and candy store in a restored 1889 building. The homemade candies and other bakery items will be sure to satisfy your sweet tooth.

Morse Reservoir (all ages) 🌊 🚶 🍁

Highway 9. Take Meridian Street (Highway 31) north from Indianapolis to Highway 32. Turn right onto route 32 (west), and pass through Westfield to Noblesville. In Noblesville turn left (north) onto Highway 9 and follow signs.

If your family enjoys water sports, you will want to go to Morse Reservoir. This is a 1,500-acre lake with 33 miles of shoreline. The county owns a park on the lake that is the perfect place for picnicking, sunbathing, and swimming for children of all ages. Boat rentals are available, too. You can take a hike on many of the paths and county roads at the reservoir, and don't forget your camera. The panoramic views are breathtaking.

Conner Prairie (all ages) 🏛 🚻 🍴 🍁

Allisonville Road south of Noblesville; (317) 776–6006, (800) 966–1836; www.cornerprairie.org. Historic area open April to October, Tuesday through Sunday; and November, Wednesday through Sunday. Closed from December through March except for special events. Open Tuesday through Saturday 9:30 A.M. to 5:00 P.M. daily and Sunday 11:00 A.M. to 5:00 P.M. $$. Museum center and museum shop open daily throughout the year with a few exceptions. Call the 24-hour general information line for more specific information about special activities and events.

It is always 1836 at this historically accurate living-history museum. History comes alive right before your eyes as you talk to settlers reenacting life in a nineteenth-century Midwest village. Conner Prairie has thirty-nine buildings in its historic areas along with a modern log cabin that serves as a nature center. Start your journey into the past at the

65,000-square-foot museum center, where you'll view an award-winning film presentation to orient yourself to the changes you must make to step back in time. After the orientation film, you will begin your walk to the 1836 village of Prairietown, where there is no evidence of the modern conveniences that you have left behind in the museum center. If everyone is quiet and listens carefully as you walk down the path, the clanking of a blacksmith working in the village can be heard.

Soon you will start meeting the residents of Prairietown as they go about their daily duties. Everyone is encouraged to interact with the residents and to talk to them about their lives. Ask them about their political views, family values, or the latest town gossip, and you'll be interacting with the past. Conner Prairie is one of a few living-history museums that does "first-person" interpretation. When you visit the Pioneer Adventure Area just around the corner from the village, you will become actively involved in the daily life of that time. You will be taking part in the making of soap and candles, cooking over an open fire, and trying to use the drop spindle or loom. There are plenty of games for children of all ages to try. Most children will find walking on stilts a real challenge. Energetic children can try their hand at household chores and find out what it is like to do them without modern-day products. At Connor Prairie, there are many special programs during the year that are especially fun for families. In December families can take part in a candlelight walk through the 1836 village to see how Christmas was celebrated more than 150 years ago. They can also attend a sumptuous holiday buffet at the Prairie Town Cafe. At the Christmas celebration at William Conner's home, you can explore early Christmas traditions and values while making a fancy tree ornament to take home. The spirit of Christmas will come alive as you sing festive songs, play parlor games, and taste delicious holiday treats. Reservations are needed for these events, which charge a fee. In December families can also enjoy the Festival of Gingerbread. Visions of sugarplums will dance in your head after you see all the breathtaking gingerbread house creations. On many October evenings, Conner Prairie has wagon rides through the village where you may see the Headless Horseman as Washington Irving's tale *The Legend of Sleepy Hollow* comes to life. Families will also enjoy music, dancing, and pumpkin/face painting for the children. This event lasts from 6:00 to 9:00 P.M., and discount coupons are available at local stores. No advance registration or reservations are necessary.

Many families enjoy having an evening picnic at Conner Prairie during the months of July and August as they listen to the Indianapolis Symphony Orchestra. The orchestra performs as the sun sets on the prairie. As the gates open at 5:30 P.M. and the concert does not start until 7:30 P.M., you will have plenty of time to enjoy a picnic supper and visit Prairietown before the performance. There are special Independence Day concerts on July 3 and 4. Different activities are always going on at Conner Prairie, from weddings to canoe trips. Enjoy the best of both worlds when you enter the Museum Center with all the amenities of modern life. The spacious gift shop is well-stocked with a wide variety of interesting items from the days of the early settlers. In the store you will find shelves full of food items such as pumpkin and plum butter, old-fashioned crackers, and herbs as well as pioneer recipe books for squash, zucchini, and berry breads. Place mats and blankets made by Prairie's own weavers are sold in the shop. Children will be fascinated by the

Indiana **Trivia**

How wide is the state?

Where was the first transistor radio receiver manufactured?

Where is the Indiana Transportation Museum?

160 miles, Indianapolis, Noblesville

1830 doll kits, historical toy patterns for mountain harmonicas and whistles, wooden clackers, rabbit skins, and a large selection of children's books. Don't worry when everyone gets hungry—the museum center has a restaurant and snack bar where you can enjoy a variety of soups, sandwiches, salads, and entrees, or homemade breads, muffins, cookies, and pies.

Forest Park (all ages) 🏛️ 🏊 🏌️ 🍁

Highway 19 in Noblesville. Modest fees for golf, swimming, and reserving various sports courts and picnic facilities. Forest Park Golf Course (317) 773–2881; eighteen-hole course (317) 773–5043; Forest Park Inn (317) 846–7308.

This is a great place to have inexpensive family fun. You can easily spend the day there. The sixty-eight-acre park has dense woods, picnic areas, and facilities for an impressive number of sports activities. Children don't need to worry about getting a turn on the playground equipment because the park has many slides, jungle gyms, and swings. The park has an Olympic-size swimming pool and a dive pool to enjoy on hot summer days. You will also find a softball diamond; horseshoe pits; volleyball, basketball, and tennis courts; and a miniature golf course (which charges a small fee). For adults and older children, the park has an adjacent nine-hole golf course and operates a nearby eighteen-hole course. For picnics, the park has three large open-air shelter houses with tables and many other picnic tables throughout the park. Forest Park Inn is available for private banquets, and 300 people can be accommodated inside this rustic old inn that overlooks the nine-hole golf course. The smaller Forest Park Cabin seats thirty people.

Indiana Transportation Museum (all ages) 🚂 🍁

(317) 773–6000; www.itm.org. Open Memorial Day through Labor Day, Tuesday through Sunday 10:00 A.M. to 5:00 P.M. and weekends only in September, October, April, and May. $. Children under 3 free. Admission price covers entrance to museum and rides all day on the trolley car.

If your family likes trains, you must include a trip to the Indiana Transportation Museum on one of your family outings to Forest Park. The Indiana Transportation Museum was founded in 1960 and is dedicated to preserving, restoring, and operating authentic locomotives. Volunteers provide much of the labor in operating the museum. You will be able to see dozens of different railroad cars and locomotives and even have the opportunity to go inside many of the cars. Each weekend there is a different special event. The highlight of your visit will be a ride on a restored interurban trolley from the Roaring Twenties, letting you feel what it was like to ride America's favorite form of transportation before the automobile. There are special excursion trips several times a year on the fully restored steam locomotive, Nickel Plate Road No. 587 and its F7 diesel locomotives, along with the museum's fleet of stainless steel passenger coaches. Most weekends there are local excursions when the museum is open.

Stoneycreek Farm (all ages) ⬤

11366 State Road 38 East; (317) 773–3344. Admission $2.00 on weekends; free weekdays.

Leave the city and all its bustle behind and visit a family-run farm. Stoneycreek Farm has fields, farm animals, a log cabin, and a gift shop in a buggy barn. It's a place where you can picnic in the summer, enjoy a fall hayride and bonfire, or choose a Christmas tree. In October at the Pumpkin Harvest Festival, you can catch a hayride into the pumpkin fields and select your own pumpkins. On October weekends you can attend special events such as the Bluegrass Music Festival, Rendezvous 1758, and the Civil War Reenactment. Your children can also enjoy pony rides, watch a blacksmith at work, and eat great outdoor cooking. Remember when families went out into the woods and cut down a tree for Christmas? Well, the next best thing is going to Stoneycreek and selecting your freshly cut tree or a freshly dug tree that you can plant in your yard after Christmas. If it's cold during this adventure, a nice cup of hot cider or chocolate will definitely warm you up.

Canterbury Arabian Horse Farm (all ages) ⬤

1213 East 196th Street; (317) 776–0779. Free.

If you love horses, especially Arabian horses, the place to visit is the Canterbury Arabian Horse Farm. Here some of the finest Arabians in the country are raised. For an admission fee that is just right, free, you can stroll through the grounds almost any time. If your timing is right, you can watch a horse take a shower in a wash rack or a foal being born. A walk through the state-of-the-art barn will quickly change your image of what you thought a barn should be.

Whispering Meadows Equestrian Center (ages 5 and up) ⬤ ⬤

2140 State Road 37 North; (317) 342–1880.

Horses can be rented here for those who yearn to ride through the countryside. Call ahead and make reservations for your family to ride in the large outdoor arena or on one of the scenic trails. If you feel that your family is really adventurous, everyone will enjoy a Saturday night barbecue and overnight camp out. Your family can even rent horses and ponies for birthday parties and other special events. If any family member needs riding lessons, this is the place to get started.

Where to Eat

SunShine Cafe. 250 West Conner; (317) 773–5245. Everyone will enjoy eating at this casual, full-service family restaurant. Complete menu featuring hometown favorites. Breakfast, lunch, and dinner. Children's menu and senior discounts available. Open twenty-four hours.

For More Information

Hamilton County Convention and Visitors Bureau. 11601 Municipal Drive, Fishers, IN 46038; (800) 776–8687; www.hccvb.org.

Carmel

The Museum of Miniature Houses (all ages) 🎭

111 East Main Street, just north of Indianapolis; (317) 575–9466. One block east of Range Line on Main Street in Carmel. From I–465 take Keystone exit north 4 miles to 131st Street (Main Street) and turn west past high school. Headed south on U.S. 31, take the east branch (Keystone, U.S. 431) when it splits. Go south to 131st Street and turn west past high school. Open Wednesday through Saturday 11:00 A.M. to 4:00 P.M. and Sunday 1:00 to 4:00 P.M. $. Museum members **free.**

Here you'll see an exhibit of antique and contemporary dollhouses, room boxes, vignettes and accessories, traveling exhibits, special collections, and seasonal displays. The museum exhibits a changing selection of miniature houses, rooms, and single pieces. Also featured are personal collections of all kinds. Some of the regular features include:
- An antique dollhouse built in 1861 and documented by the English builder
- A large, scratch-built replica of a Cincinnati home lovingly created by the grown-up child who lived there
- A wonderfully preserved and refurbished house bought in a thrift shop for $15 in 1936
- A ½-scale "museum" within the museum
- A large house all ready for the daughter's wedding and reception
- Other houses and vignettes representing several scales and many architectural styles
- Special collections ranging from cars and cannons to silhouettes, dolls, and teddy bears
- The dollhouse featured in the Dandy Doll House Stories
- A small gift shop offering fine handcrafted miniatures as well as books and periodicals

After leaving the museum you are very close to Illusions (see page 115), the restaurant that will entertain you with magic as you eat.

For More Information

City of Carmel. www.ci.carmel.in.us/.

Westfield

Westfield Summerfest (all ages)

Held in June: parade, booths, Lion's Club chicken BBQ, VFW bingo, 5K Run/Fun Walk, exhibitions, contests, merchant give-a-ways, and carnival.

Annual Little Eagle Creek Bluegrass Invitational (all ages) ♫

Rynearson Farms, 16840 Little Eagle Creek Avenue; (317) 896–2985. Admission charge.

Held in July and September since 1976. Family-oriented Bluegrass music, camping, and fun-filled weekend. Hayrides, campfires, horseshoe-pitching contest, and national bluegrass bands; held in barn if it rains.

For More Information

Town of Westfield. www.westfield town.org.

Zionsville

Zionsville is located just twenty minutes northwest of Indianapolis. Take Michigan Road north and you can experience a step back in time in Zionsville, a village that has been restored to its turn-of-the century charm. First you should stop by The Greater Zionsville Chamber of Commerce, 135 South Elm Street, (317) 873–3836; www.bremc.com/zionsville.

Have your children ever seen a brick street? If not, take a stroll down Main Street in Zionsville and you will be back in the nineteenth century. The town is filled with incredible shops. You will discover interesting antiques stores, art galleries, clothing stores, and specialty shops. Stop by the **P. H. Sullivan Museum** at 225 West Hawthorne Street, which is dedicated to the preservation of Indiana history and has a complete genealogy library.

If your family would enjoy a picnic or just spending time outdoors, Zionsville has three parks. You can go to **Lincoln Park, Starkey Park,** or **Lion's Park.**

Many events take place in Zionsville throughout the year that your family might enjoy. The **Country Market** is held the first Saturday after Mother's Day. This is a day when you will enjoy seeing antiques and different crafts and have good old-fashioned fun. There are **free** rides from the parking lots to the market. If you need more information, call (317) 873–3836. The Fourth of July celebration is an entire day full of family activities, and there is a fireworks display in the evening when it gets dark. The **Traders Point Hunt Charity Horse Show** runs the first full week of August. This show is a national event, and people in the Indianapolis area don't often get the opportunity to enjoy a horse show of this caliber with competitors from around the country. The **Fall Festival** is held the first weekend after Labor Day. There is a parade in town and games along with a flea market. The **Village Tour**

of Homes takes place during the first weekend in October. You have the opportunity to visit many of the different charming turn-of-the-century homes throughout the village that have been restored. **Christmas in the Village** is on the first Saturday and Sunday in December. The village has a large Yuletide celebration with a Christmas tree in the middle of Main Street.

Don't worry when you get hungry in Zionsville; there are more than fifteen restaurants that your family will be able to select from. You will be able to find quaint restaurants such as **Gisela's Kaffeekranschen** as well as hamburger and pizza places.

Where to Eat

Adam's Rib & Seafood House. 40 South Main; (317) 773–3600. Rustic 160-year-old building on the brick street in Zionsville. Prime rib, barbecue ribs, steaks, fish, chicken, pasta. Reservations recommended. Open for lunch Tuesday through Saturday 11:30 A.M. to 2:00 P.M.; dinner Monday through Thursday 5:00 to 9:00 P.M., Friday and Saturday until 10:00 P.M.

Zorba's Restaurant. 30 North Main; (317) 733–0633. Offering menus that tempt you with tantalizing Greek and Middle Eastern delicacies. Open for lunch Tuesday through Saturday 11:00 A.M. to 2:00 P.M. Dinner served Monday through Saturday 5:00 to 9:00 P.M.

Where to Stay

The Brick Street Inn. 175 South Main Street; (317) 873–9177. Discover a warm, friendly atmosphere in this charming 1865 inn situated in the heart of Zionsville. Unwind in front of the cozy fire.

Country Gables Bed and Breakfast. 9302 East State Road 334; (317) 873–5382. Your family can enjoy staying in this Victorian farmhouse that was built in the late 1800s.

For More Information

Greater Zionsville Chamber of Commerce. www.zionsvillechamber.org/.

Sheridan

Stuckey Farm Market (all ages) 🐘

19995 County Line Road; (317) 769–4172. Open 9:00 A.M. to 5:00 P.M. daily except Sunday. Small fee for tours.

At the Stuckey Farm Market your family can see how a family-owned and -run apple orchard with more than 4,000 trees operates. The cider-making process, an observation honeybee hive, a wagon ride to the pumpkin patch, and some small animals are all available to be seen. Children will be able to learn about different apple varieties and their various uses, from baking to just plain munching. The Stuckey Farm Store, which sells a variety of produce and package goods, is open from strawberry season to Thanksgiving.

Eastern Indiana

Eastern Indiana is a marvelous direction to head for a family getaway! What would your family enjoy—historic covered bridges, quaint Amish villages, live theater, pioneer and Native American heritage, fascinating museums, zoos, or a scenic excursion train? Everyone knows that the sun rises in the east. This is the "funshine" section of Indiana that warms up first every day. Here you'll be able to watch a professional football team prepare for the NFL season, take Indiana's longest scenic train ride, visit an authentic fort, and have a vacation on a houseboat. You'll have the opportunity to visit museums honoring Hollywood legend James Dean in Fairmount and forty-fourth vice president Dan Quayle in Huntington, as well as cartoonist Jim Davis, who sketches Garfield in his Muncie studio. And there's much more: You'll find a town that actually puts on a circus each year and have the opportunity to ride in a tank. Your family will definitely create memories when you visit Eastern Indiana.

TopPicks for fun in Eastern Indiana

1. Whitewater Valley Railroad, Connersville

2. Whitewater Memorial State Park, Liberty

3. The Fort Wayne Children's Zoo, Fort Wayne

4. Amishville U.S.A., Berne

5. Swiss Heritage Village, Berne

6. Indiana Basketball Hall of Fame Museum, New Castle

7. Me's Zoo, Parker City

8. Ouabache State Park, Bluffton

9. Historic Forks of the Wabash, Huntington

EASTERN INDIANA

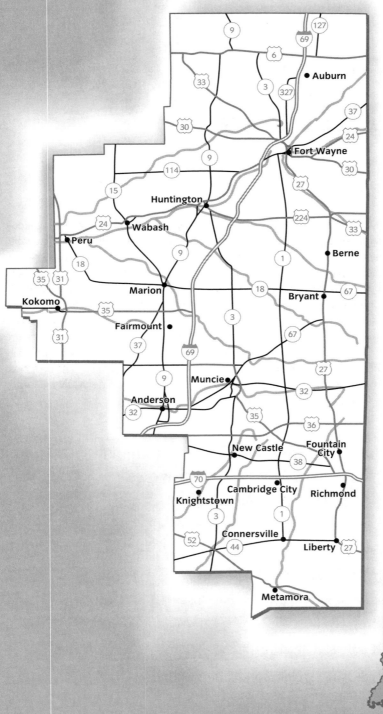

Marion

Wilson House (also known as "Hostess House") (ages 5 and up)

723 West Fourth Street; (765) 664–3755. Open Monday through Friday 10:00 A.M. to 4:00 P.M. Donations accepted.

This Classical Revival mansion was designed by the renowned African-American architect Samuel Plato. Open to the public for lunch Monday through Friday; visitors can wander through the beautifully decorated rooms or browse in the resale shop. Listed on the National Register of Historic Places.

Mississinewa Battlefield and Reenactment (ages 8 and up)

Located on the banks of the Mississinewa River, near Grant County. Mailing address: P.O. Box 1812, Marion, IN 46952; (800) 822–1812; www.mississinewa1812.com. $$.

Let your older children experience a little history by taking them to see the re-created Battle of the Mississinewa the second weekend of October. The living-history weekend includes food, arts, and culture of the period.

Deano's Sports Complex (ages 5 and up)

800 East Third (State Road 18); (765) 664–7207. Open April 15 through October 15 and other weekends, weather permitting.

This is a great place for the whole family. Enjoy go-carts, batting cages, arcade, bumper boats, and slam-dunk basketball.

River's Edge Family Golf Center (ages 5 and up)

1921 North Huntington Road; (765) 662–2805. Open April 1 through October 1.

Where everyone can enjoy miniature golf, batting cages, sand volleyball, driving range, and basketball.

Ancient Battlefield

During the War of 1812, Tecumseh urged the Miami Indians to join with the British. In December 1812 General William Henry Harrison marched against the Native American villages along the Mississinewa River. The battlefield stands as a reminder of these conflicts between the American settlers and Native Americans.

Where to Eat

Your whole family will be able to enjoy home-cooked meals at the following restaurants:

Jim Dandy Restaurant. 1229 North Baldwin Avenue;(765) 664–6702. Jim Dandy is a full-service family restaurant open for breakfast at 6:00 A.M. Monday through Saturday and 7:00 A.M. on Sunday. Complete breakfast, lunch, and dinner menus available. Daily breakfast buffets are featured, along with several homemade specialties.

Richards Restaurant. 864 East Forty-fifth Street; (765) 677–8254. Richards is a family-style restaurant—they love serving children. A full menu is offered. Chicken and fish are the specialties. Come as you are: You are always welcome at Richards! Open daily from 5:30 A.M. to 9:00 P.M.

The Super Scoop Restaurant. 1421 East Thirty-eighth Street; (765) 674–4044. Homemade biscuits and sausage gravy, breakfast platters, blueberry pancakes, breakfast biscuits, sweet rolls (served 7:00 to 10:30 A.M.). Then the family dining starts, and what member of your family wouldn't enjoy a homemade waffle cone, hand-dipped ice cream, frozen yogurt, a shake, sundae, or a blitz? Open 7:00 A.M. to 9:00 P.M. Closed Sunday and major holidays.

Where to Stay

Hampton Inn. 1502 North Baldwin Avenue (State Road 9N); (765) 662–6656. Seventy-three rooms including seven in-room hot-tub suites. **Free** breakfast bar; fitness center with indoor pool, hot tub, and gym; nonsmoking rooms; microwave; refrigerator; hair dryer; coffeemaker; and data-port phones in all rooms.

Golden Oak Bed and Breakfast. 809 West Fourth Street; (765) 651–9950. Four rooms; children are welcome here and there is a baby crib, high chair, and even a room especially for children. Pets are not allowed and neither is smoking.

Comfort Suites. 1345 North Baldwin Avenue; (765) 651–1006. Take exit 64 off I–69, travel 7 miles west to North Baldwin Avenue, hotel is 1½ miles north on the left. Complimentary continental breakfast (including coffee), exercise room, **free** newspaper, indoor pool. Close to shopping, dining, jogging track/trail, cross-country skiing, tennis, lake, baseball field, and basketball court. Handicapped-accessible rooms. Pets are allowed.

Camping

Mar-Brook Campground. 6690 East 600 South; (765) 674–4383. Two hundred sites with hookups (water, electric, sewage), swimming, fishing, hiking, volleyball, basketball, horseshoes, hayride, arcade, miniature golf, firewood, and ice. Open April 15 through October 15.

Sports Lake. 7230 East 400 South (½ mile east of I–69 at exit 59); (765) 998–2558. Open May 1 through September 30. Primitive, modern, and deluxe accommodations. Stocked eleven-acre lake, in-ground pool, miniature golf course, playground, bathhouse, boat rental, arcade, dump station, basketball court.

For More Information

Marion Grant County Convention and Visitors Bureau. www.jamesdean country.com.

Treaties at **the Fork**

Before arriving in Huntington, share some facts with your family about the town's history. Huntington is closely tied to the forks of the Wabash and Little Rivers, where three significant Indian treaties were signed. Miami Indian Chief J. B. Richardville built a house at the forks, and the house served as tribal headquarters. You can visit this restored house. You can also stop for a visit at the Samuel Purviance House at 326 South Jefferson, which is listed on the National Register of Historic Places. This house features a winding cherry stairway and unusual fireplaces.

Huntington

The Dan Quayle Center and Museum (ages 5 and up)

815 Warren Street; (260) 356–6356; www.quaylemuseum.org. Open year-round Tuesday through Saturday 10:00 A.M. to 4:00 P.M.; Sunday 1:00 to 4:00 P.M. Closed Monday. $.

Learn about former vice president Quayle's life growing up in Huntington to his years in the White House. Besides a film, there are photos and artifacts, including his report card with his spelling grade. There is a permanent exhibit about Quayle as well as different exhibits about his life that are displayed every two to three months. The center opened in 1993 and is housed in a former Christian Science Church built in the Greek Revival style in 1919. It is the only vice-presidential museum in the country.

Huntington Historical Museum (ages 5 and up)

315 Court Street; (260) 356–7264. Open Tuesday through Friday 10:00 A.M. to 4:00 P.M.; Saturday 1:00 to 4:00 P.M.

While driving through the center of downtown Huntington, you will want to point out the courthouse to your children. Built in 1904, it is one of Indiana's most striking courthouses. If you have time and older children, you can all unload and visit the wonderful museum where you'll find Miami Indian artifacts found in the county and clocks and pictures of the town from almost 150 years ago.

Historic Forks of the Wabash (all ages)

3010 West Park Drive; (260) 356–1903; www.historicforks.com. Open May through September, Saturday and Sunday 1:00 to 5:00 P.M. Admission charge.

While in Huntington you will need to take time to visit this living-history museum and park and learn the story of the relations between the Miami Indians and the early settlers on the Indiana frontier. The park has a hundred historic acres where your family will be able to visit a log schoolhouse, immigrant's log house, Miami chief's house, canal, and visitors center. You can also take a tour of the historic homes on the site or visit during the **Festival of the Whippoorwill Moon** held the first weekend in May. The whole family will enjoy attending the **Forks of the Wabash Pioneer Festival** during the last weekend in September, where demonstrators portray life from the past at **Hier's Park.** The pioneer village comes alive with buckskinners, an encampment, historical demonstrations, children's games, antiques, crafts, antique motorcars and tractors, and entertainment. Hier's Park again becomes an action-packed place for family fun on the third weekend in June during **Huntington Heritage Days.** This festival is truly family-oriented, with more than fifty events, including a celebrity concert, powerboat races, children's games, arts and crafts, and antiques.

Wings of Freedom Museum (ages 5 and up) 🛬

State Road 5, Municipal Airport; (260) 356–1945. Open Saturday 10:00 A.M. to 4:00 P.M. and Sunday 1:00 to 4:00 P.M. $.

Older children can view documents, photographs, artifacts, and aircraft tracing the history of military aviation. The central focus of the museum is a P-51D Mustang, Scat VII flown during World War II.

J. Edward Roush Lake/Huntington Lake (all ages) 🏊 👫 🚲 ⛺

517 North Warren Road; (260) 468–2165. Open year-round Monday through Friday from 11:00 A.M. to 6:00 P.M., Saturday, Sunday, and holidays 10:00 A.M. to 7:00 P.M.

Everyone will enjoy this 900-acre lake surrounded by 8,400 acres of preserved land. Rich in Miami Indian history, **Huntington Lake** and the surrounding area have a lot to offer. Walk the same trails that Little Turtle (war chief of the Miami) once roamed or visit the grave site of Little Turtle's granddaughter, Kil-So-Quah, in Huntington County. Older children will enjoy the mountain bike trails, shooting range, archery range, model airport, fishing, boating, swimming, and camping. There are also hunting (in season) and interpretive programs.

Where to Eat

Pizza Junction. Located at the railroad tracks in a restored train depot, 201 Court Street; (260) 356–4700. Open Sunday through Thursday 11:00 A.M. to 11:00 P.M., Friday and Saturday 11:00 A.M. to 1:00 A.M. Closed on Christmas, Thanksgiving, and Easter. A great time to take the children is around 6:00 P.M., when three trains go past. Feast on breadsticks, pizza, salads, and sandwiches. Prices range from $2.50 to $14.95.

BK Drive-In. 1218 South Jefferson; (260) 356–6920. Many young children have not had the wonderful experience of a drive-in. Here everyone can place their orders from the car and enjoy their meals just sitting in the car.

Where to Stay

Comfort Inn. 2207 North Jefferson Street; (260) 356–3434; www.comfortinn.com. Take the exit for U.S. 224 West off I–69 and travel 8 miles to the hotel, which is located at the intersection of U.S. 224 and bypass U.S. 24 and State Road 5. **Free** continental breakfast (including coffee), **Free** newspaper, exercise room, indoor pool, nearby hiking/nature area, hunting, jogging track, lake, picnic area, playground, tennis, bicycle rental, miniature golf, golf driving range, fishing, and boat rentals. Handicapped-accessible rooms.

Days Inn. 2996 West Park Drive; (260) 359–8989. Continental breakfast, outdoor pool, and pets are allowed.

Huggy Bear Motel. Interchange State Road 5 and I–69; (260) 375–2503. Forty-eight rooms. Playground and nonsmoking rooms available. Small pets may be approved upon request.

For More Information

Huntington Visitor and Convention Bureau. 407 North Jefferson Street; (260) 359–TOUR or (800) 848–4282; www.visithuntington.org.

Wabash

On the banks of the Wabash River, you'll find the small town of Wabash. Its downtown historical area reflects the city's development as a port city on the Wabash and Erie Canal. Wabash is known for being the first city to be illuminated by electricity, and you can see one of the first electric lights in the courthouse lobby. To take a walking or driving tour of Wabash, stop at the Honeywell Center, at 720 North Wabash Street, to pick up a map. If you are in town you can find the Visitors Bureau at 111 South Wabash Street; (800) 563–1169. There you can obtain information about the many different places of interest and festivals going on in the town. Wabash County has more than 6,000 acres of lakes where your family will be able to enjoy swimming, fishing, hunting, boating, and other water activities.

Amazing Indiana Facts

Wabash was the first electrically lighted city in the world. "From the towering dome of the Court House at 8:00 p.m. on March 31, 1880, burst a flood of lights that made world history. More than 10,000 people witnessed the event. For a mile around, houses and yards were distinctly visible, while far away the Wabash River glowed like a band of molten silver."

Honeywell Center—Wabash (all ages) 🎵 🍽

275 West Market Street; (800) 626–6345. Open year-round daily 8:00 A.M. to 10:30 P.M. Free.

Everyone traveling in your car will enjoy getting out and stretching their legs here because there are things that will interest the very young through senior citizens. This Art Deco cultural recreation and conference center features Ford Theater, where different shows are presented, a restaurant, outdoor plaza, galleries, and a year-round roller rink. Do call for a lineup of the shows coming to the Ford Theater, because they have performances especially for children as well as many different musicals.

Wabash County Historical Museum (ages 5 and up) 🔍

89 West Hill Street; (260) 563–0661. Open Tuesday through Saturday 9:00 A.M. to 1:00 P.M. Free.

This museum is a memorial to Civil War veterans. It contains Indian and pioneer articles and Civil War records. If you're interested in tracing your relatives, this museum has a splendid genealogical collection. The collection contains the following:

- **Natural History**—fossils, shell collections, mastodon bones, rock collections
- **Indian Artifacts**—projectile points, Godfroy and Slocum materials, pictures, clothing, family photographs
- **Pioneer Periods**—furniture, tools, dishware, coverlets, photographs
- **Clothing**—costume doll collection by decades from 1835

If you're a fan of country singer Crystal Gayle, who grew up in Wabash, you'll also enjoy the display honoring her.

Wabash Marketplace Historic District (all ages) 🏛

Downtown in front of the courthouse on Jefferson Street; (800) 563–1169.

Victorian, Romanesque, and Italian architecture. Many unique specialty shops. Honeywell Center and Paradise Spring Historic Park.

D Shoppe (all ages)

1876 bank building at 2 West Market Street in historic downtown Wabash; (260) 563–1420. Open Monday through Saturday 9:00 A.M. to 5:00 P.M., open Friday until 6:00 P.M., closed Sunday.

An interesting place for everyone looking for a special memento of the trip, the D Shoppe features many fine gifts, collectibles, and unusual one-of-a-kind items. Truly a specialty shop.

Mississinewa Reservoir (all ages) 😊 ⚠️ 🚴

County Roads 625 East and 500 South, Miami County; (765) 473–6528.

A good place to get out of the car and enjoy some water sports, such as swimming, boating, and fishing, because the lake covers 3,200 acres and there are 14,000 additional recreational acres where you can enjoy camping and picnicking.

Miami County Historical Museum (ages 5 and up) 🏛️

51 North Broadway; (765) 473–9183. Open Tuesday through Saturday 9:00 A.M. to 5:00 P.M. Admission $.

One of the largest county museums in the state, this place was founded in 1916, and today the museum's collection includes 75,000 articles of local interest. Exhibits interpret the area's rich history from 12,000 years ago, when mastodons and early man inhabited the region; later the Miami Indians contributed greatly to the area. In the collection are not only Native American and pioneer artifacts but also Cole Porter memorabilia: The composer and songwriter was born in Peru on June 9, 1891, and his awards and personal items are displayed here. Because Peru is a circus town, you'll find circus heritage items here, too. In the building—a renovated 1900s department store—are Victorian rooms and much more.

Where to Eat

Wabash Sweet Shop. 35 West Market; (260) 563–1312. Open Monday through Friday 6:00 A.M. to 4:00 P.M., Saturday 7:00 A.M. to 3:00 P.M., closed Sunday (except for three Sundays in December). Established in 1938, this unique old-fashioned soda shop serves homemade breakfasts and lunches. Large ice-cream selection. Greek items, thirty-six different kinds of sandwiches (all come with chips), and kids' menu.

Mr. Happy Burger. 3131 East Market, (260) 753–6418 (has ice-cream parlor); and 900 West Market, (260) 753–4016 (does not have ice-cream parlor). Great lights outside make the restaurant look like a carousel, and every child will be fascinated with the very large ceramic cow that sits out front. Inside kids can sit in a trolley and experience an old-fashioned ice-cream parlor and perch on bar stools at the counter to enjoy their meal. Food includes roasted chicken, burgers, and pizza. Open Monday through Thursday 10:45 A.M. to 10:00 P.M., Friday and Saturday 10:45 A.M. to 11:00 P.M. Closed Sunday.

Where to Stay

Lamp Post Inn Bed & Breakfast. 261 West Hill; (260) 563–3094. Children are welcome at this Romanesque-style house built in the 1890s, but you should call to make arrangements. In fact, once an entire junior high basketball team stayed here! There are four bedrooms and two baths (one room has a private bath). Call ahead to be sure your pet is welcome.

Indiana **Trivia**

Howe Sewing Machine Company opened a branch factory in 1870 in what Indiana city?

What was the name of the 1986 basketball movie filmed in rural Indiana?

Where was the first pneumatic rubber tire made?

Peru, Hoosiers, Kokomo

Wabash Inn. 1950 South Wabash Street; (800) 626–7103 or (260) 563–7451. One hundred three rooms ranging from $49.50 to $54 (single occupancy) to $54 to $59 (double occupancy). Executive rooms are also available for $60 to $66 per night. Pets are allowed, but not inside. There is a kennel outside where your pet can stay if desired. Outdoor pool.

Camping

Salamonie Lake. Mailing address: 9214 West Lost Bridge, West Andrews, IN 46702–9731; (260) 468–2125. Offers 2,000 acres of campsites, including one modern campground and two horse campgrounds (the remaining sites are primitive).

Mississinewa Campground. 6440 East 500 South, Marion, IN 46953. There are 386 RV and tent sites. Camp year-round, but the water is shut off in October. Golf course, swimming, fishing, and boating available.

Art's Country Park. County Roads 4071 East and 1000 North, North Manchester; (219) 982–4790. There are 128 grass campsites. Fishing, swimming, and recreation area available.

Lukens Lake. County Roads 9771 North and 725 West, Roann; (317) 833–7801. One hundred sites offering tent and RV camping, including water, electric, and dump station. Quiet spot on nice lake. Open May 1 through October 1.

For More Information

Wabash County Visitors Bureau. (260) 563–7171, (800) 563–1169; www.wabash countycvb.com.

Peru

Circus City Festival (all ages) 🎵

Call the festival office at (765) 472–3918 for show times, dates, and prices; www.peru circus.com. $$.

"Ladies and gentlemen, children of all ages" go to Peru for a great family experience—the Circus City Festival. Every year in mid-July, the children of Peru, ranging in age from seven to twenty-one, put on a circus with the help of adult volunteers. Thousands of people from all over the United States come to see the ten performances of these children, who appear to be professional circus talent as they perform daring acts on the high wire, the flying trapeze, and more. The festival also features a giant midway, arts and crafts, food booths, games, and Indiana's second-largest parade.

Circus City Festival Museum (all ages) 🎵

154 North Broadway; (765) 472–3918. Open October through March, Monday through Friday 9:00 A.M. to 1:00 P.M. and 2:00 to 4:00 P.M. Hours are extended until 5:00 P.M. during the rest of the year. During circus performance dates, the museum is open until show time. Donations are accepted.

Throughout the year you can visit the Circus City Festival Museum; however, the well-known circus performances by children and other young adults in the community are given only in July. The museum traces the history of professional circus performers going back to the early 1900s through pictures, equipment, and costumes. There are also pictures and costumes of today's young performers who have kept the circus tradition alive in Peru.

International Circus Hall of Fame (all ages) 🏛

Route 124, 3 miles southeast of Peru; (765) 472–7553; www.circushalloffame.com. Open April 1 through September 30, 9:00 A.M. to 3:00 P.M. Free for preschoolers.

Circus memorabilia is on display at the old circus headquarters, which is now a National Historic Landmark. Here you'll find a history of the circus through photos, miniatures, and displays as well as a huge collection of circus wagons. There's even a circus with professional circus performers on the grounds late June through Labor Day in a big tent. Try to come early to hear a calliope performance and let your children enjoy a magic show and petting zoo.

Where to Eat

China Inn Restaurant. 70 South Broadway; (765) 473–7293. Chinese, Cantonese, and American food. Open Monday through Friday 11:00 A.M. to 9:00 P.M., Saturday 4:00 to 9:00 P.M., and Sunday 11:30 A.M. to 9:00 P.M. Lunch buffet is served Monday through Friday.

Deb's Diner. 178 North Broadway; (765) 472–0688. Homestyle cooking, homemade soup served every day, and breakfast served all day. Open Monday through Saturday 5:00 A.M. to 7:00 P.M., Sunday 6:00 A.M. to 2:00 P.M. Closed for major holidays.

Harvey Hinkleyers. 14 East Eighth Street; (765) 472–4341. Sandwiches, pizza, Mexican, and Italian food. Open Monday through Thursday 10:00 A.M. to 11:00 P.M., Friday and Saturday 10:00 A.M. to midnight. Closed Sunday. Children's menu also available.

Where to Stay

Knights Inn. 675 U.S. 31 South; (765) 472–3971; fax: (765) 472–3971; www.knightsinn.com. Thirty rooms, nearby fishing, golf, and shopping. **Free** coffee, breakfast available on-site for a charge. Pets are allowed.

Lincoln Square. Corner of U.S. 31 and Business 31; (765) 472–4131.

Shelton Motor Inn. 829 West Main Street; (765) 472–1925.

Best Western Circus City Inn. 2642 South Business 31;(765) 473–8800. A new hotel meeting the needs of business or family travelers. It offers luxury suites, a beautiful full-service lounge, indoor pool, exercise room, and elevator. Located near museums and historic Peru, "Circus Capital of the World," with a public golf course rated one of the top ten by *Golf Digest*.

For More Information

Peru/Miami County Chambers of Commerce. (765) 472–1923; www.miami cochamber.com.

Amazing
Indiana Facts

The town of Peru is on the same land that was once occupied by a Miami Indian village. Today, however, the town calls itself the circus capital of the world. From the early 1800s through the decline of that form of entertainment in the 1960s and 1970s, Peru was the winter quarters for several famous professional circus shows, as well as famous performers, including the clown Emmett Kelly.

Kokomo

Kokomo Fine Art Center (ages 5 and up)
525 West Ricketts Street; (765) 457–9480. Open Tuesday through Friday 1:00 to 5:00 P.M. and Saturday 1:00 to 4:00 P.M. Admission is **free.**

Stop here at this small brown bungalow housing an excellent art collection to learn about Hoosier artists past and present. Each month a different exhibit is displayed, and in the fall, local artists get the chance to display their works.

Grissom Air Museum (all ages)
Grissom Air Force Base, 1000 West Hoosier Boulevard; (765) 688–2654; www.grissomair museum.com. Outdoor air park is open 7:00 A.M. to dusk. Indoor museum is open 10:00 A.M. to 4:00 P.M. Tuesday through Sunday. Closed mid-December to mid-February. **Free** admission.

The family will love visiting this outdoor air park featuring fifteen historic aircraft from World War II through Desert Storm; and the indoor museum displaying military memorabilia including flight trainers, uniforms, armaments, and aviation equipment.

Elwood Haynes Museum (ages 5 and up)
1915 South Webster Street; (765) 456–7500. Open Tuesday through Saturday 1:00 to 4:00 P.M., Sunday 1:00 to 5:00 P.M.

This former home of the inventor and manufacturer of America's first commercially successful car features Haynes's possessions, industrial inventions, and antique autos.

Howard County Historical Society/Seiberling Mansion (ages 5 and up)
1200 West Sycamore; (765) 452–4314. Open February through November, Tuesday through Sunday 1:00 to 4:00 P.M.; December, Tuesday through Friday 10:00 A.M. to 6:00 P.M. and Saturday and Sunday 1:00 to 4:00 P.M. Admission $. Children age 12 and younger get in **Free.**

This ornate mansion was built in 1892 and houses historical artifacts of the area. It is listed on the National Register of Historic Places. Guided tours are available for private parties and events.

Kokomo Opalescent Glass Factory (ages 5 and up)
1310 South Market Street; (765) 457–1829; www.kog.com. Open Monday through Friday 9:00 A.M. to 5:00 P.M. and Saturday 9:00 A.M. to 1:00 P.M. May through September, and Monday through Saturday 9:00 A.M. to 5:00 P.M. October through April. Tours are conducted Wednesday and Friday at 10:00 A.M. Closed Sunday.

Here you and your family will be able to take a fascinating tour of this "Gas Boom" era factory. One hundred types of glass used in stained-glass art are made here and shipped around the world.

Festivals

Haynes-Apperson Festival. Downtown Kokomo; (800) 456–1106. July 4th weekend, 10:00 A.M. to 10:00 P.M. Your family will be able to enjoy celebrating automotive history with car shows, a parade, fireworks, carnival, food, crafts, country music talent contest, a sports festival, and more. More than 100,000 people attend each year and the number is growing.

Kokomo Park Band Summer Concerts. 105 West Sycamore; (765) 457–7479. Mid-June through early August, every Wednesday at 8:00 P.M. **Free.** The forty-five-member Kokomo Park Band provides open-air concerts in Highland Park. Picnic in the park with different music each week including patriotic, jazz, and popular as you relax in your lawn chairs.

Where to Eat

Pastarrific. 3001 South Webster; (765) 455–1312. Italian food with seafood, chicken, and veal dishes. Open Monday through Thursday 11:00 A.M. to 9:00 P.M., Friday 11:00 A.M. to 10:00 P.M., Saturday noon to 10:00 P.M., and Sunday 11:00 A.M. to 4:00 P.M.

Ruby Tuesday. 515 East Southway Boulevard; (765) 453–0396. Sandwiches, burgers, salad, and entrees. Children's menu available. Open Monday through Thursday 11:00 A.M. to 11:00 P.M., Friday and Saturday 11:00 A.M. to midnight, and Sunday 11:00 A.M. to 10:00 P.M.

Where to Stay

The Signature Inn. 4021 South La Fountain; (765) 455–1000; www .signatureinn.com. There are 101 rooms, indoor pool, fitness center with hot tub, and complimentary breakfast buffet. No pets allowed.

Holiday Inn Express. 511 Albany Drive; (765) 453–2222; www.holiday-inn.com. There is a 3:00 P.M. check-in time, 11:00 A.M. check-out time. Whirlpool, indoor pool, kitchenette, and suites available.

The Super 8. 5110 Clinton Drive; (765) 455–3288; www.super8.com. There is a 3:00 P.M. check-in time, noon check-out time; two floors, fifty-six rooms. Heated pool and continental breakfast. Children under 17 stay for **Free!** Pets are allowed. Handicapped-accessible rooms.

For More Information

Kokomo Visitors Bureau. (800) 837–0971; www.kokomo-in.org.

Auburn

Auburn Cord Duesenberg Museum (ages 10 to 12) ⓜ ⓖ

1600 South Wayne, Auburn 46706; (260) 925–1444; www.acdmuseum.org. The museum is open daily from 9:00 A.M. to 5:00 P.M. $$. Family and group rates are available.

When you visit the museum you will be getting a taste of the past when Indiana was actually the automobile capital of the United States. On display in the original 1930 Art Deco showroom and administration building of the Auburn Automobile Company are 140 vintage, antique, classic, and special interest automobiles. You will be able to see and learn more about Auburns, Cords, and Duesenbergs as well as steam, electric, prototype, domestic, and foreign cars. The Duesenbergs were the luxury cars back in the 1930s that were driven by such celebrities as Greta Garbo and Clark Gable. There is even a 1956 Bentley that was owned by John Lennon. For a special treat, plan to visit on Labor Day weekend when Auburns, Duesenbergs, and Cords from all over the United States return for a festival and a collector car auction is held.

Where to Eat

The Bread Basket. 115 North Main Street; (260) 925–4257. Open Monday through Friday from 9:00 A.M. to 5:00 P.M. and Saturday from 10:00 A.M. to 2:00 P.M. Bakery/Deli coffeehouse with a one-of-a-kind setting; second floor overlooking historic downtown Auburn.

The Auburn House Restaurant. 131 West Seventh Street; (866) 925–1102; www.theauburnhouse.com. Open Monday through Saturday 6:00 A.M. to 8:00 P.M., Sunday 7:00 A.M. to 2:00 P.M. Serving breakfast, lunch, and dinner. Menu includes salads, sandwiches, and specialty burgers. Check out the daily specials.

Where to Stay

Country Hearth Inn. I–69 and State Road 8, exit 129; (260) 925–1316; www.country herth.com. Seventy-eight rooms, outdoor pool, children under 18 stay with parents. **Free** InnCredible breakfast.

Super 8. 225 Touring Drive; (260) 925–8800; www.super8.com.

For More Information

Auburn Chamber of Commerce. (260) 925–2100; www.auburn-in.com.

Fort Wayne

Start your day in Fort Wayne by seeing the downtown area aboard an old-time trolley or take a horse-drawn carriage ride. Then you may wish to visit Glenbrook Square at 4201 Coldwater Road. It is Indiana's largest shopping mall with more than 1.4 million square feet of shopping, dining, and entertainment. Visit the **Fort Wayne CVB Visitor Center** located at 1021 South Calhoun Street or call (260) 424–3700 or (800) 767–7752 to learn more about Fort Wayne, which was founded by General Anthony Wayne to protect settlers from hostile Indians.

The Fort Wayne Children's Zoo (all ages)

In Franke Park at 3411 Sherman Street; (260) 427–6800. The zoo is open from late April to mid-October from 9:00 A.M. to 5:00 P.M. $$.

Simply forty-two acres of family fun. More than 1,000 animals live in a naturalistic setting at the zoo. You can go on a family safari in the African Veldt, the twenty-two acres of grasslands where the animals are all roaming free. Travel through the grasslands in protected electric cars or walk on the elevated boardwalk. You'll think that you are really in Africa on safari as you see giraffes, ostriches, cheetahs, antelopes, gazelles, cranes, and storks. Then you will get to experience an African Village where you'll learn about rare and endangered species. From the African Veldt, you can jet to Australia for an adventure. In the award-winning Australian Adventure area of the zoo, you will see the exotic Tasmanian Devil, kangaroos, wombats, fruit bats, brush turkeys, lorikeets, parakeets, dingoes, spiny anteaters, and many more animals from the continent down under. Then you will have an opportunity to explore the "outback" in a dugout canoe on the Herbst River. You will also

A Gisler **Adventure**

Since we are all animal lovers, another favorite day trip of ours in the eastern part of the state is to one of the ten best zoos in the country, the Fort Wayne Children's Zoo. We love taking the journey into the jungles of the Indonesian Rain Forest, traveling to Africa in our own motorized jeep, strolling among eastern gray kangaroos in the Australian Adventure, touring through the park on an 1860 miniature train, and riding on the world's one endangered species carousel. We especially like walking on the elevated boardwalk through the grasslands, seeing giraffes, ostriches, cheetahs, antelopes, gazelles, cranes, and storks. At the end of the walk is an African Village, where we learn about rare endangered species. We can never leave the park without stopping by the aquarium's 20,000-gallon coral reef exhibit, or the farm area where we can pet and feed the animals.

want to see the aquarium's 20,000-gallon coral reef exhibit. You won't want to skip the Indonesian rain forest in a glass dome and the walk-through aviary. One of the highlights of your adventure will be tasting Australian food in Matilda's Fish and Chips Restaurant. You are not done yet with the zoo; there are also horse trail rides, pony rides, a ride on an 1860 miniature train, and a farm area where your children will be able to get close to the animals. This is truly an exciting zoo experience.

Science Central (all ages) 🔊

1950 North Clinton Street; (260) 424–2400; www.sciencecentral.org. Science Central is open Tuesday through Saturday 10:00 A.M. to 5:00 P.M., Sunday noon to 5:00 P.M., closed Monday. $$.

Science Central is Indiana's center for science, mathematics, technology, and hands-on family fun. You will find intriguing exhibits, spell-binding science demonstrations, and educational programs. Hands-on fun is the rule at Science Central. You can create your own earthquake, bend your own rainbows, or ride around a track 20 feet up in the air on the high-rail bike! The kids can hold a starfish, make a tornado, or walk like an astronaut over a moonscape where they weigh next to nothing. After experiencing the exhibits, check out The LaboraSTOREy—A Store for Science that offers merchandise that is fun, educational, affordable, and unique.

Special **Kids' Stuff**

1. **Me's Zoo** in Parker City delights youngsters with more than 300 exotic animals including camels, llamas, zebras, and bears.
2. **Fort Wayne Children's Zoo** will entertain and fascinate children of all ages as they have the opportunity to see more than 1,000 species of animals. Riding a train, exploring the Great Barrier Reef Aquarium, venturing forth on an African Veldt, and experiencing an Australian Adventure are some of the exciting things your family will enjoy if you select to visit the Fort Wayne Zoo.
3. **Science Central** is "kid central," especially designed for children from ages two to seven.
4. **Whitewater Valley Railroad** will entice children to venture back in time as they climb aboard for a 16-mile trip along the Whitewater Canal.
5. **Muncie Children's Museum** will let your children have the experience of climbing a giant anthill, petting a snake, holding a bunny, building a sand castle, and laughing at the funny antics of Garfield.

Historic Fort Wayne (all ages)

211 South Barr Street; (260) 427–6000. The park is open year-round. Buildings are open to the public during reenactment events. Call for reenactment dates. Admission is free; donations accepted.

This is a full-scale authentically reconstructed military garrison and is patterned after the last fort built at Fort Wayne. The First U.S. Light Artillery stages reenactments during the first weekend of the Three Rivers Festival. When you enter the fort, you will be stepping back into the year 1816. As you begin to explore the fort, you will be experiencing first-person living history at its best. You will find yourself in the homes of costumed civilian and military personnel who were assigned to Fort Wayne in 1816. Take the time to talk with Major Whistler about the details of his command at Fort Wayne. Listen to the gossip of the soldiers' wives and daughters as they perform their daily chores of baking, spinning, and dipping candles. Watch the officers and soldiers as they conduct their musket drills and fire cannons. You will also be able to visit the Indian Agency and other re-created buildings on the site. At the fort you will learn about the proud heritage of the early frontier and discover how it shaped American history.

You can also take a **Historic River Cruise** while visiting the fort along the Three Rivers and listen to the fascinating history that shaped today's Fort Wayne. Cruise season begins Memorial Day weekend and lasts through September. For more information about the river cruise, just call (260) 426–2882.

Genealogy Research Department at the Allen County Public Library (ages 10 and up)

900 Webster Street; (260) 421–1200. Open Monday through Thursday 9:00 A.M. to 9:00 P.M., Friday and Saturday 9:00 A.M. to 6:00 P.M., Sunday until 1:00 P.M. Closed on Sunday during the summer months from the Sunday before Memorial Day through Labor Day.

If you are getting your older children involved in their heritage, bring them here. They will be able to discover their roots at the country's second largest genealogy department. Professional counselors are available to assist in searches.

Black Pine Animal Park (all ages)

349 West Albion Road; (260) 636–7383; www.blackpineanimalpark.com. Hours are seasonal. Call for times. $. Children under 3 are free.

Here children young and old will enjoy seeing lions, tigers, bears, snow leopards, and more at Black Pine Animal Park. Only forty-five minutes from Fort Wayne. Park season extends May 1 through Labor Day. Call for hours and tour arrangements.

Fort Wayne Firefighter's Museum and Old #3 Firehouse Cafe (all ages)

226 West Washington Boulevard, in historic Engine House #3; (260) 426–0051. Open Monday through Friday 10:00 A.M. to 4:00 P.M. and Saturday 10:00 A.M. to 3:00 P.M.

What child has not wanted sometime in his or her life to be a firefighter? Here is the

Indiana **Trivia**

What famous American known for going around planting apple seeds died in Fort Wayne in 1845?

What famous late-night talk show host attended Ball State University in Muncie, Indiana?

Johnny Appleseed, David Letterman

opportunity for children to see the equipment and also enjoy lunch in a firehouse when you take them to visit this museum that showcases artifacts used by some of the city's earliest heroes. Dine among the artifacts in the cafe while enjoying a Hook & Ladder, Lifenet, or the Chief!

Perfection Bakery, Inc. (all ages) 🍽

350 Pearl Street; (260) 424–8245. Open Monday, Wednesday, Thursday, and Friday morning. No admission. Call ahead to make arrangements for a tour.

You and your family will be able to breathe in the aroma of freshly baked bread, view state-of-the-art robotic bakery equipment, and see how some of your favorite breads are produced. Founded in 1901, Perfection Bakery is credited with being the first bakery in Indiana to start wrapping bread. The Fort Wayne bakery produces about 170,000 loaves each day.

Foellinger-Freimann Botanical Conservatory (all ages) 🌺

1100 South Calhoun Street; (260) 482–6440; www.botanicalconservatory.org. Open Monday through Saturday from 10:00 A.M. until 5:00 P.M. and on Sunday from noon until 4:00 P.M. $.

When you visit here, you will be at one of the Midwest's largest passive solar conservatories. It is home to rare exotic plants and seasonal showcase displays. The conservatory has three unique display houses: a Sonoran desert exhibit, a collection of exotic tropical plants, and a showcase featuring six seasonal floral displays each year.

Johnny Appleseed Park (all ages) 🏕

Coliseum Boulevard at Harry Baals Drive; (260) 427–6000.

Remember Johnny Appleseed, the legendary pioneer, who distributed apple seeds and sprouts? You can visit Johnny Appleseed Park. It's a great place to rest before or after visiting the six museums in the area around the park. This park is the burial site of John Chapman, who became known as Johnny Appleseed. The park is in a wooded area adjacent to St. Joseph River and is the site of the annual Johnny Appleseed Festival (260–427–6003).

Fort Wayne **Festivals**

Children of all ages enjoy festivals, and they make for a great family outing. For a complete Calendar of Events happening in Fort Wayne call (800) 767–7752 or look them up on the Internet at: www.visitfortwayne.com. An up-to-date quarterly calendar of events is listed so that you will know what is going on at the theaters, ballet performances, philharmonic concerts, professional sports games, museum exhibits, and consumer shows in Fort Wayne. Here is just a sample (be sure to call for exact dates of these events):

MID-JANUARY THROUGH EARLY MARCH

"Garden Railway" Winter Floral Display—A combination of winter-flowering azaleas and other plants with a garden-scale model railway as the focal point. $. Hours: Monday through Saturday 10:00 A.M. to 5:00 P.M., Sunday noon to 4:00 P.M. Location: Botanical Conservatory, (260) 427–6440.

EARLY JUNE

New Haven Canal Days—Downtown. Enjoy free nightly entertainment and midway, arts, crafts, talent show, 10K run, and 3-on-3 basketball. Kids day parade and car cruise and show. Call (260) 749–2972.

Germanfest—A weeklong celebration of Fort Wayne's rich and varied German heritage. Join the German Heritage Society for Mannerchoir performances, rugby and fencing, and dancing. Contact Jim Sack at (800) 767–7752.

LATE JUNE

Greek Fest—Greek food, music, and group dancing to live bands, all among beautiful, colorful ethnic clothing and decorations. Contact Holy Trinity Greek Orthodox Church at (260) 489–0774.

MID-JULY

Three Rivers Festival—An annual summer festival that celebrates Greater Fort Wayne's sense of community. Only the Indy 500 draws more people! Ten days of raft races, hot-air balloons, Macy's-type parade, carnival rides, and fireworks. Enjoy **"Not All Junk Food Alley"** or **Club TRF's** national entertainers. Contact Three Rivers Festival Office at (260) 745–5556.

Allen County Fair—Allen County Fairgrounds. Annual 4-H events, tractor pulls, agricultural displays and competition. Crafts, food, and music. Call (260) 449–4444.

LATE JULY

Berne Swiss Days—Various locations in the city of Berne. Swiss yodeling, folk dancing, polkas, concerts, quilt and art show, sidewalk sales, and more. Contact Deb Horton at (260) 589–8080.

Indiana Highland Games—A little bit of Scotland at Zollner Stadium. Food, music, dancing, and Scottish athletics. Contact Dr. Ronald and Jo Phillips at (260) 489–0990.

EARLY AUGUST

Muddy River Run—Allen County Fairgrounds. Come out and enjoy two days of street rods galore, real muscle cars, and pre-1957 cars on display. Contact Dick Sordelet at (260) 497–0161.

AUGUST

Auburn-Cord-Duesenberg Festival—World's largest car collector show. International museum and festival host thousands at the large car auction, parade of classics, and many other fun-filled events. Call (260) 927–3600.

SEPTEMBER

La Grande Fiesta—A celebration of Hispanic-American Heritage. Contact Benito Juarez Cultural Center at (260) 422–2651.

Grabill Country Fair—Downtown Main Street, Grabill. Enjoy one of the finest arts and craft festivals in the Midwest. Activities for young and old, free entertainment, buggy rides, great food, exhibition tents full of artwork and needlework; parade on Saturday. Call (260) 627–5227.

MID-SEPTEMBER

Johnny Appleseed Festival—Join in a celebration of the pioneer spirit of John Chapman, the folk hero known as "Johnny Appleseed." Enjoy the sights, sounds, smells, and flavors of the early 1800s at the festival, which includes special roving entertainers, festival musicians, Settlers' Pioneer Village, Native American Village, a Cavalry Encampment, Farmers' Market, and Traders' Market. There are demonstrations of crafts of an 1800s tinker, weaver, soap maker, potter, painter, wood carver, leathersmith, metalsmith, herbalist, and blacksmith. The pioneer spirit of John Chapman is celebrated around Johnny Appleseed's grave site with historic entertainment, craft demonstrations, trappers and traders, antiques, and great food. More than 150 vendors plus a children's area. Contact Fort Wayne Parks and Recreation at (260) 427–6003.

LATE NOVEMBER–EARLY DECEMBER

Festival of Trees, Embassy Theatre—Professionally decorated Christmas trees on display throughout the theater. Call (260) 424–4071.

Wonderland of Wreaths, Botanical Conservatory—More than seventy-five hand-crafted wreaths decorate the conservatory. Call (260) 427–6440.

LATE NOVEMBER–MID-DECEMBER

Festival of Gingerbread—Old City Hall Historical Museum. Fantasyland of more than one hundred gingerbread houses created by kids and professionals. Hours are Monday through Friday 9:00 A.M. to 5:00 P.M.; Saturday and Sunday noon to 5:00 P.M.; (260) 426–2882.

Jack D. Diehm Museum of Natural History (ages 5 and up)
600 Franke Park Drive; (260) 427–6708. The museum is open late April through mid-October on Wednesday through Sunday from noon to 5:00 P.M. There is a modest charge for admission.

Satisfy your curiosity about the natural habitats of North American animals at the Jack D. Diehm Museum of Natural History. Here you will be able to see dioramas of mounted animals. Minerals and gems are displayed here, too, as well as Far East artifacts. To enhance your enjoyment of the museum, there are written and audio descriptions of the exhibits.

The Lincoln Museum (ages 8 and up)
200 East Berry; (260) 455–3864. You can visit the museum Tuesday through Saturday 10:00 A.M. to 5:00 P.M. and Sunday 1:00 to 5:00 P.M. Admission is free.

When you see Lincoln documents, letters, personal possessions, and original photographs, you gain a far greater understanding of our sixteenth president. The Lincoln Museum depicts the life of Abraham Lincoln in more than sixty exhibits drawn from the world's largest private collection of Lincoln memorabilia. You will become better acquainted with Lincoln as you study his possessions and see what his law office was like and a War Department telegraph room. This museum is also a research library for those studying Lincoln.

Glenbrook Square (all ages)
4201 Coldwater Road; (260) 483–2119; www.glenbrook sqr.com. Open Monday through Saturday 10:00 A.M. to 9:00 P.M. and Sunday noon to 5:00 P.M.

Everyone will enjoy shopping in Indiana's largest enclosed mall with more than 180 shops.

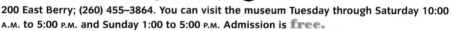

Old City Hall Historical Museum (all ages)

302 East Berry Street; (260) 426–2882. Open Tuesday through Friday 9:00 A.M. to 5:00 P.M., Saturday and Sunday noon to 5:00 P.M. $.

By visiting this museum you will again be able to venture back into Fort Wayne's history from the Ice Age to the Space Age at this architectural landmark.

Fort Wayne Barr Street Market (all ages)

Downtown Fort Wayne, between Berry and Wayne Streets; (260) 426–2882. Open May through October, Wednesday and Friday 10:00 A.M. to 4:00 P.M.

Great place to stop and get some fresh fruit for a family picnic or just a snack. Who wouldn't enjoy a great caramel apple in the fall?

Hilger Farm Market and Restaurant (all ages)

7 miles west of Fort Wayne on U.S. 30 or 7 miles east of Columbia City on U.S. 30; (260) 625–3030.

Besides good fruits and vegetables there is "Fantasy Land," hayrides, a petting zoo, the "Pumpkin Festival," and tours.

Where to Stay

Best Western Luxury Inn. 5501 Coventry Lane; (800) CLASS–4–U; www.bestwestern.com.

Baymont Inn. 1005 West Washington Center Road; (260) 489–2220; www.baymontinns.com.

Canterbury Green Executive Suites. 2613 Abbey Drive; (260) 485–9619.

Coliseum Inn. 1020 North Coliseum Boulevard; (260) 424–0975.

Comfort Suites. 5775 Coventry Lane; (260) 436–4300; www.comfortinn.com.

Courtyard by Marriott. 1619 West Washington Center Road; (800) 321–2211; www.courtyard.com.

Days Inn. 1161 West Washington Center Road; (260) 969–0381. Exit 111B, right on West Washington Center Road. Completely renovated in summer 2002, there are forty-eight rooms, free continental breakfast, and free local calls. Each room is tastefully appointed and includes a hair dryer, dataport phone, and alarm clock radio.

Don Hall's Guesthouse. 1313 West Washington Center Road; (800) 348–1999.

Fairfield Inn by Marriott. 5710 Challenger Parkway; (260) 489–0050; www.marriott.com.

Fort Wayne Hampton Inn & Suites. 5702 Challenger Parkway; (260) 489–0908.

Fort Wayne Hilton at the Convention Center. 1020 South Calhoun Street; (260) 420–1100; www.hilton.com.

Fort Wayne Marriott. 305 East Washington Center Road; (800) 228–9290; www.marriott.com.

Hampton Inn. 8260 West Jefferson Boulevard; (800) HAMPTON; www.hamptoninn.com.

Holiday Inn Express Hotel & Suites. 5915 Ellison Road; (260) 459–1888; www.holiday-inn.com. New as of January 2003. Located in the Village of Coventry area, close to fine dining and shopping. One of the newest malls in Fort Wayne, Jefferson Point, is nearby and offers entertainment and dining as well as unique shops. There are eighty-three guest rooms, suites and public areas are equipped with high-speed Internet access, and all rooms feature a spacious work desk with two speaker phones, voice mail, and data port. Suites include a microwave and refrigerator. Coffeemakers and iron/ironing boards are also standard in all guest rooms.

Holiday Inn Hotel & Suites. Downtown 300 East Washington Boulevard; (260) 422–5511; www.holiday-inn.com.

Hometown Inn. 6910 U.S. Highway 930 East; (260) 749–5058.

Lee's Inn. 5707 Challenger Parkway; (800) 733–5337; www.leesinn.com.

Residence Inn by Marriott. 4919 Lima Road; (260) 484–4700; www.marriott.com.

Signature Inn. 1734 West Washington Center Road; (260) 489–5554; www.signature.com.

Super 8 Motel. 522 Coliseum Boulevard East; (260) 484–8326; www.super8.com.

Travelodge. 4606 Lincoln Highway East; (260) 422–9511; www.travelodge.com.

Willows of Coventry. 4499 Coventry Parkway; (260) 432–9566.

For More Information

Fort Wayne/Allen County Visitors Bureau. (800) 767–7752; www.visitfortwayne.com.

Muncie

Muncie, east of I–69 on State Road 67, derives its name from the Munsee tribe of the Delaware Indians. A former Indian campsite can be see at Walnut Road and Minnetrista Boulevard and is marked by a statue of an Indian and his pony. Muncie is well known for being the home of the Ball Corporation, makers of glass canning jars. Through the contributions of the Ball brothers, Ball State University was founded here in 1918. Like all other college campuses, the campus of Ball State University, at Riverside and University Avenues, offers a wealth of interesting things to do—most of them **free.**

Christy Woods (all ages)

(765) 285–8820. Open Monday through Friday 8:00 A.M. to 4:30 P.M., Saturday 8:00 A.M. to 4:00 P.M., Sunday (April through November) 1:00 to 5:00 P.M. Free.

You can visit Christy Woods, where you'll find an orchid greenhouse, an arboretum that has recorded messages as you walk along the trails, flower gardens, and a nature center.

Ball State Museum of Art (ages 8 and up)

Fine Arts Building, 2000 Riverside Avenue; (765) 285–5242; www.bsu.edu/cfa/artmuseum. Open Monday through Friday 9:00 A.M. to 4:30 P.M., Saturday and Sunday from 1:30 to 4:30 P.M. No children's exhibits. Admission is free.

This museum features Italian Renaissance and American nineteenth-and early twentieth-century art, plus a collection of ancient glass.

Muncie Children's Museum (all ages)

515 South High Street; (765) 286–1660. Open Tuesday through Saturday 10:00 A.M. to 5:00 P.M. and Sunday 1:00 to 5:00 P.M. $$.

While museums aren't always the favorite place for children to visit, this museum is clearly an exception. This hands-on museum was created especially for preschool and elementary children, and its exhibits are designed to arouse their curiosity and stimulate their imagination. Children delight in exhibits that have them climbing a giant anthill, weaving a rug, donning Indiana clothes, testing the hardness of rocks, holding a snake or bunny, learning about fire safety, building a sand castle, cooking a meal, participating in a fossil dig, or sailing on the Cutty Sark. The museum also offers a variety of programs throughout the year.

Minnetrista Culture Center (ages 5 and up)

1200 North Minnetrista Parkway; (800) 428–5887; www.mccoak.org. Open Monday through Friday 9:00 A.M. to 5:30 P.M., Saturday 9:00 A.M. to 8:00 P.M., and Sunday 11:00 A.M. to 5:30 P.M. Admission rates vary.

This center has exhibits about history, art, science, and industry. These exhibits represent the local area as well as national and international areas. You and your family will enjoy seeing lasers, holograms, and virtual reality bears! Throughout the summer, outdoor concerts and theme festivals are also scheduled at the center.

Me's Zoo (all ages) 🐘

County Road 500 South; (765) 468–8559. Open April through October on Tuesday, Wednesday, Thursday, and Saturday 10:00 A.M. to 6:00 P.M. and Sunday noon to 6:00 P.M. Also open late November through Christmas Eve Thursday through Sunday 5:30 to 10:30 P.M. $.

Me's Zoo is one of the largest privately owned zoos in the United States. On its thirty-plus acres are buffalo, deer, antelopes, tigers, leopards, camels, bears, llamas, monkeys, kangaroos, zebras, and prairie dogs. Also there is an animal petting area. You can have a picnic in the picnic area but may want to call ahead to reserve a picnic table; soda machines and snacks are available.

Oakhurst Gardens (all ages) 🏛️ 🌿

600 West Minnestrista Boulevard; (800) 428–5887, ext. 107. Open Tuesday through Saturday 10:00 A.M. to 5:00 P.M. and Sunday 1:00 to 5:00 P.M. Extended hours sometimes held for special exhibits. $.

At Oakhurst Gardens you can stroll through exquisitely landscaped gardens, then visit the elegant Victorian home of a canning jar heiress.

Where to Eat

Applebee's Neighborhood Bar and Grill. 1423 West McGalliard Road; (765) 284–7008. This well-known neighborhood bar and grill serves a variety of appetizers, delicious American entrees, and delectable desserts. It is open daily for lunch and dinner.

Bruner's Family Restaurant. 2200 West Kilgore Avenue; (765) 288–2711.

J.R. Brooks. 1101 McGalliard Road; (765) 282–1321.

MCL Cafeteria. 3501 North Granville Avenue; (765) 289–2955. Enjoy hearty, home-cooked meals at this restaurant that features more than one hundred different food items that change daily. It serves lunch and dinner daily.

Where to Stay

Radisson Hotel Roberts. 420 South High Street; (765) 741–7777.

Signature Inn. 3400 Chadam Lane; (765) 284–4200.

Lees Inn. 3302 North Everbrook Lane; (800) 733–5337.

For More Information

Muncie Visitors Bureau. (800) 568–6862; www.munciecvb.org.

Anderson

Older children will enjoy stepping back into history when they visit Anderson. They will learn that in the late 1800s Anderson was known as the "Queen of the Gas-Boom Era" because of the way it grew after the discovery of natural gas. Today you can take a walking or driving tour and see more than one hundred Newport-style gaslights illuminating blocks of beautiful Victorian homes built between 1870 and 1920 on **Historic Eighth Street.** Try to drive through this area after dark so your family can get a picture of what this street looked like at night a century ago. Christmas is an especially great time to see this area. The **Historic Home Holiday Tour** gives you a chance to visit Victorian homes decorated for the holidays.

Another excellent time to visit Historic Eighth Street is the second weekend in June, when the **Gaslight Festival** is held there. This festival has been going on for a generation and is one of the few nationwide dedicated to celebrating the grand Victorian era. There are special events like **Victorian Tea Time,** which requires purchasing tickets in advance. You will also be able to enjoy a **Gaslight Parade** and arts and crafts booths. People in period costumes will add to the flavor of the festival as will the period entertainment, which includes barbershop quartets. You might even meet "Thomas Edison" strolling the streets and celebrating his many inventions. For added fun, you can take a romantic **horse-drawn carriage ride** or tour some of the homes. To add to your knowledge of this special time in history, you can attend lectures. Call (800) 533–6569 for more information about Historic Eighth Street and its festivals.

Plum Retreat Bed-and-Breakfast (ages 12 and up) 🏛 ⊖
926 West Eighth Street; (765) 649–7586.

If you would like to stay in one of these Victorian homes, your wish can be granted at the Plum Retreat Bed-and-Breakfast. Plum Retreat welcomes you with candle-lit windows and gives you the feeling that you have come home. You will enjoy touring both the inside and outside of this fantastic house with its stained-glass windows and doors, fireplaces, leaded crystal chandeliers, immense tapestry in the front foyer, and an eclectic collection of antiques. This house beckons your exploration. You can tour the home and even have the special treat of a Victorian tea, but you must call ahead. Outdoors, the enclosed yard offers privacy and the opportunity to enjoy nature and the beautiful rose gardens and a variety of flower beds. Be sure to call ahead for reservations for a stay, a tour, or tea.

The Giant (ages 5 and up) 🏛
2928 West Larry Street; (765) 778–2757. Open May 1 through mid-October. $$.

The Giant is a house that blends technology with environmental awareness. Powered by solar energy and built with scavenged wood and stones, the do-it-yourself home in the woods is the creation of Anderson native Vic Cook. Reservations for tours must be made at least twenty-four hours in advance.

Greunewald House 🏛

626 Main Street; (765) 648–6875. The house is open from April through December on Tuesday through Friday from 10:00 A.M. until 3:00 P.M. There is an admission charge, and appointments need to be made for group tours and a living history tour.

The Greunewald House is a twelve-room French Second Empire structure built in 1872. Take the living history tour of the house and you will experience it as the home of a successful German businessman. You may wish to add to your holiday enjoyment by attending the **Victorian Open House** the second Sunday before Christmas. This gives your family the chance to see how the Christmas season was celebrated in the 1800s. Refreshments are served.

Tom St. Clair Studio Glass (ages 12 and up)

6360 Pendleton Avenue; (765) 642–7770. The studio is open on Monday through Saturday 10:00 A.M. to 5:00 P.M.

This is the place where older children will be able to see molten glass hand-shaped into art—glass paperweights, vases, animals, Christmas ornaments, lamps, perfume bottles, and free-form sculptures.

Historical Military Armor Museum 💂

2330 North Crystal Street; (765) 649–TANK. Open Tuesday, Thursday, and Saturday 1:00 to 4:00 P.M. $. Be sure to call if you want a tour or tank ride.

Older children who like history will enjoy visiting the Historical Military Armor Museum. One of the most complete collections of light armor vehicles in the United States dating from WWI to the present can be seen here. You can have a ride in a tank for $5.00 per person if you call ahead. Your group can also eat in a mess hall if you call ahead. Besides seeing armor that goes back to World War I, you can see the latest armor from Desert Storm. Although you can't climb all over the tanks, you may be the one on the tour to demonstrate how a tank's gun turret works.

U.S. Merchant Marine Museum (ages 8 and up) 💂

2418 Poplar Street; (765) 643–6305. Open Tuesday through Friday 1:00 to 4:00 P.M. or by appointment. The museum is closed during the month of January. $.

This museum is best suited for older children—especially any children who are considering becoming a sailor. The museum is dedicated to the WWII merchant seamen who volunteered to deliver men and supplies. You will be able to see uniforms, medals, pins, papers, insignia, ships' instruments, and a reference book and video library.

Indian Trails Riverwalk and Festival (all ages) 🏃 🐟 ⛺ 🚲

Starting on Grand Avenue at Broadway; (765) 754–7725. The festival is held the second weekend in October.

You'll be walking along the White River on a trail that Indians once took when you follow the Indian Trails Riverwalk. The White River is also the focus of the Indian Trails Riverwalk Festival the second weekend in October. A few markers along the boardwalks and paved pathways of the Riverwalk will acquaint you with the past. The trail goes to the **Wetlands Nature Preserve,** where it connects to a trail around **Shadyside Park and Lake;** there you can put boats in the river and fish. There are several other hiking, bicycling, and canoeing trails along White River; most of these travel through **Mounds State Park.** You should park your car at Grand Avenue to start the walk.

Anderson University (ages 8 and up) 🏛 🔔

1100 East Fifth Street; (765) 649–9071; www.anderson.edu. There is no admission charge to visit places on the campus.

At Anderson University you will find a lovely campus with valleys and wonderful trees, grounds, and flowers. Check out these great stops:

- A different art collection every six weeks at the **Krannert Fine Arts Center.** You'll also find a collection of Boehm birds and an unusual collection of 1,500 napkin rings at the center.
- In the **Bible and Near Eastern Museum,** you can see history through the artifacts from the Holy Land.
- The observatory is open for astronomy buffs, and the **Broadcast Center** is also available for tours.

Mounds State Park (all ages) 🏕

Off I–69 and Mounds Road, just east of Anderson; (765) 642–6627. Open daily 7:00 A.M. to 11:00 P.M.

One of the unique features of Mounds State Park is the ten distinct "earthworks" built by a group of prehistoric Indians known as the Adena-Hopewell people. The largest earthwork, the "Great Mound," is believed to have been constructed around 160 B.C. Archaeological surveys seem to indicate it was used as a gathering place for religious ceremonies. The nature center is located in the Bronnenberg House, which is considered to be one of the oldest buildings constructed as a dwelling in Madison County. There you will be able to enjoy an informative educational display. The park has camping, fishing, hiking trails, naturalist services, picnicking, a swimming pool, and bridle trails.

Where to Eat

Grindstone Charleys. 5627 South Scatterfield Road; (765) 644–5021.

Shouts Pub & Eatery. (Inside Bowling Alley) Coopers Sports Bowl, 1920 East 53; (765) 642–9336. Wonderful food, lively, and a fun place to eat.

Where to Stay

Lees Inn. 2114 East Fifty-ninth Street; (800) 733–5337.

Motel 6. 5810 Scatterfield Road; (765) 642–9023.

Plum Retreat Bed-and-Breakfast. 926 West Eighth Street; (765) 649–7586.

For More Information

Madison County Visitors Center and Convention Bureau. 6335 South Scatterfield Road; (800) 533–6569; www.madtourism.com. Open 8:30 A.M. to 4:30 P.M.

Berne

When you enter the town of Berne, you will see bright window boxes overflowing with colorful flowers, picturesque balconies, clock towers, and more. The rich heritage of Switzerland is clearly evident here. The town was settled in 1852 by a group of seventy Mennonite immigrants who left their home in Switzerland to settle in this country. If you want to live more simply, a visit to Berne will acquaint you with the Amish way of life. Here you will see buggies both in town and on the roads and meet people who live wholesome lives without modern conveniences including plumbing, television, and cars.

Do you enjoy celebrations? Then you will like attending Swiss Days and other festivals that celebrate Berne's heritage. Here's a chance to hear yodeling, sample Swiss food, enjoy dancing, take tours, and more. The Swiss Heritage Society sponsors fun and educational family activities to help everyone have a better understanding of its people, places, and traditions. Special events take place in April, June, July, August, October, and December. You will want to contact the Society at (260) 589–8080 to find out about these yearly events.

The Swiss/Amish Community of Berne (all ages) 🏛
Web site: www.bernein.com; e-mail: tourism@bernein.com or contact the Chamber of Commerce at 175 West Main; (260) 589–8080.

Here families and children of all ages can see Swiss architecture, the Swiss Heritage Village, specialty shops, Amishville, Pine Lake, a covered bridge, lodging, and Bearcreek Farms.

Indiana **Trivia**

In what Indiana city was Shelley Long born?

The pioneer highway known as the National Road today is what U.S. highway?

In what Indiana city are you still able to take a ride aboard a 1900s steam train?

How many counties are in Indiana?

Fort Wayne, U.S. Highway 40, Connersville, Ninety-two

Swiss Heritage Village (all ages) 🏛

1200 Swiss Way; (260) 589–8007. Open from May through October Monday through Saturday 9:00 A.M. to 4:00 P.M.

Show older children Berne's Swiss cultural and religious heritage. Children will see a restored village containing twelve buildings, including a unique cider press and a bird sanctuary.

Amishville U.S.A. (all ages)

844 East 900 South; (260) 589–3536. Open late March through mid-December Monday through Saturday 9:00 A.M. to 5:00 P.M. and Sunday 11:00 A.M. to 5:00 P.M. $. Home tours are free for children under 5; buggy rides are free for children under 2.

To get to Amishville U.S.A., take U.S. 27 off I–69, go east on 950 (the road will eventually wind into 900). Three miles down the road you will pass a covered bridge and an Amish schoolhouse. You could also take highway 218 off I–69 and go through Berne. There is a sign to Amishville U.S.A. When you get to the T, turn left onto 900. You will pass several Amish homes on the way. You could also take I–69 off U.S. 27. Go east on 950, wind into 900—3 miles down the road. On the way you will pass several Amish homes.

A visit to Amishville U.S.A. will give children of all ages a glimpse into the life of one of the country's most conservative Amish settlements, on an operating 120-acre farm. Visitors can tour the Amish farmhouse and barns, see chores being done, watch an authentic mid-1800s gristmill grind grain into flour, and take a ride in an open horse-drawn buggy just like the Amish use every day. You will be able to taste homemade breads and see crafts being made. A meal at Essen Platz Restaurant is an opportunity to feast on home-cooked food. If your family likes camping, you will be able to select primitive or modern campsites. The campgrounds are open from March through December. There's also a beautiful, stocked lake where you can swim in a special area and enjoy the large beach. If you are at the campgrounds on Sunday morning, you can attend the casual-attire church services. Call for camping reservations and information.

A Gisler **Adventure**

Our family enjoys learning about other cultures, especially when they exist in our own home state. One of our most exciting trips was to Amishville U.S.A., where our family spent the entire day learning about the Amish. We toured the 120-acre operating farm, house, and barns, saw daily chores being done, watched a mid-1800s gristmill grind grain into flour, and took a ride in an open horse-drawn buggy. We also watched craftsmen hard at work in their one-room shops making everything from farm tools to candles and other needs for the home. Our family especially enjoyed tasting the homemade breads, hot from the oven. After a day filled with learning, we headed to Essen Platz Restaurant to feast on home-cooked food.

Ouabache State Park (all ages) 🏊 🛶 ⛺ 👫

4930 East State Road 201; (260) 824–0926. Open year-round from 7:00 A.M. to 11:00 P.M. Office hours are 8:00 A.M. to 4:30 P.M. Monday through Friday November through March and 8:00 A.M. to 4:30 P.M. daily from April 1 through October 31. $.

At the park you and your family will be able to enjoy swimming, climbing, hiking, fishing, picnicking, playing tennis and basketball, cross-country skiing, and boating. Boat and canoe rentals are available in the park.

From the town of Bluffton, which is only five minutes away, you can connect to a bike trail at River Greenway along the Wabash and bike right to the park's entrance.

Where to Eat

Essen Platz Restaurant/Amishville U.S.A. 844 East and 900 South; (260) 589–3536. March through December open Sunday through Thursday 11:00 A.M. to 7:00 P.M., Friday and Saturday 11:00 A.M. to 8:00 P.M. Closed in winter. With Geneva, Amish, and Swiss recipes and the Country Harvest Buffet, the Essen Platz Restaurant is home cooking at its best.

The Gathering House. 105 West Main Street; (260) 589–8466. Open Monday through Saturday, 8:00 A.M. to 5:00 P.M. Closed Sunday. Relax and enjoy a cup of gourmet coffee and a fresh-baked specialty. Stroll two floors of quality antiques and beautiful handmade gifts. Open year-round.

Where to Stay

Black Bear Inn & Suites. 1335 U.S. 27N; (260) 589–8955. Forty-five rooms, including nine suites with Jacuzzis, indoor swimming pool, continental breakfast. Prices start at $54.

The Schug House. 706 West Main Street; (260) 589–2303. This 1907 twin-tower queen inn features Victorian architecture, inlaid floors, open staircase, pocket doors, wraparound porch laden with wicker furniture, and indoor furnishings that date from the 1850s to the turn of the century. Every room has a private bath and air-conditioning. Continental breakfast is offered and so is the option of renting the entire house.

For More Information

Bluffton Chamber of Commerce. (260) 824–0510.

Bryant

The Country Fair at Bearcreek Farms (all ages) ⊖ ⓦ ⓛ ⓦ
50 miles south of Fort Wayne, take 27 south out of Fort Wayne; 8839 North 400; (260) 997–6822, (800) 288–7630; www.bearcreekfarms.com. Open mid-May to mid-September. Admission is **free,** but tickets must be purchased for individual rides.

In Bryant you will find a place to make wonderful memories for kids, parents, and grandparents as you escape to the country for old-fashioned family fun.

Bearcreek Farms was purchased in 1973 by the owners of the Richards Restaurant chain to provide an escape from the hectic day-to-day pace of the restaurant business. At that time, the 200-acre farm consisted of a barn and a few outbuildings. Things have been changing constantly ever since.

The farm has lodging, dining, campsites, shopping, and recreational activities. At the Bearcreek Country Fair children from ages two to ten can enjoy a variety of rides, and what child doesn't enjoy a carousel or kiddie rides! There's also miniature golf, a train ride, and more. You'll stroll through Bloomfield Village and enjoy a walk down Main Street on your way to see the Bearcreek Singers/Dancers performing live musical revues at the Goodtimes Theater. There is plenty of entertainment at the farm, with shows every day and special outings on featured holidays that include a show and a meal served family-style for one price. Call to find out about special events taking place at Bearcreek Farms.

Limberlost State Historic Site (all ages) 🏛

200 East Sixth Street, Geneva; (260) 368–7428. Open mid-March through mid-December Wednesday through Saturday 9:00 A.M. to 5:00 P.M. and Sunday 1:00 to 5:00 P.M. Admission is free, though donations are accepted.

Limberlost, named for a nearby swamp, is the Geneva home of author, naturalist, and photographer Gene Stratton-Porter. The family is bound to enjoy a tour of this log home that includes a stuffed bird collection, a butterfly and moth collection, swamp things, stenciled ceilings, and period furnishings. The recently restored dining room and bedroom are the highlights of the tour, which takes about a half hour. Annual events here include a nature photography contest in August and a Christmas Open House.

Pine Lake Water Park (all ages) 🏊 ⛵

3½ miles west of Berne on U.S. 218; (260) 334–5649. Open Memorial Day to Labor Day Monday through Saturday 10:00 A.M. to 8:00 P.M., Sunday noon to 8:00 P.M. $.

Pine Lake Water Park offers recreation for the entire family. During a visit you can swim, sunbathe on a sandy beach, picnic under the pines, or paddle a boat on the lake. Pine Lake Water Park also offers two large water slides, three levels of platforms off a 30-foot tower, a cable ride, a lily pad walk, and a playset for younger children.

Richmond

Richmond is located near the Indiana and Ohio border on the Old National Road, which once stretched from Cumberland, Maryland, to St. Louis, Missouri. The town was founded in 1806 by Quakers from North Carolina and German immigrants. Its downtown area was largely destroyed in a fire in 1968, but the area now has an exciting **Downtown Promenade** on Main Street between Fifth and Tenth Streets. Here you'll find sixty specialty shops in five interconnecting blocks of brick walkways, shady trees, and flowing fountains. Also, you can take a self-guided tour through the **Old Richmond Historic District,** containing more than 213 structures of historical importance. The **Schoot House,** at 126 North Tenth Street, is one of Indiana's great Victorian homes; an ornate cupola is in the center of the building. When you tire of walking, stop at one of the quaint restaurants nestled in and among the fine residential structures. Pick up a tour guide at the Wayne County Convention and Tourism Bureau at 5701 National Road East, or call (800) 828–8414 for tourist information.

Glen Miller Park (all ages) 🏛️ 🌼

U.S. 40, 2200 National Road East; (765) 983–7275. Open daily 6:00 A.M. to 11:00 P.M. Free.

Stop at Glen Miller Park, which has more than 1,600 rosebushes in its Hill Memorial Rose Garden. The park also has a small zoo. At the entrance to the park is *The Madonna of the Trail,* a statue erected in commemoration of the pioneer mothers of covered-wagon days. The statue is the ninth link in the Great National Shrine erected by the Daughters of the American Revolution along the National Road Trail (U.S. 40).

Hayes Regional Arboretum (all ages) 🏛️ 🚶

801 Elks Country Club Road; (765) 962–3745. Open Tuesday through Saturday 9:00 A.M. to 5:00 P.M. $.

Owing to the vision of city forefathers in Richmond, large areas of rolling hills were set aside in the heart of the growing community to preserve scenic beauty. The Hayes Regional Arboretum is a 355-acre nature preserve containing 179 woody plants native to this region. The preserve also contains Indiana's first solar greenhouse, an 1833 dairy barn converted into a nature center, a bird sanctuary, hiking trails, and a 3-mile auto nature tour. This is a wonderful area for your family to enjoy the outdoors and at the same time learn about local flora and fauna.

Where to Eat

Ryan's. 5703 National Road East; (765) 966–5878. Buffet.

Cracker Barrel. 6050 National Road East; (765) 935–0881.

Garfield's Restaurant and Pub. 3801 National Road East; (765) 962–2882.

Where to Stay

Best Western Imperial Motor Lodge. 3020 East Main Street; (765) 966–1505. Forty-four rooms. Outdoor pool, cable with HBO, free continental breakfast, nonsmoking rooms, free local calls, restaurants, and shopping nearby. Refrigerators in twenty-five rooms. Fax service. $5.00 for pets. AAA discount.

Holiday Inn Holidome. 5501 National Road East; (800) 548–2473; www.holiday inn.com.

Lees Inn. 6030 National Road East; (800) 733–5337.

For More Information

The Old National Road Welcome Center is a great place to begin your adventure. When you stop by this unique building, you'll get a taste of Richmond/Wayne County's rich heritage and all the visitor information you need about Indiana. (800) 828–8414; www.visitrichmond.org.

Wayne County Convention and Tourism Bureau. 5701 National Road East; (800) 828–8414; www.visitrichmond.org. or www.waynet.org.

Liberty

Have you ever considered a family vacation on a houseboat? You can have one in Indiana at Kent's Harbor on Brookville Lake in Liberty. Call (765) 458–7431 to obtain all the information you need. While in town, check out the **Union County Historical Society Museum,** on Railroad Street. The museum is housed in a restored 1886 railroad depot. Open June through August, Saturday and Sunday 2:00 to 4:00 P.M. Also open holidays (same hours) or by appointment. Call (317) 458–5030 for specifics. Admission **free.**

Whitewater Gorge Park (all ages)
64 Waterfall Road; (765) 983–7275. Always open.

Whitewater Gorge Park at Brookville Lake is a great place for an outdoor adventure that includes fossil collecting and lots of hiking. Brookville Lake is located in the middle of the Whitewater River Valley, one of the most picturesque and historically significant areas in Indiana. The lake is located in Franklin and Union Counties on the East Fork of the White-water River. The dam is about 1½ miles above Brookville, Indiana, and 36 miles northwest of Cincinnati, Ohio. Here three branches of the Whitewater River converge in a spectacular geologic gorge formed during the last Ice Age. The gorge provides miles of hiking trails, scenic vistas, picnic areas, vertical cliffs, and the beauty of Thistlewaite Falls. You can play geologist here as you collect fossils, and helpful geologic information to assist you in examining and collecting fossils is available at the park.

Whitewater Memorial State Park and Brookville Lake (all ages)
1418 South State Road 101; (765) 458–5565. Closed from 11:00 P.M. to 7:00 A.M., except to admit campers. $.

A great picnic stop on any trip, where you and your family can enjoy waterskiing, horse-back riding, camping, swimming, fishing, and more.

Middlefork Reservoir (all ages)
Sylvan Nook Drive off U.S. 27; (765) 983–7293. Open April through October during daylight hours. Free.

Water fun can be had at Middlefork Reservoir. Its 405 acres, including a 177-acre fishing lake, offer an ideal location for fishing and boating. The lake is stocked by the Indiana Department of Natural Resources—you can expect to catch some fish here. A public fishing pier, a fish cleaning station, and rowboat and paddleboat rentals are available, so you can easily get out on the lake and enjoy yourself. Relaxing picnic areas and hiking areas, as well as a live bait and concession operation, are here, too. For children the Super Park offers a fully accessible, state-of-the-art playground system.

Where to Eat

Liberty Bell Restaurant. 216 South Main Street; (765) 458–6115.

Liberty Restaurant. 7 West Union; (765) 458–5223.

Where to Stay

The Sagamore Resort on Brookville Lake. 15179 Old State Road 101; (765) 458–7431; www.kentsharbour.com.

Liberty Motel. Main Street; (765) 458–6894.

Connersville

From the minute your family boards the **Whitewater Valley Railroad** train in Connersville, a fun-filled excursion for folks of all ages begins. The station for Indiana's longest scenic railroad is on State Road 121. You will travel 16 miles along a route that follows the towpath of the **Whitewater Canal.** Along the track, you will see remnants of old canal locks, **Laurel Feeder Dam,** and the **Whitewater River.** While you are sightseeing, you can enjoy your own picnic lunch aboard the train. Your destination is **Metamora,** where you are given two hours to explore a true 1800s town. Then it's time to board the train for the return trip. The train operates on Saturday and Sunday from the first Saturday in May to the last Sunday in October and on Memorial Day, the Fourth of July, and Labor Day. It departs Connersville at 12:01 P.M. and returns by 6:00 P.M. The train runs some special trips as well as a dinner train. You can have a shorter trip if you board the train at Laurel. Call (765) 825–2054 for more information on train times and fares or browse its Web site: www.whitewatervalleyrr.org.

Connersville also hosts a **Summerfest** the last weekend in August.

A Gisler **Adventure**

Another day trip we enjoy as a family is the Whitewater Valley Railroad train ride from Connersville to Metamora. We are always amazed at the sights as we travel the 16-mile scenic railroad following the towpath of the Whitewater Canal. We bring along a picnic lunch to enjoy along the way. Once we reach Metamora, we hop off the train to explore life in a true 1800s canal town. We walk through the more than one hundred arts and crafts shops that line the streets in town. Our favorite time to enjoy this town is the annual Christmas Walk. The family found the sights interesting as luminaria are everywhere lighting the canal banks, roads, and walks. Of course, we can't board the train without first stopping by one of the family-style restaurants and having dinner.

Mary Gray Bird Sanctuary (all ages)

County Road 350 West, 3½ miles west of State Road 121 (follow the signs); (765) 825–9788. Open daily dawn to dusk. Admission by donation.

The Mary Gray Bird Sanctuary, a 684-acre nature preserve, is owned by the Indiana Audubon Society. Besides offering hiking on more than 6 miles of trails in the preserve, this is an excellent spot for a picnic lunch.

Manlove Park Campground (all ages) Ⓐ

6632 North Manlove Park Road; (765) 478–4080. Free.

If you like to camp, the Manlove Park Campground may be an excellent choice for you. The campgrounds cover more than 123 acres, including an eighteen-acre lake. While you camp, your family can enjoy boating, hiking, basketball, horseshoes, the playground, a horse track, a nature center, and a lodge.

Connersville Armed Forces Day Parade (all ages)

Main Street; (765) 825–2561.

This parade salutes the men and women who have served their country in the armed forces. The parade starts at Roberts Park and proceeds south to downtown Connersville. There are bands, dignitaries, and floats from all over the United States.

Where to Eat

Burger King. 2132 North Park Boulevard; (765) 825–0300. Children's playroom.

The Hot Pot Restaurant. 319 West Thirtieth Street; (765) 825–7096.

Where to Stay

The Over House Bed-and-Breakfast. 1826 Indiana Avenue; (765) 825–2371.

For More Information

www.southerninn.com/pages/counties/fayette/index.html.

Cambridge City

Cambridge City is one of the many towns that emerged along the National Road in the 1800s. Here, in the **Museum of Overbeck Art Pottery** at 33 West Main, you can see Overbeck pottery, which was produced between 1911 and 1955. This art form has been recognized as an important part of the cultural history of the United States. The museum is dedicated to preserving the creative art of the six Overbeck sisters, who lived and worked in Cambridge City. Admission is **free,** and you can visit the museum Monday through Saturday 10:00 A.M. to noon and 2:00 to 5:00 P.M. To learn more about the museum, call (317) 478–3335.

Huddleston Farmhouse Inn Museum (ages 5 and up) (m) (k)
838 National Road; (765) 478–3172. Open February through December Tuesday through Saturday 10:00 A.M. to 4:00 P.M. Also open Sunday 1:00 to 4:00 P.M. May through August only. Closed in January. Admission Free; donation requested.

The Huddleston Farmhouse was built between 1839 and 1841 when the National Road was young. Today the Huddleston Farmhouse Inn Museum includes the restored farmhouse, springhouse, smokehouse, and barn. Make believe you and your family are going west, just like those who traveled the National Road, and you are stopping at the farm for food and shelter. Here you can imagine what the experience would be like for an early Hoosier farming family and the visiting pioneer travelers.

Where to Eat

Burger King. 1598 North State Road 1; (765) 478–9741.

Cambridge City Inn Truck Stop. 1534 North State Road 1; (765) 478–5550.

K&J Drive Inn. 1200 National Road, Mount Auburn; (765) 478–3998.

Lumpy's Restaurant. 20 South Foote Street; (765) 478–6510.

Lakeview Restaurant. 1219 National Road, Mount Auburn; (765) 478–3661.

Where to Stay

Cambridge City Inn. 1534 North State Road 1; (765) 478–5550. A real truck stop—no televisions in the rooms.

R&R Motel. U.S. Highway 40, Dublin; (765) 478–6374.

For More Information

Cambridge City/Western Wayne County Chamber of Commerce. www .cambridgecityindiana.org.

Indiana **Trivia**

On April 16, 1867, Wilbur Wright was born near what Indiana City?

New Castle

Fairmount

James Dean Gallery

425 North Main Street; (317) 948–3326; www.jamesdeangallery.com. Open 10:00 A.M. to 5:00 P.M. daily.

Are you a James Dean fan? Have you enjoyed his major roles in movies such as *East of Eden, Giant,* and *Rebel Without a Cause?* If so, be sure to visit the James Dean Gallery. This is heaven for Dean fans; it contains the world's largest collection of memorabilia and archives of this famous Indiana native. You can see film clips from Dean films as an added treat. James Dean was a young, talented actor when he died in a highway accident in California. He attended school in Fairmount and graduated in 1949 from Fairmount High School before taking off to California to start a career in acting. In the gallery you will see items from the private collection of Dean archivist David Loehr. He has collected clothing from Dean films, Dean's high school yearbooks, original movie posters, books, and magazines from around the world. After touring the house, you may want to stop at the gift shop and take a memory home with you.

Where to Eat

Ivanhoe's Restaurant. 979 South Main Street (I–69 north to Upland exit); (765) 998–7261. This restaurant is really worth the stop. It has a menu of one hundred shakes and one hundred sundaes; fourteen salads including fresh fruit, taco, pasta, chef, and chicken salads; eighteen sandwiches including hamburgers (ground fresh daily), its own recipe chicken salad, grilled chicken breast, grilled tenderloin, and hand-breaded tenderloin. Fresh strawberry shortcake in season.

In Fairmount

Taco Bell Express. 150 West Eighth Street; (765) 948–3378.

Point Pizza. 704 North Main Street; (765) 948–5299.

Dot's Diner. 421 West First Street; (765) 674–8602.

Fountain City

Levi Coffin House State Historic Site

U.S. 27 North; (765) 847–2432. Guided tours on Tuesday through Sunday 1:00 to 4:00 P.M. from June until September, and from then through October on Saturday only. There is a modest admission charge.

Runaway slaves needed to find safe havens along the way as they struggled to leave the South and cross into freedom. You will see one of their refuges when you visit the Levi Coffin House State Historic Site. This was the home of Levi and Catherine Coffin, who helped more than 2,000 slaves reach safety. Once slaves reached this home, they would stay for several weeks until they gained sufficient strength to continue their journey. One of the slaves who stayed at this house was "Eliza," whose story Harriet Beecher Stowe immortalized in Uncle Tom's Cabin. The Coffins were the Simeon and Rachel Halliday characters in the book. The eight-room brick house is in the Federal style, with furnishings typical of the mid-nineteenth century. A visit to this house provides your older children with an excellent lesson in history and background for reading *Uncle Tom's Cabin*.

Knightstown

Does your family enjoy a train ride? The **Carthage, Knightstown, and Shirley Railroad Excursion Train** will give folks of all ages a memorable trip in vintage coaches. The depot is at 112 West Carey Street. You and your family will climb on board the vintage coach, caboose, and covered open-platform car that was formerly a New York Central freight and passenger station. All aboard! Sit back and enjoy a one-hour-and-fifteen-minute train ride through the countryside as you make a scenic 10-mile round-trip from Knightstown south over the Big Blue River to Carthage and back. On the trip the train will be traveling south, crossing U.S. 40 (National Road), passing under the old "Pennsy" railroad bridge, and through scenic countryside. The track that you will be traveling on was once part of the Cleveland, Cincinnati, Chicago, and St. Louis Railroad. In Carthage you can enjoy the display of old railroad equipment and have a small snack before returning to Knightstown. When you get back to Knightstown, put on your walking shoes and go over to the old academy where some of the scenes from the basketball movie *Hoosiers* were filmed. In that same area, you can enjoy watching the coppersmiths as they practice their trade much the same way as their ancestors did generations ago. Trains run May 1 through October on Friday at 11:00 A.M. and Saturday, Sunday, and holidays at 11:00 A.M., 1:00 P.M., and 3:00 P.M. $. Children under 3 ride free. The train is available for charter excursions. The depot can be visited Friday through Sunday 10:30 A.M. to 4:30 P.M. Learn more about the train at (765) 345–5561. There is a covered open-platform car equipped with ramps for up to twenty wheelchairs. The company looks forward to serving its visitors who have special needs.

Metamora

You can drive to Metamora or take the Whitewater Valley Railroad Train from Connersville. No matter how you get there, you'll be stepping back in time to a nineteenth-century canal town. The town buildings are located along the canal or, in Old Metamora, in reconstructed, reproduced, or actual pre–Civil War buildings, within which are a variety of art, craft, and specialty stores and restaurants. Old Metamora shops and restaurants are open between mid-April and mid-December except on Monday. Hours are 10:00 A.M. to 5:00 P.M.; 9:00 A.M. to 6:00 P.M. on weekends and holidays. Throughout the year special events are held in the town. The **Christmas Walk** is especially interesting, as luminaria are everywhere, lighting the canal banks, roads, and walks. Learn more about the town and its special events by calling the visitors center at (765) 647–2109.

Kennedy Covered Bridges (ages 5 and up)
(765) 629–2892.

The Kennedys built fifty-eight bridges. Six bridges were built from 1873 to 1916 and these bridges are still standing. Call for more information about the bridges and the date of the Bridge Festival.

Whitewater Canal State Historic Site (all ages)
19083 Clayborn Street, Metamora; (765) 647–6512. Mill open mid-March through mid-December 9:00 A.M. to 5:00 P.M. Tuesday through Saturday, 1:00 to 5:00 P.M. Sunday. Free.

The nation's only working covered aqueduct, the Whitewater Canal Historic Site includes the Whitewater Canal and the **Metamora Grist Mill,** where cornmeal, grits, and flour are ground for sale. Browse through 120 antiques and craft shops. Annual events include May Days the first weekend in May, Strawberry Days the first weekend in June, Canal Days in October, and the Christmas Walk in December. If you take a boat ride through the canal, the cost is $1.00 per person; 3 and under are **free.** Boat rides are given on the hour from noon to 4:00 P.M. Tuesday through Sunday and on Monday holidays from May 1 to October 31.

Whitewater Canal **State Historic Site**

Originally Metamora was located along a 76-mile canal built between 1836 and 1847. When you visit the Whitewater Canal State Historic Site, along the canal south of town, you'll be able to ride on a horse-drawn canal boat on a restored section of the canal. Your ride will last about thirty minutes, and you'll go through a restored lock, as well as an 80-foot-long covered wooden aqueduct that carries the canal 16 feet above a creek. A gristmill on the site grinds grain, and you can buy cornmeal, grits, and flour there. Throughout the season performances offer everything from barbershop quartets to cloggers. Admission to the site is **free,** except for a modest fee for canal boat rides. You can take boat rides between May and October starting on the hour. Call (765) 647–6512 for days and times of operation and for an entertainment/educational schedule.

Where to Eat

Note: With the exception of Hearthstone, all restaurants are closed in the winter months.

Cappuccinos. 10544 Main Street; (765) 647–3072. Coffee bar, pastries, and sandwiches.

Hearthstone Restaurant. 18149 U.S. Highway 52; (765) 647–5204. Family-style dining. Closed Monday. From January through March open only Thursday through Sunday.

Mr. Fudge's Confectionery. 19036 Main Street; (765) 647–4956. Try a soda from the antique soda fountain or some of its fourteen different kinds of fudge. Get a scoop of ice cream in a waffle cone (sugar-free ice cream is available). Open Monday through Friday 10:00 A.M. to 4:00 P.M., Saturday and Sunday 10:00 A.M. to 5:00 P.M.

Thorpe House Country Inn. 19049 Clayborn Street; (765) 647–5425. Lunch daily, weekend breakfast buffet.

Duck Creek Palace. 19066 South Main Street; (765) 647–6802. Home cooking.

Where to Stay

Hospitality House. 19010 Main Street; (765) 647–1270. Air-conditioned rooms in summer. Breakfast is served in your room or in the cafe. Children under ten **free.** Features a special breakfast for children.

The Grapevine Inn. 10083 Bridge Street; (765) 647–3738.

Camping

Maclyn Campground. U.S. Highway 52; (765) 647–2541. Water and electrical hookups, dump station, showers.

For More Information

www.metamora.com.

Indiana **Trivia**

In what Indiana town did General Ambrose Burnside grow up?

The Indiana Football Hall of Fame is located in what city?

Liberty, Richmond

New Castle

Henry County Convention and Visitors Bureau, 2020 South Memorial Drive. Located three minutes north of I–70. Stop in to see what's happening in Henry County! Open Monday through Friday 8:30 A.M. to 5:00 P.M.; (888) 676–4302; www.henrycountyin.org.

Summit Lake (all ages) Ⓐ ⓣ ◒

5993 North Messick Road; (765) 766–5873. Open year-round. Free.

A great family fun spot for fishing and camping. More than 2,550 acres, including a large lake. Facilities include 125 Class "A" campsites, three boat ramps, a beach bathhouse, and two large open shelters that can be reserved for family picnics and other events.

Indiana Basketball Hall of Fame Museum (all ages)

One Hall of Fame Court; (765) 529–1891; www.hoopshall.com. Museum and gift shop open Tuesday through Saturday 10:00 A.M. to 5:00 P.M. and Sunday 1:00 to 5:00 P.M. Closed Monday, Thanksgiving, Christmas, and New Year's Day. $.

To discover exactly what Hoosier hysteria over basketball is, everyone needs to take a trip to the Indiana Basketball Hall of Fame Museum. Here you'll find enough Indiana basketball memorabilia to satisfy the most ardent fan, in addition to lots of appealing hands-on exhibits. Surely no true basketball fan in the world hasn't wondered if he or she could make the winning shot in a basketball game. At the Hall of Fame Museum, everyone gets a chance to try—for only 25 cents. You'll also have the opportunity to compare your jumping ability to basketball legend Oscar Robertson's and get an idea of what coaches say in the locker room by listening to a speech by UCLA Coach John Wooden, who won more NCAA championships than any other coach. If you're truly curious about Hoosier high school basketball, use the computer to find out such details as scores of championship games and why Felix the Cat is one team's idol. All the legends of the game that you learn about here will have one thing in common: They're Hoosiers. There is also a well-stocked gift shop.

Henry County Historical Museum (all ages) ⓖ

606 South Fourteenth Street; (765) 529–4028. Open Monday through Friday 1:00 to 4:00 P.M., Saturday 1:30 to 3:30 P.M. Closed Sunday and holidays. Free.

This museum is dedicated to promoting and preserving the history of Henry County. It is located in the home of General William Grose, who commanded the 36th Indiana Regiment during the Civil War. Victorian-era items fill the museum, including a clothing exhibit, musical instruments, taxidermy specimens, and domestic tools.

Where to Eat

Applebee's. 109 South Memorial Drive; (765) 521–4275.

Bob Evans. 111 South Memorial Drive; (765) 521–4641.

The Maxwell House Restaurant. 1326 Broad Street; (765) 521–8296.

Where to Stay

Best Western Raintree Inn. 2836 South State Road 3; (765) 521–0100.

New Castle Inn. 2005 South Memorial Drive; (765) 529–1670.

Walnut Ridge Resort and Country Haven Inn Bed-and-Breakfast. 408 North County Road 300 West; (765) 533–6611.

Steve Alford All-American Inn. 21 East Executive Drive; (765) 593–1212. Features a basketball theme with memorabilia, meeting and game rooms. Fifty-four rooms and one suite available.

Additional Attractions in the East

Grabill

Here you will be able to let your family experience a small town. Nestled in the midst of a large settlement of Old Order Amish, the small village has kept much of its turn-of-century charm. There are antiques and collectibles, Amish crafts and wares, art galleries, and a general store with a candy counter. The **Grabill Country Fair** is held the first weekend after Labor Day. For more information you can write Grabill Promotions, P.O. Box 7, Grabill 46741 or call (800) 939–3216. Visit the Grabill Web site at www.grabill.org.

St. Joe

Children can learn firsthand how pickles are processed and packaged at **Sechler's Fine Pickles,** founded in 1923 by Ralph Sechler. The business sells forty different varieties of pickle products in more than fifteen states. The pickles are hand harvested, most within a 100-mile radius of St. Joe. The operation includes 30,000 square feet of buildings for production and warehousing and capacity for 90,000 bushels of pickles in brine. Group tours can be scheduled between 9:00 A.M. and 2:00 P.M. weekdays from April 1 through October 31. Call a week or more in advance for reservations. For more information on visiting the factory, call (260) 337–5461 or (800) 332–5461. Visit its Web site at www.sechlerpickles.com. **Free.**

Millville

Your family will get to experience history when you visit the **home of Wilbur Wright,** the American pioneer of aviation who was born on April 16, 1867, in Indiana, where he lived as a child for eighteen months before moving to Dayton, Ohio. The replica of the house where he lived sits on about five acres and has period furnishings. An F-84 jet stands out front, as well as a shelter house with picnic tables. See a full-scale replica of the 1903 Wright Flyer, which took ten years to build. Open Monday through Saturday 10:00 A.M. to 5:00 P.M. and Sunday 1:00 to 5:00 P.M. Call (765) 332–2495. $.

Western Indiana

G o west, and you will find a wide variety of things to see and do in Indiana. Here is a part of the state where you can enjoy outdoor activities as you hike on trails, canoe, or float down rivers and streams. It's also an area that has many festivals, including the famous **Parke County Covered Bridge Festival.** And believe it or not, there's a place where you and your family can go and howl with the wolves. Also, this is Larry Bird country—where the famous Boston Celtics basketball star grew up and played high school and college ball.

TopPicks for fun in Western Indiana

1. Wolf Park, Battle Ground

2. Indiana Beach, Monticello

3. Billie Creek Village, Rockville

4. Turkey Run State Park, Marshall

5. McCormick's Creek State Park, Spencer

6. Children's Science and Technology Museum, Terre Haute

7. Purdue University, Lafayette

8. Columbian Park, Lafayette

9. Shades State Park, Crawfordsville

10. Logansport Carousel, Logansport

WESTERN INDIANA

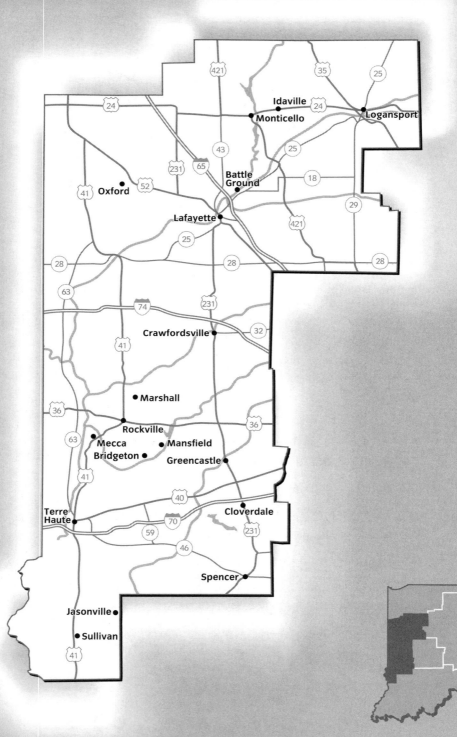

Lafayette

Lafayette is named for the Marquis de Lafayette, the famous French general. In Lafayette your family will enjoy a variety of different activities, from visiting zoos, amusement parks, and forts to touring a world-famous university in West Lafayette. The city has more than thirty hotels and 250 restaurants that cater to the most discriminating tastes and offer economical alternatives to big-city prices. Most accommodations are located just minutes from many of the city's attractions, such as the restored buildings in the unique downtown district, museums, parks, and historical sites.

Columbian Park (all ages)

1915 Scott Street; (765) 771–2221. **Zoo grounds open throughout the year 8:00 A.M. to 7:30 P.M. Monkey Island and Petting Zoo closed during winter months; Animal House open 11:30 A.M. to 7:30 P.M. Free admission to zoo and park; a small fee for pool and rides.**

Columbian Park is truly the perfect place for family fun and frolic. You can swim, play tennis or horseshoes, visit a zoo, enjoy an amusement park, and have a picnic all in this one spot. The zoo exhibits are located throughout the park. The park zoo has a large bird collection, and it is quite an experience to enjoy looking at the birds as you walk through the aviary. Everyone will have fun at A Touch of Country Petting Zoo, where you are invited to hand-feed and pet barnyard animals such as piglets, lambs, donkeys, geese, rabbits, and ducks as well as deer, fawns, and llamas. It costs only 25 cents to buy a cone full of food for the hungry animals. Remember to bring your camera because you can get some great shots when children and animals meet! The main Animal House at the zoo is where the big cats live and the monkeys stay during the winter. This is a newly constructed exhibit where both the snow leopards and the spider monkeys reside. The Columbian Park Zoo is among the first zoos to use this type of exhibit. There is also an exhibit of small mammals, reptiles, and nocturnal animals.

For even more fun there is a "Kiddieland" with seven rides for younger children, including a ferris wheel and a 1-mile train ride. There are also adult rides. Throughout the summer, there is a variety of free entertainment in the outdoor theater. If you need a snack, there is a concession stand.

Indiana **Trivia**

What university did Virgil I. Grissom, the astronaut, attend?

What county in Indiana has 34 covered bridges?

Where is Wolf Park located?

Purdue, Parke County, Battle Ground

Tropicanoe Cove (all ages)

Inside Columbian Park (765) 771–2220. Hours are seasonal; call for details. $. Children under 2 are free.

The Tropicanoe Cove is a water park with something for everyone in the family. Check out Sunfish Bay for small swimmers or Dolphin's Delight, a miniature water slide especially for little tikes. Older kids and adults can ride on the Toucan Chute water slide or the Banana Peel, which is a 300-foot twisting and turning tube slide. For the brave, take a walk at the Gator Walk, but beware of the gators! For something more relaxing, float down the gently flowing Cattail Crik in a tube or frolic in the sand playground at Crawdad Corner. Everyone will find something good to eat or drink at the Bait Shop. It serves snacks, ice cream, and meals.

Purdue University (all ages)

Visitor information center, 504 Northwestern Avenue, West Lafayette; (765) 494–INFO; www.purdue.edu. Walking tours Monday through Friday at 9:00 A.M., noon, and 2:00 P.M. and Saturday at 9:30 A.M. Reservations required. Free.

If you have older children who are starting to think about college, a trip to investigate Purdue University should be on your agenda. Purdue, an outstanding university, is home to Big Ten sports and cultural events. A walking tour can give your children a taste of what college life is like.

Greater Lafayette Museum of Art (all ages)

102 South Tenth Street; (765) 742–1128. Open Tuesday through Sunday 11:00 A.M. to 4:00 P.M. $. Children under 12 are free.

By visiting art museums, you can foster your children's appreciation of art. Spend some time with your family at the Greater Lafayette Museum of Art. The museum has three galleries with artwork from contemporary sources along with a permanent collection. Guided tours are offered that should help introduce your children to art as well as art classes for children and adults.

Clegg Botanical Gardens (all ages)

1782 North 400 East; (765) 423–1325. Open 10:00 A.M. to sunset daily. Free.

Does anyone at your house have a green thumb? Then a visit to the Clegg Botanical Gardens will be enjoyable. You can take a relaxing 1-mile walk through the woods. This is a great place to look at wildflowers when they are in season or simply enjoy the woods and the more than 250 varieties of labeled plants and trees. The view from Lookout Point lets you see for miles.

Wabash Heritage Trail (all ages)

(765) 463–2306. Open all year.

How about a family hike on the Wabash Heritage Trail? It is currently 13 miles long. Start the trail at the Tippecanoe Battlefield and walk along Burnett's Creek as it flows into the

Wabash. Cross over the old Davis Ferry Bridge and end this section at Davis Ferry Park. The Wabash Corridor Section begins at Davis Ferry Park and follows the river to the Lafayette Municipal Golf Course. The hike serves as a nature walk. Watch for sycamore and cottonwood trees and the woodchucks and squirrels that make their homes in the woods. Parking is available at Tippecanoe Battlefield, Davis Ferry Park, and the golf course.

Feast of the Hunters' Moon (all ages) 🏛
Fort Ouiatenon, South River Road; (765) 743–3921; www.tcha.mus.in.us.

If you want a day's escape into the past with your family, then you must spend time at the Feast of the Hunters' Moon held for two days each fall at **Fort Ouiatenon.** It is considered one of the best festivals in the country, drawing more than 60,000 people each year. At the Feast of the Hunters' Moon, you will be part of the re-creation of an eighteenth-century French and Indian gathering. There will be more than 8,000 costumed actors showing life as it was at an outpost during the fur-trading era. The sounds of cannons, French folksingers, chanting, and tom-toms add a realistic touch to the drama. Your pulse will throb to the beat of the drums as the Indians perform their traditional dances, and you will be part of the excitement that was felt by the early French settlers. At the celebration you will have the opportunity to eat traditional French foods cooked over an open fire, such as onion soup, pork chops, crepes, herb teas, pastries, Indian fry bread, buffalo stew, corn soup, and dozens of other foods. All are prepared from eighteenth-century recipes. Along with the fragrances from the kettles simmering over the open fires and the pungent smell of the wood smoke, the air is filled with the smell of molten pewter, hot iron, and wet clay being molded into pottery. There's also the acrid haze of blackpowder mixed with the scent of melting candle wax.

Park **It!**

The West Lafayette Parks and Recreation Department at 609 West Navajo runs the six developed parks in the area, and any one of these parks would make a great spot for family bonding through picnics and recreational activities. You don't even have to take any sporting equipment because you can pay a cash deposit and check out the equipment you need for volleyball, badminton, football, kickball, and more. If you want additional information about these parks, you can call (765) 755–5110. The department can also send you a **free** brochure about the parks and more than one hundred recreational activities.

You can enjoy **free** and continuous entertainment such as French and Indian music and dance, fife-and-drum corps performances, military drills, and puppet shows. You'll see canoe races, tomahawk throws, colonial fashions, a military encampment, merchants selling their goods, and blanket traders selling replicas of eighteenth- and early nineteenth-century trade goods from blankets or skins spread on the ground. For the children, there is special entertainment including puppet shows, pantomime, singers, and jugglers. They can try on costumes, make candles and pottery, and play Indian hand games. The secret of this festival's success is its authenticity.

There is limited **free** parking near the festival grounds. You may wish to take advantage of the shuttle buses running from the Purdue University Stadium parking lot from 8:00 A.M. to 6:00 P.M.

Tickets may be purchased in advance at Fort Ouiatenon, the Battlefield Museum, the Historical Museum, the Tippecanoe County Historical Association at 909 South Street, (765) 476–8411, and many locations throughout the Lafayette area. Prices at the gate are slightly higher. There is no public camping available at Fort Ouiatenon. A list of campgrounds, motels, and hotels in Tippecanoe County can be obtained by contacting the Greater Lafayette Convention and Visitors Bureau at (800) 872–6648.

Children's Imagination Station (all ages)

600 North Fourth Street; (765) 420–7780. Open Friday 9:00 A.M. to 5:00 P.M. and Saturday and Sunday 1:00 to 5:00 P.M. $. Children under 2 free. There is also a family membership for people planning to visit the museum frequently.

Some of the larger exhibits that you will see are a 1928 fire truck, a 1910 Maxwell Car, a flight simulator, a butterfly house, rock collections, a 36-inch sailplane, and a 21-inch steel bridge.

There is also a museum store.

Where to Eat

Applebee's Tippecanoe County Mall. Sagamore Parkway; (765) 448–1999.

Arni's. Market Square Shopping Center, between Elmwood Avenue and Greenbrush Street; (765) 447–1108. A special place for kids.

Christo's Family Restaurant. 1018 Sagamore Parkway, (765) 497–3164. Christo's serves homemade soups and has daily specials. Breakfast, lunch, and dinner.

Where to Stay

Fairfield Inn. 4000 State Road 26 East; www.fairfieldinn.com. Continental breakfast, indoor pool, and game room.

Ramada Inn. 4221 State Road 26 East; (765) 447–9460; www.ramada.com.

Signature Inn. I–65 and State Road 26; (765) 447–4142; www.signature.com.

Battle Ground

Wolf Park (all ages) 🏕️ 🐗

R.R. #1; (765) 567–2265; www.wolfpark.org. **Open May 1 through November 30, 1:00 to 5:00 P.M. Closed Monday and holidays. Lectures daily. All activities subject to weather. $. Kids under 6 are free.**

Listening to the wolf's captivating song is a rare treat. At Wolf Park in Battle Ground, you don't just listen to the wolves, you can howl along with them every Friday night May through December and Saturday night all year-round beginning at 7:30 P.M. First you see the wolves in the early evening, when they are most active. Then you learn about wolves and how they communicate by howling. Later you learn to howl and join in the chorus with wolves and coyotes. A count of one, two, three is made. You and the wolves begin to howl, making a noise that can be heard 10 miles away. This should appeal to most children.

Wolf Park was founded in 1972 by Dr. Erich Klinghammer, a retired professor of animal behavior at Purdue University. The mission of the park is to educate people about wolves, as well as to conduct behavioral research on wolves. By being able to look at the wolves so closely, visitors can gain a greater appreciation of the intelligence that the wolves possess. Currently, the park has approximately seventeen wolves in packs or functioning singly. The wolves are kept in a seminatural situation and are fed carcasses of deer, calves, cows, and horses. All of the wolves in the park are hand-raised from the time they are very small. This reduces stress from living in captivity, makes it possible to handle them, and allows medical treatment with minimal trauma. In spite of this, the wolves maintain all their natural behavior patterns. The fact that the wolves are tame enables volunteers to greet and interact with them as a reward for their help at the park.

At Wolf Park visitors can see the wolves at close range and hear lectures about wolves in general and park research results specifically. These are presented by researchers or docents in front of the wolf enclosures.

You can develop a special relationship with a wolf by becoming a sponsor in the Adopt-a-Wolf Program. You can follow special events in your wolf's life and as a sponsor receive letters four times a year that update the social status of your wolf. Plus you have the opportunity to personally meet and interact with your wolf.

Not only can you see wolves at Wolf Park, you can also see a small herd of American bison at close range. Each Sunday there is a demonstration showing how bison protect themselves and their calves from wolves, and how the wolves test the bison for signs of weakness. Wolves are placed in a seventeen-acre enclosure with a herd of healthy American bison. While the wolves are not permitted to injure the bison, visitors see how the two species interact. Since the bison are healthy, they are quite capable of defending themselves and they are not killed or wounded. This presentation can only be seen each Sunday during open season, weather permitting. The presentation starts at 1:00 P.M., followed by the demonstration at 2:00 P.M.

For centuries, livestock guarding dogs have been used in Europe to protect sheep,

A Gisler **Adventure**

Our family has always enjoyed spending a summer day at Wolf Park in Battle Ground. After observing the wolves in their natural environment, our family gained a greater appreciation of a wolf's intelligence. We also enjoyed going on the guided tours through the park and learning more about the wild creatures' lifestyle. The children really like how close they could get to watch the animals interact with each other and other animals such as American bison and coyotes. Of course, we could never leave the park before it gets dark because that is when the real fun takes place. After dusk is when a park guide will tilt back his or her head and let go a howl into the night. Soon the resident wolf pack will howl right back. It is a sight and sound that our family will never forget.

goats, and cattle from predators. At Wolf Park, you will learn how these dogs are raised to perform this job. Wolf Park has an Italian Maremma guarding its sheep.

If you are really interested in wolves, you may want to participate in a six-day wolf behavioral seminar—a family vacation not soon forgotten! The seminars are usually held in May, August, and October and are based on the behavioral research carried out at Wolf Park since 1972. They consist of lectures, discussions, films, video and slide presentations, extensive observations of wolf behavior, and hands-on experience with wolves in a pack situation and, when possible, with pups.

The North American Wildlife Park Foundation, which maintains Wolf Park, offers opportunities for study not only to researchers but also to students and anyone else who may wish to observe wolves. There is usually a donation requested for this privilege. For more details, contact the foundation at Wolf Park, Battle Ground 47920.

The visitors center sells unique items that pertain to the wolves, such as books, handmade jewelry, and T-shirts. Photographs for sale are of the wolves who lived in the park before they were moved to zoos around the country. You can pick up a **free** Wolf Park newsletter in the center and brochures about special wolf seminars.

Tippecanoe Battlefield National Historic Landmark (all ages) 🏛

Prophet's Rock Road; (765) 567–2147; www.tcha.mus.in.us/battle.htm. Open 10:00 A.M. to 5:00 P.M. Tuesday through Saturday and noon to 5:00 P.M. Sunday. Closed Monday during the month of January, Thanksgiving, Christmas, and New Year's Day. $. Special group rates are available.

Here is a living history lesson for your children. This is the actual site of the 1811 battle in which General William Henry Harrison, governor of the Indiana Territory, and his men

Indiana **Trivia**

What city is Purdue University located in?

Where in Indiana can you find the unique 1882 two-story cylindrical rotating cellblock jail?

Lafayette, Crawfordsville

fought against an Indian army under the Prophet, the brother of Tecumseh. The Indians' defeat ended all organized resistance to the settling of the Northwest Territory.

When you arrive at the battlefield, you are taking a step back in time. Be sure to go to the museum first to get an idea of what the battle was like. The fiber optics map will light up the positions of the soldiers and Indians. Then you can step inside one of the two theaters for a slide presentation describing the battle. Be sure to look at the special exhibits about the battle. The museum also has a collection of arrowheads, archaeological exhibits, and Indian costumes that will interest you. The exhibits are always changing, so you can learn something new with each visit.

If you want a guided tour of the site, you will have to call ahead and book the tour in advance. The price is very modest. Or you can pick up a **free** map for your self-guided tour. Some of the old trees on the battlefield were hit by musket balls. Even though they are now largely surrounded by bark, it's fun to see if you can find spots where the musket balls may be. On the battlefield you will see signs that mark where the commissioned officers died in battle. In the center of the battleground, a large monument lists the names of the enlisted men who fought and died in the battle.

The battlefield is located inside a ninety-acre park that has many scenic trails for hiking as well as a large open playing field. The picnic area has tables and grills, making it easy for you to have a great gathering. Throughout the summer, special events are held on Sunday relating to pioneer life. You may be able to join in singing folk songs, see how quilting or making lace is done, saw a log, participate in a gunny sack race, or play pioneer games.

There are no places to eat or sleep at the battlefield; however, it is only 7 miles south on State Road 43 back to Lafayette.

For More Information

Lafayette Convention and Visitors Bureau. 301 Frontage Road; (800) 872–6648; www.lafayette-in.com.

Camping

Indiana Beach Amusement Park and Camp Resort (all ages) Ⓐ Ⓐ
West side of Lake Shafer, off U.S. 24; 4 miles north of Monticello; 20 miles east of I–65 at 5224 East Indiana Beach Road; (574) 583–4141; www.indianabeach.com. Hours are from 11:00 A.M. to 11:00 P.M. $$.

Camping is fun here in the center of Indiana's largest vacationland. Here is all you would expect in a modern camp resort and, in addition, you are a guest at Indiana's largest resort and family park.

Leave your car or motor home at your site—you'll never need to move all the time you are at Indiana Beach Camp Resort. The store is well stocked; the Boardwalk at Indiana Beach offers shopping, good restaurants, and entertainment. You may travel by **free** ferry or bus to and from the Boardwalk. Boating and waterskiing are available. Bring your boat or rent; motorboats, ski boats, canoes, or jet skis are all available at Indiana Beach Campground or nearby marinas. **Free** boat launching for guests on a large, wide boat ramp and boat channel with docking area.

Where to Eat

Skyroom. 5224 East Indiana Beach Road. Enjoy breakfast, lunch, or dinner overlooking Lake Shafer and Indiana Beach Amusement Resort. Open May through September 9:00 A.M. to 10:00 P.M.

Where to Stay

Inn, Motels, Cottages (219) 583–4141. There is a private pool for hotel, motel, and cottage guests. Guests are also welcome at Sand Beach, which is open to the public. Be sure to bring a small passport-type photo for each person for your pass to the beach, pool, and **free** ferryboat rides to the Camp Resort, or have one taken at the arcade (four snapshots for $2.00).

Monticello

The Greater Monticello Chamber of Commerce is located at 116 North Main Street. Visit Monticello's Twin Lakes vacation area. Enjoy recreation, shopping, entertainment, and Indiana Beach. For more information call (574) 583–7220 for your **free** Fun Pack, or see its Web site at www.monticelloin.com.

Indiana Beach (all ages)

5224 East Indiana Beach Road; (574) 583–4141; www.indianabeach.com.

Indiana Beach is the Hoosier State's largest privately owned summer resort and family park. Located on Lake Shafer, the park has three coasters, five water slides, and a 1,670-foot-long action river along with cottages, camping, restaurants, motels, an inn, entertainment, and amusement rides. Indiana Beach offers the perfect family vacation. It is a busy place that provides fun for all ages, from adults to small children, for one day or several days. If the weather is warm, you will want to be at the Sand Beach Public Swimming Area where you can swim in clear, filtered water. While the older people in your family relax in the sand and soak up the sun, the younger ones can enjoy building sand castles. There is also a diving area and a rope crawl. For thrills and excitement, there are five 400-foot-long water slides; two are fast body slides and three are extra-wide tube slides, where you ride a tube all the way to splashdown. For the older and more adventurous, there is a toboggan ride. You can also enjoy floating on a tube on an elevated torrent of water.

If you are looking for fun but want to stay dry, your family can enjoy the Amusement Funway or Boardwalk that stretches along the lake for almost a half-mile. Here you can enjoy twenty-four major adult fun rides. There is an amusement arcade, an eight-ride Kiddyland for children, miniature golf, a large sightseeing paddle-wheel steamer, and a number of unique shops. Will you be brave enough to try the "Hoosier Hurricane"? It is the first major custom coaster to be built in Indiana in more than fifty years. With ten peaks and nine valleys spanning its 3,000-foot lakefront location, the Hurricane runs on a conventional steel-on-wood track mounted on steel supports.

Lake Shafer Boat Rentals (all ages)

2419 West Shafer Drive, 1,000 feet south of Indiana Beach entrance; (574) 583–5238. Open daily May through September.

Here you can rent fully equipped ski boats, pontoons, Yamaha wave runners, runabouts, deck boats, and fishing boats. Call anytime for information or brochure.

Shafer Shores Boat Rental and Marina, Inc. (all ages)

4599 North West Shafer Drive, 2 miles north of Indiana Beach; (574) 583– 3488. Open daily May through October 8:00 A.M. to 8:00 P.M.

Boat rentals, pontoons, ski, fishing, and waverunners are available here.

Festivals

Indiana Beach Venetian Night.
5224 East Indiana Beach Road; (800) 583–5306.

Venetian Night, held in mid-May, features a lighted boat parade seen along the shores of Lake Shafer as well as from the reviewing stand at Indiana Beach. The weekend also includes a crafts festival along the boardwalk, boat show, and a country music dance in the famous Indiana Beach Ballroom.

Where to Eat

Benno's by the Bay. 3000 West Shafer Street; (574) 583–7575. Open Tuesday through Thursday 4:00 to 9:00 P.M.; Friday, Saturday, and Sunday 4:00 to 10:00 P.M.

Where to Stay

Andrews Lakeside Resort. 4295 Indiana Beach Road; (574) 583–9513. Located on Lake Shafer with great view, boat docks, luxury rooms. Near Indiana Beach entrance.

The Riveria Complex. 5057 East Indiana Beach Road; (574) 583–3366. Lakeview kitchen apartments and motel rooms, kitchen, heat, air-conditioning, heated pool; adjacent to Indiana Beach. Coupons available.

Clearview Resort. 5070 East Indiana Beach Road; (574) 583–3624. Lighted piers for boat docking and fishing, picnic tables, grills, walking distance to park.

Lakeside Resort. 5824 North West Shafer Drive, 41 East; (574) 538–3291.

A Gisler **Adventure**

Another great place that our family enjoys on a hot summer day or for a long weekend is Indiana Beach Amusement and Camp Resort on Lake Shafer in Monticello. We all love the giant water park that features sand beaches, swimming, five water slides, a speed slide, and the longest action river in the United States. Also on the park grounds is the Amusement Boardwalk that offers thrilling amusement rides with three roller coasters. Our favorite is the "Hoosier Hurricane," Indiana's first and fastest super coaster. We also like seeing and taking photographs of the state's largest paddle-wheel steamer. Since we love adventure, we never miss the **free** aquatic stunt show or the "Amazing World of Animals" show, both performed daily in the summer. To end our day of family fun, we enjoy dinner at the Skyroom and then live entertainment at the Roof Lounge.

Idaville

Would you like to see what it was like to live at an early Amish settlement? Then go to **Parrish Pioneer Village,** an outdoor living-history museum at 1250 East and 50 North to catch a glimpse of early nineteenth-century life. You can watch the costumed staff demonstrate the daily activities of the original Amish settlers. The highlight will be your visit to **Abner Shafer's 1850 home.** You will be surprised to see the unique stenciling and country look throughout this home. While you are visiting the settlement, be sure to tour the new herb garden to see herbs used for seasoning, medicines, dyes, teas, wreaths, decorations, and magic at festivals. The village is open daily from May to November. For more information about the village and special events, call (574) 826–4163.

Logansport

Logansport Carousel (all ages) 🎡 🏛

1212 Riverside Drive, in Riverside Park; (574) 753–8725. Open seven days a week from Memorial Day to Labor Day; reduced hours in the fall; closed January through April. Call for exact hours of operation.

Everyone enjoys a merry-go-round, and family memories will be made when you visit this carousel. The Logansport Carousel has forty-two wooden animals, which are approximately one hundred years old. All of these animals were hand-carved by Gustav Dentzel and his artisans. The Dentzel figures are regarded today as the finest of their kind. The Dentzel workshop made primarily stationary animals like the ones that you will see in Logansport. The Logansport Carousel is not only a historic masterpiece of animal carving, but it has been and remains a working carousel that has brought joy and delight to children and adults of all ages for the better part of this century. The carousel brings a moment of magic that lives in the hearts and memories of all who ride it. It is a National Historic Landmark. If you are visiting in July, you can attend the Iron Horse Heritage Festival.

France Park (all ages) 🏊 🎣 ⛷

4505 West U.S. 24 on the Wabash-Erie Canal; (574) 753–2928. Open year-round. $.

Everyone in your family will enjoy the park's 400-acre recreation areas, located on U.S. 24, 4 miles west of Logansport. The park has a lake with rocky cliffs on three sides plus a beach, waterfall, fishing, scuba diving, hiking, camping, and water slide. In the winter, families can enjoy snowmobiling, ice skating, fishing, and cross-country skiing.

Hoosier Bikeway System–Wabash Valley Route (all ages, but more fun if everyone can ride a bike) 🚴

This bicycle route runs east-west across Cass County, 4 miles south of Logansport. The Hoosier Bikeway System is designed to provide riders with scenic bike routes connecting many of Indiana's recreation areas and cities. The Wabash Valley Route connects Shades State Park with the Mississinewa Reservoir.

The History of the **Logansport Carousel**

The Logansport Carousel is a "merry-go-round" comprised of forty-two wooden animals. These animals were hand-carved by Gustav Dentzel and his artisans. The Dentzel figures are generally regarded today as the finest of their kind. The Dentzel workshop made primarily stationary animals prior to 1890. Although the history of the Logansport animals can be definitely traced back only to 1902, much evidence exists to date the animals back to 1885. It is probable that the Logansport animals are approximately one hundred years old. The carousel was moved to Logansport from Fort Wayne, Indiana, in 1919 and operated in Logansport from that date. It was first located in Spencer Park but was moved in 1950 to Riverside Park. The last private owner died in 1969, and the carousel was closed until the Logansport Jaycees raised the funds necessary to purchase it in 1972. Because of the importance of the carousel to this community, the estate of the owner agreed to sell the carousel to the town of Logansport for the appraised price of $15,000.

Shortly after the purchase of the carousel by the Jaycees, Logansport–Cass County Carousel, Inc. was formed by interested citizens as a nonprofit corporation to manage and maintain the carousel for the community. This group has managed the carousel since that time.

The Logansport Carousel is not only a historic masterpiece of animal carving, but it has been and remains a working carousel that has brought joy and delight to children and adults in the area for the better part of the twentieth century. It is a moment of magic that lives in the hearts and memories of all those who have been fortunate enough to enjoy the carousel for these many years.

Iron Horse Museum (ages 5 and up)

300 East Broadway Street; (574) 753–6388. Open in July only, Monday through Friday 8:00 A.M. to 5:00 P.M. Free.

This vintage railroad depot houses railroad memorabilia and information.

Edson Art Center (ages 5 and up)

424 Front Street; (574) 735–2915. Open Monday and Saturday 1:00 to 4:00 P.M. and Tuesday through Friday 11:00 A.M. to 4:00 P.M. Free.

The center is home to the Logansport Art Association, which hosts art exhibits and a variety of shows; instructional classes are offered.

The Jerolaman-Long House (ages 5 and up)

1004 East Market Street; (574) 753–3866. Open Tuesday through Saturday 1:00 to 5:00 P.M. Free.

The twenty-room Italianate-style mansion was constructed by George Jerolaman in 1853. The mansion was donated to the Historical Society by Benjamin Long in 1967. The museum contains a wide variety of historical artifacts and has especially strong Civil War and American Indian collections. The museum also features several prints by nineteenth-century artist George Winters. Winters, best known for his portraits of Indian chiefs, lived in Logansport for a time and painted many Cass County landscapes. On the museum grounds are a log cabin and a log barn that have been moved to the site and restored to depict pioneer life in the 1840s. The Chick Family Cabin was built in 1866 and is furnished as it might have been in that period. The cast-iron heating stove was used in the cabin when it was first built. A Carriage Barn on the property is the Historical Society's meeting place, with seating for sixty to seventy-five people. This area is decorated with early Cass County articles.

Other Festivals in the Area

Macy Community Christmas Event.

Third Saturday in December in Macy; (574) 382–3985.

Holiday celebration with live nativity scene and festive decorations.

Squirrel Village Festival and Rendezvous.

First weekend of May and first weekend of October in Peru; (765) 689–8169.

Native American displays, arts and crafts, and more.

Iron Horse Festival.

Held annually in July, in and around the downtown area of Logansport; (574) 753–6388.

The festival features steam train rides, arts and crafts, food booths, home tours, and special guest entertainment.

Where to Eat

Mr. Happy Burger. 3131 East Market Street, East Gate Plaza; (574) 753–6418.

B-K West. 1101 U.S. Highway 24 West; (574) 753–3917. Open February through September. Great cheese fries.

Ponderosa Steak House. 3101 George; (574) 722–2646.

Where to Stay

Super 8 Hotel Motel. 3801 East Market Street; (574) 722–1273.

Manor Hotel. 3315 U.S. 24; (574) 722–4885.

Holiday Inn. 3550 East Market Street; (574) 753–6351.

For More Information

Logansport/Cass County Chamber of Commerce. 300 East Broadway, Suite 103, Logansport, IN 46947; (574) 753–6388; www.logan-casschamber.com.

Oxford

Ride 'em cowboy! During **Dan Patch Days** in Oxford, your family can watch a rodeo, a toy tractor pull, and a draft horse pull. Dan Patch Days are held annually the first weekend after Labor Day to celebrate the famous horse Dan Patch, who was foaled in Oxford. Dan was one of the greatest pacers of all time. In 1905 he paced a mile in 1 minute, 55.25 seconds—a record that lasted until 1938. When your family watches the rodeo, you will see several of the top fifteen cowboys and cowgirls in the nation compete, as this is an International Professional Rodeo event for championship points. When you watch the toy tractor pull, you will see teens driving lawn tractors in an event that is sponsored by the Future Farmers of America. Children of all ages should really be able to relate to this competition. The draft horse pull pits local horse owners against each other. Besides these events, which you really don't get to see very often, especially if you live in a large city, there are a softball tournament, bingo, a parade, a flea market, and entertainment. Before or after attending Dan Patch Days events, you will want to explore the small town of Oxford, noting the brick streets and 1800s buildings on the town square as well as some of the older homes in the town. There is a moderate charge for some of the events at this festival sponsored by the Oxford Lions Club. The celebration begins on Friday and ends on Sunday. Call (765) 385–2935 to find out the times of events.

Crawfordsville

Would you enjoy visiting a city that is rich in Victorian charm? Then you should head to Crawfordsville. Park your car and stop at the visitors bureau at 218 East Pike Street for information about all of the town's activities and places to visit and stay; (800) 866–3937; www.crawfordsville.org. From there you can easily walk to two of the town's museums and see some beautiful Victorian homes along the way.

Old Jail Museum (all ages) 🏚️

225 North Washington Street; (765) 362–5222. Open April, May, September, and October, Wednesday through Saturday 1:00 to 4:30 P.M. In June, July, and August open Tuesday and Sunday 1:00 to 4:30 P.M. and Wednesday through Saturday 10:00 A.M. to 4:30 P.M. Free.

One of the stops on your museum walking tour will be the Old Jail Museum. Here you can see the first jail that had rotary cell blocks. The sheriff could sit at his desk and see each of his prisoners by just turning a crank that rotated the cells. When you go down to the basement, you can see the huge gears that turned the circular cell block. This jail was actually used until 1973. The sheriff's residence, which is attached to the jail, is now an exhibit area. You will hear the guide tell about the public hangings here or maybe the story about the town drunk who would prevent rotation of the cells by sticking his peg leg through cell bars. As the story goes, the only thing that stopped him was the sheriff threatening to saw off the leg. If you visit Crawfordsville over Labor Day, there will be a Labor Day Break-Out at the jail, with food, a variety of entertainment, and tours of the museum.

Ben Hur Museum (all ages) 🏚️🏛️

Wallace and Elston Avenues; (765) 362–5769; www.ben-hur.com. Hours are seasonal; call or visit its Web site for details. $. Children under 6 free.

Perhaps you have read *Ben Hur* or seen the movie based on this famous story. At the Ben Hur Museum you can see where General Lew Wallace actually wrote this book. He wanted peace and quiet for his writing, so he designed the building for that purpose. It sits behind a brick wall on four acres of grounds and is a National Historic Landmark. On display in the museum you can see memorabilia of Wallace's life as a soldier in the Civil War and Mexican War, his artwork, items from the *Ben Hur* films, and items connected to his work as a state senator, lawyer, and writer.

Indiana **Trivia**

Where is Turkey Run State Park located?

Where did Indiana's tenth governor, Joseph Wright, start practicing law?

What is Crawfordsville called?

Marshall, Rockville, "Athens of the Hoosier State"

Wabash College (all ages) 🏛
West Wabash and Grant Avenues; (765) 361–6100.

Take a stroll through Wabash College, which has an extremely attractive campus with buildings dating back to 1882. This small college for men, with only 850 students, has an outstanding reputation for the intellectual pursuits of its graduates. It ranks sixteenth in the United States for college graduates going on to earn their Ph.D. degrees.

Shades State Park (all ages) 🧗 🛖 🚲 ⛺
County Road 800 South, off State Road 234; (765) 435–2810. Open dawn to dusk. $.

You will have to do some real hiking to appreciate the different trees, geologic formations, and eleven waterfalls in this 3,000-acre park. The beauty of this park is incredible in the spring, when the dogwoods and redbuds are blooming, and in the fall, when the leaves are turning. Within the park is the Pine Hills Preserve, which will delight you with its rugged hills and deep gorges. Caution is advised when climbing the four backbone ridges rising more than 75 feet above the valley floor. Sugar Creek, considered one of the prettiest streams in the state, runs through the park and is a fabulous stream for canoeing. You can put your canoe in at the park and have a great day trip down to Turkey Run State Park. If the water level is low, you can have fun tubing. As this creek can be dangerous at flood stage, you must check conditions at park headquarters before beginning any trip on Sugar Creek. For all-day fun and overnight stays, the park has campsites, picnic areas, bicycles for rent, and a naturalist in the summer.

Festivals! Festivals! **Festivals!**

Venture to Crawfordsville to attend one of the many festivals held there. The **Strawberry Festival** is always held the second weekend in June and is the town's most popular event, attracting more than 25,000 visitors. Outdoor stage entertainment, food, crafts, children's activities, art, antiques, and a classic auto show highlight the three days of festivities. At Christmas, you may want to attend the **Christmas Candlelight Tour of Crawfordsville's Historic Homes.** If you want to stay overnight, there are two historic bed-and-breakfast inns in Crawfordsville. **The Yount's Mill Inn,** built in 1851, is situated on a bluff overlooking Sugar Creek. The **Davis House** is located on the west side of Crawfordsville. You can enjoy a gourmet breakfast and deluxe accommodations at either inn.

Clements Canoes, Inc. (ages 3 and up) ⊕

613 Lafayette Avenue; (765) 362–2781; www.clementscanoes.com. Trips offered daily April 1 through September, water and weather permitting. Reservations required.

When the water is too high for canoeing or tubing, there is an appealing alternative for people of all ages. Clements Canoes, Inc. in Crawfordsville offers guided raft trips. You can take a trip for a few hours or overnight. Up to eight people plus a trained guide fit in one raft. You will have a memorable journey down scenic Sugar Creek. Make sure you call ahead for reservations. Clements Canoes also provides equipment, facilities, and service for tubing, canoeing, and kayaking trips.

Where to Eat

SunShine Cafe. 1605 U.S. 231 North; (765) 362–6808. Every country-style meal is cooked with pride here. The whole family will enjoy the 180-item menu. Carry-out and children's menus available. Open 6:00 A.M. to 11:00 P.M. daily. Closed Christmas.

The Forum. 1410 Darlington Avenue; (765) 361–8751. Casual family dining. Serving breakfast, lunch, and dinner.

Where to Stay

Day's Inn. 1040 Corey Boulevard; (765) 362–0300; www.daysinn.com.

Sugar Creek Queen Anne Bed-and-Breakfast. 901 East Market; (800) 362–6293. Victorian home, deluxe continental breakfast. Rates begin at $65.

Holiday Inn. 2500 Lafayette Road (I–74 and U.S. 231); (765) 362–8700; www.holiday-inn.com.

Marshall

If your family loves wilderness activities, then **Turkey Run State Park** on State Road 47 is the place to go. You'll want to explore the deep sandstone ravines, walk along the stands of aged forest, and enjoy the scenic views along Sugar Creek. Your family can rent bicycles and tackle some of the 27 miles of the **Hoosier Hills Bicycle Route,** go fishing, enjoy horseback riding, or discover more about the park from the park naturalist. For more fun, there are tennis courts, a swimming pool, a nature center, and a planetarium. You can fish on the 230-acre lake, or rent a paddleboat, canoe, or rowboat. If you are there for the day, there are many picnic areas. For longer stays, there are camping, cabins, and the Turkey Run Inn. The inn has combined all of today's modern conveniences with the rustic country charm of yesteryear. It even has an indoor pool! Special events at the park include a Pumpkin Show the last weekend in September and a Bluegrass Festival on the first weekend in October. To learn more about the park or make reservations, call (765) 597–2635.

Hit the **Water!**

Does your family want the challenge of a canoe trip? If the answer is yes, there are companies that offer rentals and provide transportation so you can enjoy the wilderness areas of Sugar Creek and see abundant wildlife, sandstone cliffs, and historic covered bridges. Your family will marvel at the natural geologic wonders of this beautiful park, nestled along State Road 47 southwest of Crawfordsville, as you hike along its famous trails. Everyone will want to explore the ravines, walk along the stands of aged forests, and enjoy the scenic views along Sugar Creek. You will also want to visit the Colonel Richard Lieber Cabin, which commemorates the contributions of the father of Indiana's state park system. On weekends you may need to make reservations.

Turkey Run Canoe Trips offers a variety of trips from a minitrip that is only 4 miles long to a gentle 12-mile trip and a 15-mile white-water trip or a combination of the two longer trips involving an overnight stay. Call (765) 569–6705 or (765) 597–2456 for information or stop by Turkey Run Canoe Trips, on Highway 41 a mile from the park. Across from Turkey Run State Park Campground is Sugar Valley Canoe Trips, Ltd., which offers canoe trips through Turkey Run State Park and a trip through Shades and Turkey Run parks. Call (800) 422–6638 or (765) 597–2364 for more information or reservations. Both of these companies also offer tube rentals. Remember to check at park headquarters to make sure there are no dangerous flood conditions before embarking on a trip.

Where to Eat/ Where to Stay

Cabins and the Inn at the state park along with the restaurant at the Inn. (See above for more information.)

Turkey Run Inn. Rural Route 1, Box 444; (765) 597–2211.

Rockville

A highlight of fall in Indiana is the **Parke County Covered Bridge Festival,** celebrated annually in Rockville for ten days starting the second Friday in October. Parke County is the covered bridge capital of the world, with thirty authentic bridges—most can be driven over because they are in such good condition. All of the bridges are listed on the National Register of Historic Places. What a treat it will be for your family to drive across these bridges as you leisurely explore the Hoosier countryside and small towns of Parke County and savor the vibrant fall colors. There's a **Clydesdale farm** in Tangier, as well as big, juicy roast beef sandwiches made with beef cooked in a pit and a cemetery to view in Rosedale. Bloomingdale is a Quaker community; you can learn about its interesting history at **Dennis Hall.** You will want to stop at several towns as well as walk across a few of the bridges. If you bring a picnic, you will find a spot along the way to enjoy your meal.

Begin your visit to the Covered Bridge Festival at the tourist information center on the town square in Rockville or at the visitors bureau 3 blocks east in an 1883 railroad depot. At either spot, you can pick up festival information and maps of the five covered bridge routes. You can either drive or take a guided bus tour of the covered bridges. Rockville and the Parke County covered bridge area can be visited throughout the year. You may wish to see this area when it is less crowded. For festival information and information about the covered bridges, lodging, recreation, and special events throughout the year, call (765) 569–5226 or visit its Web site: www.coveredbridges.com.

The heart of the covered bridge festivities is Rockville Town Square. Here you will be able to sample real country cooking. Choose from such popular items as pork chops, biscuits and gravy, corn on the cob, hobo stew, oxtail soup, freshly cooked crullers, apple cider, homemade ice cream, and more. You will also want to wander among the many shops and tents filled with art, crafts, antiques, country food items, and farm products. The variety of products will absolutely astound you. Local artisans work throughout the year to produce this bounty.

Once you have visited the town square, hop on a **free tractor-pulled shuttle** or walk to **Billie Creek Village.** This re-creation of an early twentieth-century village is in a beautiful wooded area with a stream running through it. There are three covered bridges here, a farmstead, and thirty historic buildings moved from other sites in Parke County. During the festival you can watch America's largest gathering of crafters demonstrating their turn-of-the-century skills. There will also be people making apple cider, ice cream, and herb teas. Your children will be busy every minute, riding the antique carousel, watching entertainment, and having fun on horse-pulled wagon rides. You can shop at the booths or the general store, which is one of the Midwest's largest handmade consignment craft shops. If you don't wish to visit Billie Creek during the crowded Covered Bridge Festival, it is open most of the year. Many weekends there are special events such as Civil War Days, School Days, Maple Fair, Halloween Fright Nights, and Sorghum and Cider Making. At times there is an admission fee at the village. To learn more about all the year-round activities, call (765) 569–3430 or visit its Web site at www.billiecreek.org.

Where to Eat

Abalon. U.S. 41; (765) 569–9496.

White Horse Café. U.S. 41; (765) 569–9450. Travel back to the days of cowboys, cattle drives, and chuck wagons. Try the "Texas-sized" tenderloin.

Weber's Family Restaurant. 105 South Jefferson; (765) 569–6153; www.dineat webers.com.

Where to Stay

Billie Creek Village and Inn. Rural Route 2, Box 27; (765) 569–3430.

Motel Forrest. 868 North Lincoln Road; (765) 569–5250.

Park Bridge Motel. 304 East Ohio Street (U.S. 36 East); (765) 569–3525.

Indiana **Trivia**

What movie did Indiana director Robert Wise receive two Oscars for in 1961?

Where do you have to go to visit Saint Mary-of-the-Woods College, the oldest Catholic liberal arts college for women?

What was the speed limit if you were driving your car on Indiana state highways in 1925?

West Side Story, Terre Haute, 35 mph

Mecca

Mecca is proud of its newly restored **covered bridge** over Big Raccoon Creek. Because no vehicles are allowed on this bridge, you have an opportunity to walk through it. At the end of the bridge is a **one-room schoolhouse,** which is in session during the Covered Bridge Festival. No matter when you visit Mecca, stop at the post office. You will be amazed at how tiny this old post office is.

Mansfield

Mansfield is a charming village that you can visit during the hustle and bustle of the Parke County Covered Bridge Festival, when the streets are filled with vendors selling food and craft items, and there's a flea market, too. You might enjoy an **Old-Fashioned Christmas** here during the early part of December and the popular **Mushroom Festival** that is held late in April. Or you can choose to visit on an ordinary day and savor the sights. Overlooking Big Raccoon Creek is the rustic old **Mansfield Roller Mill,** which is still in operation and has been grinding with waterpower since 1820. You can watch the mill grind corn and make cornmeal you can take home. There is a breathtaking view of the waterfall, and the grassy bank behind the mill is a perfect place for picnics and snapshots. Plus you are welcome to swim, fish, and explore the grounds as much as you like. You will enjoy walking through the majestic covered bridge that will transport you to a quieter, simpler time.

Bridgeton

Bridgeton is a tiny town filled with foodstuffs, artists, and craftspeople with their handmade wares during the Parke County Covered Bridge Festival. The town's beautifully preserved **covered bridge** has a 245-foot double span. Alongside the bridge is the **Weise Mill,** which was built in 1823. During the festival, the mill will be open and grinding grain. The mill water thunders over a dam and under the bridge. This magic spot has been called the Brigadoon of Parke County. It is especially great at any time for a picnic, fishing, or just wading in the water.

Terre Haute

Terre Haute was founded in 1816, the same year that Indiana was admitted to the Union. Because the city is located above the high-water mark on the east bank of the Wabash River, the French named the city *Terre Haute,* which means "high land" in French. Today this city of more than 60,000 people is one of the largest in western Indiana. You'll find it a great city to visit as it has more than 1,550 hotel rooms, 125 restaurants, fifteen movie screens in five theaters, ninety bowling lanes, 1,000 acres of parks, five public golf courses, and sixty tennis courts. With five colleges, it's quite an educational center, too. Don't forget to pack a picnic when you visit Terre Haute, because the city takes pride in its many city parks that offer so many activities from cool dips in pools and **free** concerts in the summer, to walks under trees with brightly colored leaves in the fall, to cross-country skiing during the winter. If you like to do your sightseeing by foot, pick up a map and guide to the **Downtown Terre Haute Historic Tour,** a walking tour of some twenty-one buildings. Contact the Visitors Bureau (634 Wabash Avenue, 812–234–5555) for more information.

Vigo County Courthouse (all ages) 🏛
South Third Street between Ohio and Cherry Streets; (812) 234–5555.

Would you like to stand in the same spot where soldiers enlisted to fight in the Civil War? Well, if you visit the Vigo County Courthouse, you can. On the front lawn of the court-house is the **Soldiers and Sailors Monument** where the soldiers enlisted. Although the courthouse was built in 1888, it is still being used today. The courthouse and monument are part of the Downtown Terre Haute Historic Tour (see above).

Farrington Grove Historic District (ages 8 and up) 🏛
Next to the downtown area; (812) 235–9717.

This tour gives you a chance to exercise as you tour the more than 800 nineteenth-century historic buildings, mainly houses, in this area. The oldest home is a classical Greek Revival structure at 900–904 South Fourth Street that was built in 1849. You will also see other styles of homes; however, most of the homes are Victorian. While you are taking this tour, you will pass by an area where Senator Stephen A. Douglas, the man who debated Abraham Lincoln, once spoke. In December your family might enjoy taking part in a **candlelight tour** of the district.

For more information about these tours, visit the Terre Haute Convention and Visitors Bureau, located in an old building at 634 Wabash Avenue; (812) 234–5555.

Indiana State University (all ages) 🏛
217 North Sixth Street; (800) 742–0891; www.indstate.edu.

This is the largest college in Terre Haute. It has more than 12,000 students and offers more than 250 different degree programs. This is an urban campus located on ninety-one acres next to the north side of Terre Haute's downtown business district. The campus, however, is beginning to look more like a traditional campus with the closing of some city streets and the addition of a fountain and a greenway. There is also a multistoried student union. Visit this campus with your children to help them become better acquainted with what colleges are like. You also might want to attend an event at the college, which has an award-winning theater program, many musical programs, and a convocation series. Plus there are always sports for you to view on campus. The university participates in fourteen intercollegiate sports, with both men's and women's teams. Many sports heroes have attended the school, including Larry Bird of basketball fame, world-champion gymnast Kurt Thomas, and Olympic gold medalist wrestler Bruce Baumgartner. Sports information is available at (812) 237–4160.

John C. Hook Astronomical Observatory (ages 6 and up)
Indiana State University campus; (812) 237-2444. Open Tuesday and Friday evenings 8:00 to 10:00 P.M., weather permitting. The observatory is in the Science Building, to the east of the student union. You enter the building and climb the stairs to the roof to reach the observatory. Free.

For an enjoyable evening, gaze at the night skies and check out the stars and planets at the Hook Astronomical Observatory, on the Indiana State University campus. The observatory is usually open even when the university is closed.

Historical Museum of the Wabash Valley (all ages)
1411 South Sixth Street; (812) 235-9717. Open Tuesday through Sunday 1:00 to 4:00 P.M.; closed in January.

History buffs need to visit this museum to learn more about the history of the valley and the Midwest. The museum is housed in the former home of William H. Sage. It was built in 1868 and has twelve different exhibit rooms on three floors. Much of the collection has been donated by local residents. The museum has a good collection of military memorabilia from the Revolutionary War to World War II. When you climb up to the third floor, you'll feel like you've gone back a century because the rooms are decorated in Victorian style. Your children will be interested in seeing a child's nursery and toy shop. You will be fascinated by the personal effects of the wealthy of this period. In the gift shop, a golden sculpture of Mercury that once was atop a downtown building in Terre Haute can be seen. You will also discover a jolly Punch that once stood guard outside an old cigar and tobacco shop. Many interesting items are for sale in the gift shop. Sunday is a good day to visit because the museum has craft demonstrations and special feature films. There are also special displays, such as the spring egg tree. Call to learn about special events.

Allen Memorial Planetarium (ages 5 and up)
3737 South Seventh Street; (812) 462-4272. Be sure to call ahead for tours, especially during the school year.

Enjoy looking at the stars, planets, and other heavenly bodies with your children at the Allen Memorial Planetarium. The planetarium has shows for the public around Christmas, in the spring, and in the fall. Also, the director welcomes you to call and ask if there's room for you to attend a showing at other times when the planetarium is having shows for the public schools.

Children's Science and Technology Museum (all ages)

523 Wabash Avenue; (812) 235–5548; www.cstm.org. Open Tuesday through Saturday 9:00 A.M. to 4:00 P.M. $.

Inquisitive people of all ages enjoy visiting a museum like the Children's Science and Technology Museum. There are lots of hands-on exhibits here that your family will enjoy playing with as you learn more about science. Some of the permanent exhibits are a shadow wall, lasers, a stoplight, model trains, holograms, fossils, human-powered electricity, a television studio, marble runs, and floating rings. At other times, there will be exhibits like one that lets you work with pulleys, cranes, and wheels to make things move. Call to find out about special exhibits.

Eugene V. Debs Home (ages 8 and up)

451 North Eighth Street; (812) 232–2163. Admission is free. Open Wednesday through Sunday 1:00 to 4:30 P.M.

When you visit the Eugene V. Debs Home, you are stepping into the home of a man who ran for president five times as the Socialist party nominee and was a well-known labor leader, writer, and humanitarian. Debs was born in Terre Haute in 1853. His home is an official landmark of the State of Indiana and a Registered National Historic Landmark. Debs built the home for himself and his wife in 1890, and it is a good example of Midwest mid-Victorian architecture. The home's eight rooms still have much of their original furniture, including art objects and other memorabilia. When you are in the attic, take a look at the John Joseph Laska wall murals and plaques honoring historic labor leaders.

Paul Dresser Birthplace Memorial (all ages)

First Street and Dresser Drive; (812) 235–9717. Open mid-May through September Wednesday 1:00 to 4:00 P.M. Free, but donations are accepted.

When Hoosiers sing the state song "On the Banks of the Wabash," they are singing a song written by Paul Dresser, who lived in Terre Haute. You can see the Paul Dresser Birthplace Memorial at First Street and Dresser Drive. Unlike other homes, the Paul Dresser Birthplace Memorial home shows how the working class—90 percent of the people—really lived in Indiana during the pre–Civil War period. The main living quarters on the first floor consist of a kitchen, bedroom, and parlor. Upstairs there are two bedrooms that could only be reached by an outside staircase. The furnishings are sturdy—not fancy.

Fowler Park (all ages)

Bono Road; (812) 462–3392. Open late May to mid-October weekends and by appointment. Free.

In Fowler Park on Bono Road, your family can enjoy swimming, fishing, boating, picnicking, and playing on a playground. But there is one extra feature at this park—Fowler Park Pioneer Village. It is an 1840s village that has nine log homes and shops, a smokehouse, barn, sorghum mill, evaporator house, church, blacksmith shop, carpenter's shop, and gristmill. There is also Indiana's oldest covered bridge. You can take a guided tour or your own tour during Pioneer Days in October or the Christmas Walk in December. Call to get more information on the village, special events, and hours of operation.

John G. Dobbs Memorial Grove (all ages)
5170 East Poplar Drive; (812) 877–1095. Open 9:00 A.M. to 5:00 P.M. Monday through Saturday and 12:30 to 5:00 P.M. Sunday. Free.

Being outdoors and enjoying nature is easy when you are at the John G. Dobbs Memorial Grove. Although your family can enjoy fishing, boating, picnicking, and winter activities in the park, a special feature they should enjoy together is a walk on the nature trails. There are four relatively short trails for exploration. As you walk along, you can learn about nature through observation, from park brochures, and from informative markers. The park also has a nature center that is open throughout the year.

Swope Art Museum (all ages)
25 South Seventh Street; (812) 238–1676; www.swope.org. Open Tuesday through Friday 10:00 A.M. to 5:00 P.M. and weekends noon to 5:00 P.M. Tours by appointment. Free.

You can introduce your children to the work of several fine American artists at the Swope Art Museum. The permanent collection here includes works by Grant Wood, Thomas Hart Benton, Edward Hopper, Mary Fairchild MacMonnies, Charles Burchfield, Ansel Adams, Andy Warhol, Marc Chagall, and many more.

Saint Mary-of-the-Woods (all ages) 🏛
(812) 535–5151; www.smwc.edu.

Before leaving Terre Haute, you should visit Saint Mary-of-the-Woods. First-time visitors are often overheard saying that they could never imagine a place so beautiful hidden in the cornfields of western Indiana. Saint Mary-of-the-Woods is the home of the Sisters of Providence, a congregation of religious Catholic women, and of Saint Mary-of-the-Woods College, which is more than 150 years old. You will want to take a leisurely walk through the woods to see the shrines and grottoes. There is the Our Lady of Lourdes Grotto, which is a replica of the internationally known Lourdes Shrine in France. When you step into the Church of the Immaculate Conception, you will believe that you have actually stepped into a European cathedral. If you are visiting on Sunday, the Sunday Brunch at the Woods starts serving at 10:30 A.M. and stops at 1:30 P.M. Call (812) 535–5151 if you want a tour of the Providence Center.

Festivals and Special Events (all ages)
In Terre Haute and the Wabash Valley, there are plenty of festivals and special events that will appeal to the entire family.

The **Riverfest** is a festival that offers a fun-filled day of outdoor activities designed to generate family entertainment. It is sponsored by the Wabash Valley Region of Ivy Tech to increase awareness of that institution's adult education programs and to promote the quality of life in the Wabash Valley. Some of the special events include raft racing on the Wabash River, a children's fair, singing, and craft sales.

You can also choose from the **Maple Sugarin' Days** in Prairie Creek Park in February and March; the **Strassenfest** and the **Easter Egg Hunt** at Deming Park in April; the **Wabash Valley Festival** in Fairbanks Park in May; the **Kids' Fishing Rodeo** in Dobbs Park and **Lightning on the Wabash** at Fairbanks Park in June; the **Vigo County Fair** in July; **Run for Fun** at Deming Park in August; the **Oktoberfest** in September; **Pioneer Days** at Fowler Park, the **Ethnic Festival** at Fairbanks Park, the **Contemporary Music Festival** at Indiana State University, and **Old-Fashioned Day** at Collett Park in October; **A Taste of Terre Haute** at the Hulman Center in November; and the **Great Midwest Racing Weekend** at Hulman Regional Airport, **Christmas-at-the-Woods** at Saint Mary-of-the-Woods College, **Christmas Walk** at Fowler Park, and **Christmas in the Park** at Deming Park in December. For more information about these festivals and the Riverfest, call (812) 238–TALK to get the visitors bureau information line.

For More Information

Terre Haute Convention and Visitors Bureau. 634 Wabash Avenue; (812) 234–5555; www.terrehaute.com.

Cloverdale

Travel to **Cagles Mill Lake** in Lieber State Recreation Area on State Road 243 for some different and unusual activities. At Easter time, your children can hunt eggs outside and win lots of prizes. Then one Saturday night around Halloween, everyone can take the **Haunted Trail** through the woods from 6:30 to 11:00 P.M. As this trail is quite scary, it is not appropriate for all children. Between Memorial Day and Labor Day, there are activities galore, including fun things to do such as watching Civil War reenactments, learning how to line dance, and participating in sand-sculpture contests. On Wednesday and Sunday, you can take three-hour pontoon boat tours to **Cataract Falls,** the largest waterfalls in the state. There are two sets of waterfalls and a final drop of more than 80 feet. Some nights at 10:00 P.M., there is an **Owl Tour** on the boat, which features ghost stories. You'll need reservations for these popular boat tours. Your recreational needs will be fully met at this park, for there is hiking, swimming, water-skiing, picnicking, horseshoes, volleyball, basketball, fishing, and more. There is also camping. Be sure to call (765) 795–4576 to learn about all the recreational programs.

Where to Eat

Chicago Pizza. 1004 North Main Street; (765) 795–4070.

Torrs Restaurant. Junction of State Road 231 and U.S. 40; (765) 653–2666.

Cloverdale Travel Plaza. 1032 North Main Street; (765) 795–3220. Truck stop.

Where to Stay

Cloverdale Days Inn. 1031 North Main Street; (765) 795–6400.

Holiday Inn Express. 1017 North Main Street; (765) 795–5050; www.holiday inn.com.

Ramada Inn. 1035 North Main Street; (765) 795–3500; www.ramada.com.

For More Information

Putnam County Convention and Visitors Bureau. (800) 829–4639.

Spencer

McCormick's Creek State Park (all ages) 🏕️ 🚻 🎣 🏊

Open dawn to dusk. Admission is $3.00 for in-state cars and $5.00 for out-of-state cars.

McCormicks's Creek State Park has unique limestone formations and scenic waterfalls. This was the first state park in Indiana. It is located along the White River and has beautiful hiking trails and magnificent thick wooded areas where you can roam leisurely through canyons surrounded by high cliffs. This park has just about everything for outdoor family fun. There is a saddle barn where you can rent horses for rides through the woods and a swimming pool where you can take a nice cool dip on a hot day. You could also play a game of tennis here or visit the park's nature center. Of course, you will want to bring a picnic to enjoy with your family. If you want to spend some time in the park, there is an inn, camping sites, and cabins. Find out more about the park and park activities at (812) 829–2235.

Greencastle

Greencastle has been named an All America City. Visit the historic courthouse to see one of the two World War II buzz bombs in the country on the lawn there. Drop by the Putnam County Visitors Bureau at 12 West Washington Street to get a map of the nine **covered bridges** that can be seen in the county. On Saturday nights in racing season, you can watch sprint cars, thunder cars, and modified cars race at **Lincoln Park Speedway.** For more information call (800) 829–4639.

Indiana **Trivia**

Where is DePauw University located?

Greencastle

A walking tour of the **DePauw University** campus is an opportunity to view a small university that has eleven historic sites on the campus. You will want to see the **Old Bethel Church,** built in 1807, and the **East College,** in the heart of the campus, which was built in the 1870s. Tours of the campus are given on Monday through Friday and most Saturdays between Labor Day and the end of April and can be arranged by calling ahead, (765) 658–4006.

Where to Eat

The Different Drummer. 2 Seminary Square, in the Walden Inn; (765) 653–2761.

Hathaways. Jackson Street, just off Courthouse Square; (765) 653–1228.

Almost Home. 17 West Franklin Street; (765) 653–5788.

Where to Stay

Walden Inn of Greencastle. 2 Seminary Square; (765) 653–2761.

Sullivan

If your family loves fishing, take everyone to the 1,550-acre **Turtle Creek Reservoir** on Old State Road 54 West. This place is nationally known as a great fishing spot. The reservoir has been stocked with bluegill, red-ear sunfish, black crappie, largemouth bass, and channel catfish. Perhaps everyone in the family can catch a fish here. There is also waterfowl hunting. All sporting activities are subject to Turtle Creek rules and regulations and Indiana State Fish and Wildlife laws. This reservoir is a wonderful place to observe wildlife. You will see deer, waterfowl, and game. You can camp nearby in Shakamak State Park and the Green Sullivan State Forest. For more information call (812) 665–2158.

Jasonville

Ready to relax? A trip to **Shakamak State Park** on State Road 48 is a good choice in every season. The park has more than 400 acres, with three man-made lakes that are the main attraction, as they offer fishing throughout the year plus boating fun in the summer. You can rent rowboats or paddleboats. The new family aquatic center pool has extra appeal because of its large water slide. In the summer you can also rent horses for riding. For more family fun, there are tennis courts, picnicking, seasonal naturalist services, hiking trails, and tennis courts. Of course, like all other state parks, there is the opportunity to camp. About two-thirds of the campsites are in wooded areas and offer cool shade in the summer and beautiful fall colors. Near the campsites is a great playfield area for more family fun. Information is available by calling (812) 665–2158.

General Index

M

Activities Index

Sports Facilities/Events

Entertainment/Theater

Help Us Keep This Guide Up to Date

Every effort has been made by the author and editors to make this guide as accurate and useful as possible. However, many changes can occur after a guide is published—establishments close, phone numbers change, hiking trails are rerouted, facilities come under new management, etc.

We would love to hear from you concerning your experiences with this guide and how you feel it could be improved and be kept up to date. While we may not be able to respond to all comments and suggestions, we'll take them to heart, and we'll make certain to share them with the author. Please send your comments and suggestions to the following address:

The Globe Pequot Press
Reader Response/Editorial Department
P.O. Box 480
Guilford, CT 06437

Or you may e-mail us at: editorial@GlobePequot.com

Thanks for your input, and happy travels!